COOKING WITH

A YEAR OF ITALIAN HOLIDAYS

130 CLASSIC HOLIDAY RECIPES FROM ITALIAN GRANDMOTHERS

ROSSELLA RAGO

Foreword by Adriana Trigiani

Race Point
PUBLISHING

I dedicate this book to my beloved Nonna Romana, who thinks Tupperware is a complete waste of money and expiration dates mean nothing. The whole world wishes you were their Nonna and I am so lucky you're mine.

Inspiring | Educating | Creating | Entertaining

Brimming with creative inspiration, how-to projects, and useful information to enrich your everyday life, Quarto Knows is a favorite destination for those pursuing their interests and passions. Visit our site and dig deeper with our books into your area of interest: Quarto Creates, Quarto Cooks, Quarto Homes, Quarto Lives, Quarto Drives, Quarto Explores, Quarto Gifts, or Quarto Kids.

Text © 2018 by Rossella Rago

First published in 2018 by Race Point,
an imprint of The Quarto Group,
142 West 36th Street, 4th Floor,
New York, NY 10018, USA
T (212) 779-4972 **F** (212) 779-6058
www.QuartoKnows.com

Fairy light motif on page 3 and throughout © Shutterstock.com
Photographs on pages 16 and 40 by Evi Abeler, Big Leo Productions

ISBN 978-1-63106-520-0

Editorial Director: Jeannine Dillon
Project Editor: Erin Canning
Photographer: Colin Cooke
Food Stylist: Michaela Hayes
Hair Stylist: Enza Cristino
Makeup: Gabriella Trantino

10 9 8 7 6 5 4 3 2 1

Printed in China

CONTENTS

FOREWORD

BY ADRIANA TRIGIANI

Hallelujah and pass the gravy!

Rossella Rago is back in the kitchen with Nonna Romana and an all-star team of Italian-American grandmothers with roots and recipes from every region in Italy. The dynamic duo has written the most spectacular holiday cookbook since the first loaf of Saint Rocco's bread was baked in his honor outside of Naples. Yes, we celebrate his feast day, and, yes, the recipe is in this cookbook!

Tradition, folklore, and love are blended, sifted, and baked into these timeless recipes with skill. Rossella describes how to find and use the freshest herbs, spices, and essential ingredients to create your *la bella tavola*. You will revel in the storytelling and find the inspiration to reach back in time and make your favorite dishes, *Nonna's way*.

Whether you're Italian-American, married to one, or a foodie who simply craves the occasional dish of macaroni, this cookbook is a must for your family's kitchen. As I read Rossella's beautiful stories, interviews, and recipes, I savored memories of holidays past, and looked forward to the year ahead with plans to make the profiteroles, zeppole, and risotto, à la Nonne—for starters. You can't go wrong. Rossella and the Nonne guide you through the preparation of each dish with clear instructions. You will even develop new techniques to apply to your old recipes, invigorating your family's favorite dishes.

E vero, Rossella and the Nonne have done it again, but this time, they did it wearing party hats with their aprons. And you will too! *Cooking With Nonna: A Year of Italian Holidays* gives us 130 reasons to celebrate from New Year's Day to Christmas, as we prepare these fabulous dishes for those we love. And if gorgeous Rossella and her *bella* Nonne have anything to say about it, it will be a year you will never forget.

Adriana Trigiani
New York City
Autumn 2018

INTRODUCTION

"Why does everyone always come over to our house?" I asked my Nonna Romana as I painstakingly ironed her embroidered napkins with perfect creases for the celebration the next day. "Because, Rossella, we keep the family together." She said in her Italian Nonna voice, which served to remind me that she does, in fact, know everything.

Her words made me think of how in every Italian family there is always that one house that hosts more holidays than everyone else. No matter what distances or circumstances separate people throughout the year, all it takes is one phone call from Nonna to bring everyone back to that holiday table where memories are made.

My most cherished holiday memory is surprisingly not one from my childhood, but a very recent Christmas Day. Two years ago, my parents—Vito and Angela—were hosting Christmas at their home in New Jersey so that we could better accommodate our large family. My father had about two hundred raw clams and a plethora of seafood chilling in the garage (the second refrigerator for many Italians), and my mother had perfectly arranged tables covered in Christmas tablecloths with matching napkins and holiday plates. For the past two decades, this has been the traditional setting for our holiday meals, but it never quite felt right.

You see, when I was eight years old, my parents moved us (my brother, Leo, and me) to the northern New Jersey suburbs, and while there was much more space than we were used to in our home on the corner of West 6th Street in Bensonhurst, Brooklyn, the holidays never felt the same. Before we moved, the holidays were always held in Nonna Romana's basement apartment, just downstairs from where my family lived. As far back as I can remember, I would help Nonna move furniture and arrange card tables in a zigzag pattern that would stretch all the way from the dining area to the front door. The kid table was always separate from the adult table, and we were usually stuck by the front door, or "Siberia" as I liked to call it. Whichever cousin wasn't lucky enough to get a folding chair was made to sit on Nonna's old La-Z-Boy, while the rest of us giggled at the unlucky soul who had to fumble with their broccoli rabe in the wayward recliner.

We would cover the tables with a bunch of Nonna's holiday tablecloths, none that matched, but each with its own story. "This one belonged to Nonna Regina! She bought it from Martin's department store in downtown Brooklyn the first year she was in

"We eat, we drink, and we reminisce, but most importantly, we love!"

America!" Or, "This one, Zia Commara brought back for me from her honeymoon," she would tell me as I traced the delicately embroidered holly on the matching napkins. I gathered the mismatched cutlery and the glasses, which ranged from Nonna's stemmed wine glasses for the adults to repurposed jelly jars with pictures of cartoon characters on them for the kids.

Then, of course, there was the food. Out of Nonna Romana's tiny corner kitchen would emerge enough dishes to rival the cocktail hour at Russo's on the Bay in Queens! Baked clams, focaccia, mussels marinara, calamari, and a dozen different kinds of cookies . . . oh my! Sure, my aunts and relatives would bring over a few dishes to round out the meal, but for a basement kitchen with very limited resources, it was an astonishing selection. As family began to arrive, the air in the basement would become thick and warm from the oven. The small windows barely provided any ventilation, and the circulating hot air would only intensify when my Uncle Vito started discussing politics.

We would eventually all sit down to a sea of antipasti, which would usually leave us way too full to eat anything else, though not for lack of trying! The pasta course was superfluous, but it always made an appearance, because skipping it would be downright sacrilegious. Mesmerized by the colors and flavors spread across the table, we would all eat until the tablecloths were stained with wine and Coca-Cola, and sprinkled with a delicate layer of focaccia crumbs. After the meal, we would stay up late playing *tombola* (Italian bingo) and card games, to be interrupted occasionally by a symphony of swear words in our Italian dialect whenever one of my uncles would lose—yes, even if it was a holiday. These are some of my most precious memories. Few of them are perfect, but they are all real.

But back to New Jersey. It was just a few years ago on Christmas Day: The stage had been set at my parents' home for the grandiose holiday affair, but at around nine o'clock in the morning, while I was still opening Christmas presents in Brooklyn, I received a frantic phone call from my mother. Strong winds had brought down a power line, knocking out all the power on my parents' street. "Rossè! What are we going to do? Everybody's coming! We have all the fish!" my mother wailed in despair over the phone. I could hear my father in the background, fighting a losing battle with a generator. This was not good. After a few hours, Papa Vito managed to restore power to the heating system with the generator, but without electricity, hosting and cooking for twenty people was just not going to happen. "We're coming to Nonna's," my mother said to me in a much calmer phone call. The decision was made, and for the first time in over a decade, we would spend Christmas Day in the place where we first became a family: Nonna Romana's Brooklyn basement. None of the silverware matched that day, and there may have been an old red wine stain or two on the tablecloth, but we still feasted on seafood cavatelli and played *scopa* like the good old days. Sometimes, we're guilty of trying to make each and every moment perfect and Instagrammable, so this Christmas was a beautiful return to our roots. For Italians, every holiday is a chance to come together as a family and enjoy one another. We eat, we drink, and we reminisce, but most importantly, we love!

Cooking with Nonna: A Year of Italian Holidays is a collection of holiday recipes, stories, and memories from some of the incredible Nonne who serve as the cornerstone in every Italian-American family. Whether you're baking cookies in the kitchen with your Nonna as she tells you a sweet story of holidays gone by or frantically yelling at someone because they forgot to buy lemons at the supermarket, the magic of the holidays will always bring out the passionate side of Italians.

Italy is a country rich in tradition, especially when it comes to the holidays, and I wanted this book to be a go-to guide for putting together a holiday meal, Italian-style. The chapters are organized by holiday instead of course, because every holiday has its own unique flow of ingredients and traditions behind the recipes. I had the opportunity to meet a number of incredible ladies who shared their own families' histories and heritages while I wrote this book. Many of the dishes on these pages have evolved with time and have been adapted to suit a particular family's palate or circumstances. For instance, perhaps carrots were not in the original version of any given dish because they didn't grow in the area at the time, but in America, they became a tasty addition.

Feel free to be adventurous with any of the recipes, because by doing so, you'll begin to forge holiday recipe traditions of your own. I cannot tell you how many people write to me during the holiday season feeling regret that they can't seem to get something to taste exactly like their Nonna's rendition. My response is usually the same for everyone: "That's totally fine, because I'm sure your Nonna used to say the same thing about matching her own Nonna's skills, and one day your grandchildren will say the same thing about you!"

The recipes in this book will take you through a year of Italian holidays, through the lenses of the incredible Nonne who make our holidays so special in the first place. They celebrate the meaningful moments in life, whether it be with a fabulous cookie for Christmas Day or a humble bread made as an offering to a saint. While there are over one hundred recipes in this book, I wish I could have included hundreds more to adequately represent the vast beauty of the Italian holiday landscape. Each Nonna was so excited to share her recipes and stories with me, and ultimately with all of you. I hope you adopt at least one of these recipes as your own so that it lives on with your families and creates as many special memories for you as these recipes have for me. In the words of my Nonna Romana: *"Figlia bella di Nonna, durante le feste si creano i ricordi più belli.* (Throughout the holidays, the most beautiful memories are made.)"

BASIC RECIPES

NONNA GIULIA ROTONDI'S

PICKLED MIXED VEGETABLES

Giardiniera

PREP TIME: 16 HOURS* • **YIELD: 4 JARS (32 OUNCES, OR 907 G, EACH)**

*REQUIRES 2 TO 3 WEEKS OF PRESERVING

Giardinera is a mix of vegetables preserved in a vinegar brine that Italians refer to as *sottaceto* (under vinegar). Nonna Giulia always has her pantry stocked with a few jars for when company drops by unexpectedly (which is often). They make a wonderfully effortless antipasto when paired with olives and cheeses, and she usually sends her guests home with a jar or two, like an Italian-style party favor or *bomboniera*.

3 pounds (1.4 kg) red bell peppers, stemmed and seeded, cut into ¾-inch (2 cm) dice

3 pounds (1.4 kg) green bell peppers, stemmed and seeded, cut into ¾-inch (2 cm) dice

3 pounds (1.4 kg) yellow bell peppers, stemmed and seeded, cut into ¾-inch (2 cm) dice

3 pounds (1.4 kg) eggplant, peeled and cut into ½-inch (13 mm) dice

2 pounds (907 g) celery, cut into ¼-inch (6 mm) dice

3 tablespoons (60 g) salt

Juice of 5 large lemons

14 cups (112 ounces, or 3.3 L) white vinegar

35 cloves garlic, sliced

1 cup (140 g) capers, drained

1 cup (96 g) coarsely chopped fresh mint

1 tablespoon (15 ml) red pepper flakes

4 cups (960 ml) extra-virgin olive oil, plus more as needed

1 Add the bell peppers, eggplant, and celery to a large bowl and sprinkle with the salt and lemon juice. Toss well with a spoon.

2 Cover the bowl with plastic wrap and let it rest for 4 hours at room temperature.

3 Place all the vegetables in a large colander and apply pressure to them with a dish so the liquid from the vegetables drains. Drain for about 5 minutes.

4 Discard the liquid, then transfer all the vegetables to a large bowl and cover them with the white vinegar. Let the vegetables marinate for 3 hours at room temperature.

5 Drain the vinegar and place all the vegetables in the colander once again. Put a large plate over the vegetables and place weights equal to about 40 pounds on it. Leave the weights on the plate overnight.

6 Mix the vegetables well and add the capers, mint, and red pepper flakes. Evenly divide the vegetables among the jars.

7 Fill each jar with 1 cup (240 ml) of the olive oil, adding more oil as needed to cover all the vegetables. Cover the jars and store for 2 to 3 weeks before serving. Serve chilled or at room temperature. Refrigerate the jar after opening.

PASTRY CREAM

Crema Pasticcera

PREP TIME: 5 MINUTES • COOK TIME: 10 MINUTES • YIELD: ABOUT 2 CUPS (475 ML)

Nonna Lydia makes the smoothest, most velvety pastry cream I have ever tasted. In Italy, this basic cream with light notes of citrus and vanilla is used to fill countless pastries and cakes. The secret is using cornstarch instead of flour, which can give the cream a bit of a chalky taste and is more likely to create lumps. For most desserts, you can easily make the cream the night before and store it in the refrigerator. Just let it come to room temperature before using it.

6 tablespoons (75 g) granulated sugar

3 tablespoons (23 g) cornstarch

1 cup (240 ml) whole milk

1 tablespoon (15 ml) heavy cream

3 egg yolks, beaten

1 teaspoon vanilla extract

Whole peel of 1 lemon

Nonna Lydia Says

If you made your cream the night before and you find that it has a few lumps, you can either push it through a fine-mesh strainer with a spoon or do a quick mix with an electric mixer.

1 In a medium bowl, whisk together the granulated sugar and cornstarch. Set aside.

2 In another medium bowl, whisk together the milk, cream, beaten egg yolks, and vanilla extract. Whisk until blended.

3 Place a large saucepan over a medium heat and add the milk-egg mixture and the sugar-cornstarch mixture. Stir continuously with a wooden spoon. Add the lemon peel and continue stirring until the mixture thickens, 7 to 8 minutes. Remove from the heat. Remove and discard the lemon peel, and continue to stir for another 30 seconds.

4 Take a sheet of plastic wrap and press it into the surface of the cream. Cool to room temperature.

CANNOLI CREAM

Crema di Ricotta

PREP TIME: 10 MINUTES • YIELD: ABOUT 4 CUPS (1 KG)

This classic Sicilian cannoli cream is a mixture of sheep's milk ricotta, confectioner's sugar, and maybe some semisweet chocolate chips, and is used in cannolis, among other things. Over the years, Nonna Lydia's family has tweaked the recipe to add a little more flavor with some notes of orange, vanilla, and cinnamon. This recipe also calls for *ricotta impastata*, which has been naturally drained of excess moisture to produce a smooth, velvety cream. If you're in a hurry (and to eat cannoli cream, who wouldn't be?), you can skip the straining step, but it does kick the texture up a notch.

2 pounds (907 g) ricotta impastata

1½ cups (180 g) confectioners' sugar

1 packet (½ ounce, or 15 g) Italian vanilla powder or 1 teaspoon vanilla extract

½ teaspoon cinnamon

½ teaspoon orange extract

½ cup (90 g) mini semisweet chocolate chips (optional)

1 In a large bowl, combine the ricotta impastata, confectioners' sugar, vanilla, cinnamon, and extracts. Mix well and then pass the mixture through a strainer to smooth out the ricotta's texture.

2 Fold in the chocolate chips (if using).

Nonna Lydia Says

If you like the cream a little sweeter, add a few more tablespoons (22 g) of confectioners' sugar, but don't use too much because it will melt and make a runny cannoli cream.

SWEET LEMON ZEST

Estratto di Limoni

PREP TIME: 15 MINUTES • YIELD: 1 JAR (6 OUNCES, OR 170 G)

The first time I baked with Nonna Laura, she reluctantly allowed me to shop for the ingredients she needed. I purchased a little bottle of lemon extract as she asked, but upon arriving to her darling house in Astoria, Queens, she instructed me to return it and get my money back for two reasons: 1. "It's expensive!" and 2. "I make!" She pulled a jar out of the refrigerator with a small, faded label on it that said, "Nonna Laura's Sweet Lemon Zest." It was basically a mixture of freshly zested lemons, some lemon juice, and a bit of sugar. A Nonna with her own product line? My heart melted! This little jar of heaven will save so much time zesting lemons during your holiday baking.

Zest of about 24 medium to large organic lemons

Juice of 4 lemons

2 tablespoons (25 g) sugar

1　Add the lemon zest, juice, and sugar to the jar, making sure the juice barely covers all the zest.

2　Store in the refrigerator for up to 2 months.

FIG OR WINE SYRUP

Vin Cotto

PREP TIME: 5 MINUTES • COOK TIME: 6 HOURS • YIELD: ABOUT 10 CUPS (85 OUNCES, OR 2.4 L)

Vin cotto (cooked wine) is a thick syrup made throughout southern Italy, usually out of wine, wine must, or even figs. The fig variety is technically called *cotto di fichi*, but in my family we always used the term vin cotto. It is primarily used in desserts, such as *cartellate* (page 188), and is regarded as something of a precious commodity in my family. While it is readily available these days at certain Italian specialty stores that import it directly from Puglia, it can be quite expensive for just a small bottle. In Italy, my Bisnonna Regina would always make gallons of vin cotto to be sold in her bottega for the holiday season. I still have such vivid memories of my Zia in Mola di Bari making vin cotto from the figs that bloomed in late August. This event usually heralded the end of summer vacation, and it was always my job to "smuggle" the vin cotto into the States. My aunts would fill 1.5-liter plastic Coca-Cola bottles, tightly duct tape the caps, and discreetly hide the bottles in a bundle of clothes in my suitcase. I'm not entirely proud of this (yes I am!), but in our defense, making vin cotto out of figs in Brooklyn was next to impossible! Today, my Zia Rosa is notorious for her "bootleg" vin cotto.

2 gallons (7.6 L) prune juice or
    wine must

Home for the Holidays
My mother had a store, and around the period of Christmas, we would sell so many cartellate *and* vin cotto! *The store would be full, from opening to closing, with people rushing to buy the ingredients. My whole family worked hard around the holidays, and then we still found the time to make some for ourselves.*
—Nonna Romana Sciddurlo

1 Add the prune juice to a large stockpot, cover, and bring to a boil. You want to choose a pot that has a wide surface area so that the juice will evaporate a little faster.

2 Once boiling, uncover and reduce the heat to a simmer. Simmer uncovered until the juice has reduced by two-thirds and thickens enough to coat the back of a spoon, about 6 hours.

3 Cool to room temperature. The syrup will further thicken as it cools.

4 Once cooled, pour the syrup through a fine-mesh strainer and funnel into a glass bottle. Store in a cool, dry place for up to 8 months.

NEW YEAR'S EVE AND DAY

VALENTINE'S DAY

 Home for the Holidays
Italian people make so much food for the holidays. Too much food! But it's wonderful because we have food for days, so the celebrating never stops. —Nonna Cecilia DeBellis

COTECHINO SAUSAGE WITH LENTILS

Cotechino con Lenticchie

PREP TIME: 5 MINUTES • COOK TIME: 45 MINUTES • YIELD: 6 TO 8 SERVINGS

Most Italians believe in the old superstition that eating lentils on New Year's Eve will bring wealth and good fortune for years to come, owing to their disk-like shape that resembles a coin. Nonna Rosa fiercely believes in this and never skips a year. "I no wanna take no chances, but I eat a lotta lentils and I'm still waiting for the money," she jokes as she unwraps a fresh *cotechino* sausage. Cotechino is a rich pork sausage that hails from the Emilia Romagna region. Most people buy a precooked cotechino that is vacuum-packed, but now, many butchers carry the fresh variety, which is superior in flavor and easy to prepare.

1¼ pounds (567 g) cotechino sausage, not precooked

3 tablespoons (45 ml) extra-virgin olive oil

4 cloves garlic, sliced

2 celery ribs, cut into ½-inch (13 mm) dice

1 medium carrot, cut into ½-inch (13 mm) dice

1 small red onion, cut into ¼-inch (6 mm) dice

3 or 4 leaves fresh sage

2 tablespoons (8 g) chopped fresh parsley

16 ounces (454 g) dry lentils, rinsed

5 cups (1.2 L) water

1½ teaspoons salt

Black pepper, to taste

1 Prick the cotechino all over with a fork.

2 Add the cotechino to a small heavy-bottomed stockpot. Cover the cotechino with cold water and bring the pot to a boil over high heat. Boil for 45 minutes, uncovered. In the meantime, cook the lentils.

3 Put another small stockpot with a lid over medium heat. Add the olive oil and let it heat. Add the garlic and cook for 30 seconds.

4 Add the celery, carrot, onion, sage, and parsley. Toss in the oil for 1 to 2 minutes. Add the lentils and toss in the oil for another 2 minutes.

5 Add the water, salt, and black pepper to the pot. Cover and cook until the lentils are tender and most of the water has been absorbed, about 30 minutes.

6 Transfer the cotechino to a plate. Remove the outer skin of the cotechino. Slice and serve over the lentils.

SICILIAN PIZZA

Sfincione Siciliano

PREP TIME: 1 HOUR • COOK TIME: 1 HOUR • YIELD: 6 TO 8 SERVINGS

Sfincione is a thick-crusted Sicilian pizza—or more of a *focaccia*, to be precise. Nonna Angelina prepares hers with a golden semolina crust and tops it with savory anchovies, Pecorino Romano cheese, and a delicious sauce with lots of oregano that builds incredible layers of flavor. The bread crumb topping melts into the cheese and creates a soft, creamy texture like no other. Although this dish is usually prepared through Christmas and New Year's in the Palermo area, Angelina makes two or three trays at a time for almost every holiday because it's that good! (See the photo for this recipe on page 16.)

DOUGH

2 packets (¼ ounce, or 7 g, each)
    active dry yeast
3 cups (700 ml) warm water
2 tablespoons (30 ml) extra-virgin
    olive oil, plus more for greasing
4 cups (668 g) semolina flour
    (semolina rimacinata)
2 cups (240 g) all-purpose or
    00 flour, plus more for dusting
1 tablespoon (15 ml) salt

SAUCE

2 tablespoons (30 ml) extra-virgin
    olive oil
1 medium onion, cut into ¼-inch
    (6 mm) dice
1 can (28 ounces, or 794 g)
    crushed tomatoes
½ teaspoon salt
½ teaspoon dried oregano
¼ teaspoon black pepper

1 **To make the dough:** Pour the yeast into the warm water in a small bowl and let dissolve for 5 minutes.

2 Grease a baking sheet with olive oil.

3 In a large bowl, whisk together the semolina flour, all-purpose flour, and salt. Slowly pour the yeast mixture into the bowl and stir until a sticky dough forms. Turn out the dough onto a floured work surface and knead for 7 to 10 minutes, until smooth. Add the 2 tablespoons (30 ml) olive oil to your hands and the dough, and knead for another 2 to 3 minutes, until the oil has somewhat been incorporated.

4 Transfer to the baking sheet and press the dough out with your hands, pushing out from the center until it has spread into an even layer.

5 Cover the pan with a kitchen towel and set aside to rise for 1 hour in a warm, dry place. In the meantime, make the sauce.

6 **To make the sauce:** Heat the olive oil in a large saucepan over medium heat. Add the onion and cook and stir until translucent, 5 to 7 minutes.

7 Add the tomatoes, salt, oregano, and black pepper, and stir to combine. Reduce the heat to low and cook for 15 minutes, stirring occasionally with a wooden spoon. Remove from the heat and set aside.

SFINCIONE

¼ cup (27 g) plain bread crumbs

2 tablespoons (13 g) grated
  Parmigiano-Reggiano cheese

1 teaspoon dried oregano

¼ teaspoon black pepper

18 anchovy fillets packed in
  olive oil, drained and fillets
  halved

1 cup (100 g) large-grated Pecorino
  Romano cheese

½ cup (120 ml) extra-virgin
  olive oil

Nonna Angelina Says
When I let the dough rise, I cover it with many blankets or towels. Call me superstitious or old-fashioned, but it works for me!

8 **To make the sfincione:** Preheat the oven to 400°F (200°C).

9 In a small bowl, combine the bread crumbs, Parmigiano-Reggiano, oregano, and black pepper, and mix well.

10 Arrange the anchovy fillets over the dough. Top the anchovies with the Pecorino.

11 Spread the sauce over the sfincione, leaving a 1-inch (2.5 cm) border all the way around. Sprinkle the bread crumb mixture over the top and lightly press the entire sfincione with your fingers, creating indentations that will hold the olive oil. Drizzle the olive oil over the top of the sfincione, depositing it within the indentations.

12 Bake for 30 to 45 minutes, or until the bottom of the crust is golden brown.

MOZZARELLA AND TOMATO FRITTERS

Panzerotti

PREP TIME: 1 HOUR 5 MINUTES • COOK TIME: 8 MINUTES • YIELD: 6 PANZEROTTI

Every summer I look forward to eating this special street food, which is comparable to the Italian-American calzone. With every bite, gorgeous strings of fresh mozzarella ooze from the golden crust, which is light as a feather. Families from Puglia also make these for both New Year's and Christmas Eve.

DOUGH

2 tablespoons (30 ml) extra-virgin olive oil, plus more for brushing

1 packet (¼ ounce, or 7 g) active dry yeast

¾ cup (180 ml) water

2 cups (240 g) all-purpose or 00 flour, plus more for dusting

1 teaspoon salt

FILLING

6 ounces (170 g) fresh mozzarella, shredded

½ cup (50 g) grated Parmigiano-Reggiano cheese

½ cup (75 g) cherry tomatoes, cut into ¼-inch (6 mm) dice

1 tablespoon (9 g) capers (optional)

Black pepper, to taste

Olive oil, for frying (or any frying oil you like)

> **Nonna Romana Says**
> *Fry the* panzerotti *as soon as you finish making them or else you risk the dough drying out and splitting open in the oil.*

1 **To make the dough:** In the bowl of a stand mixer fitted with the dough hook attachment, combine the olive oil, yeast, and water. Let stand until the yeast is dissolved, 5 to 8 minutes.

2 In a medium bowl, whisk together the flour and salt. With the mixer running on low speed, slowly add the flour to the yeast mixture. Mix until a smooth, supple dough forms, 8 to 10 minutes.

3 Transfer the dough to a bowl brushed with olive oil. Brush the ball of dough with more oil. Cover with plastic wrap and set aside to rise for 1 hour, or until doubled in size.

4 Transfer the dough to a floured work surface and knead for 2 to 3 minutes. Cut the dough into six 2-ounce (56 g) pieces. Roll each piece into a ¼-inch-thick (6 mm) round. (Don't worry if it isn't perfectly round; you will adjust the shape later with a ravioli cutter.) Reroll any scraps.

5 **To make the filling:** Add 2 tablespoons (14 g) of mozzarella to the center of each piece of dough. Follow with 1 tablespoon (8 g) of Parmigiano-Reggiano cheese and 1 tablespoon (10 g) of diced tomatoes. Add 4 or 5 capers (if using). Season with black pepper and fold the dough over to create a pocket.

6 Seal the edges around the filling by pressing with your fingers or with the floured tines of a fork. With a ravioli cutter, trim the edges, leaving a border about ½ inch (13 mm) wide. Add any scraps from the edges to a ball to make other panzerotti. Lay the panzerotti on a floured baking sheet and cover with a dish towel until they're ready to be fried.

7 Heat 1 inch (2.5 cm) of oil in a small heavy-bottomed stockpot over medium-high heat. Fry the panzerotti in batches until golden brown, about 2 minutes per batch.

NO-BAKE ALMOND SAN MARZANO BALLS

Palline di San Marzano

PREP TIME: 20 MINUTES • YIELD: ABOUT 48 BALLS

This incredibly easy recipe was created by my Nonna Romana and perfected by my mother, Angela. Ground almonds are mixed in cocoa powder, sugar, and San Marzano, a liqueur from Puglia that my family has been using for many years to garnish gelato. We used to have to smuggle San Marzano into the United States ourselves, but now it's becoming more readily available here. It was my mother who had the brilliant idea to use hot cocoa mix or Nesquick to easily achieve that sweet chocolaty flavor. This is the perfect, slightly boozy dessert to make if you're entertaining on New Year's Eve and don't want to spend all night in the kitchen. Be careful though, they're stronger than you think!

16 ounces (454 g) whole blanched almonds
10 ounces (283 g) hot cocoa mix
¾ cup (180 ml) San Marzano liqueur or any amaro you prefer
Granulated sugar, for rolling

Nonna Romana Says
If you can't find San Marzano liqueur, you can substitute any sweet liqueur you desire, such as amaretto, Baileys Irish Cream, or even Marsala wine.

1 Add the almonds to the bowl of a food processor and process for about 2 minutes, until finely ground. (You want the almonds to be finely ground but not a flour-like consistency.) Transfer to a medium bowl and mix in the hot cocoa mix.

2 Add the liqueur and mix well until you have a soft paste.

3 Put the sugar in a shallow dish.

4 Roll the almond paste into balls about 1 inch (2.5 cm) in diameter.

5 Roll the balls in the sugar and place on a clean plate.

6 Refrigerate for about 1 hour and serve cold.

SPAGHETTI IN WINE SAUCE

Spaghetti al Primitivo

PREP TIME: 10 MINUTES • COOK TIME: 15 MINUTES • YIELD: 4 TO 6 SERVINGS

Venturing out on Valentine's Day can be more trouble than it's worth. The restaurants are always crowded and the food tends to be subpar. It's a much better idea to stay in and make something simple that packs in a ton of flavor! Nonna Romana makes this unique pasta dish a few times a year, which I think is perfect for a romantic night in. The pasta is quickly plunged in boiling water and then finishes cooking in a sauce made with garlic, oil, red pepper flakes, and Primitivo wine, a slightly sweet wine from Puglia made with Zinfandel grapes. The spaghetti takes on a lovely reddish-purple tint, and the aroma is undeniably romantic.

1 teaspoon salt, plus more for cooking the spaghetti

16 ounces (454 g) dried spaghetti

¼ cup (60 ml) extra-virgin olive oil

4 cloves garlic, sliced

¼ teaspoon red pepper flakes

2 cups (475 ml) Primitivo wine or your favorite red wine

2 fresh basil leaves, torn

1   Bring a medium stockpot of salted water to a boil over high heat. Drop in the spaghetti. Cook until pliable, about 5 minutes.

2   While the spaghetti cooks, put a large skillet over medium-high heat and add the olive oil, garlic, and red pepper flakes. Cook for about 2 minutes, until the garlic is fragrant and golden.

3   Add the wine to the pan and bring to a boil.

4   Quickly scoop the spaghetti out of the water and transfer to the skillet along with ½ cup (120 ml) of the pasta cooking water. (Do not drain the pasta, as you may need to add more pasta cooking water to the pan.)

5   Stir in the basil and the 1 teaspoon of salt. Cook, tossing the pasta in the wine sauce, until the alcohol evaporates and the pasta is al dente, 6 to 7 minutes. If the pan gets a bit dry, add more pasta water, ¼ cup (60 ml) at a time, as needed. Taste and season with salt as desired. Serve immediately, garnished with the torn basil.

HAZELNUT HEARTS

Cuori di Pasta Frolla alla Nocciola

PREP TIME: 2 HOURS 20 MINUTES • COOK TIME: 10 MINUTES • YIELD: ABOUT 24 COOKIES

There are few things better than a heart full of Nutella! Nonna Gilda's hazelnut shortbread cookies are an easy way to show someone you love them. They're also fun to make and decorate with grandchildren.

½ cup (58 g) chopped hazelnuts

1 cup (2 sticks, or 240 g) unsalted butter, at room temperature

⅔ cup (130 g) sugar

2 teaspoons vanilla extract

2 large egg yolks, at room temperature

2 cups (240 g) all-purpose or 00 flour

1 cup (296 g) Nutella or your favorite chocolate-hazelnut spread

Sprinkles, for decorating

1 In a food processor, process the hazelnuts until fine, about 2 minutes. Set aside.

2 In the bowl of a stand mixer fitted with the paddle attachment, combine the butter, sugar, and vanilla. Beat on medium-high speed until fluffy, about 5 minutes. Turn the speed to low and beat in the hazelnuts.

3 One at a time, add the egg yolks, mixing on low speed, until each yolk is fully incorporated before adding the next one. Add the flour. Mix again until fully absorbed and a dough forms. Do not overmix. Cover the dough in plastic wrap and flatten into a disk. Refrigerate for at least 2 hours or up to 5 days.

4 Preheat the oven to 350°F (180°C). Line a baking sheet with aluminum foil or parchment paper.

5 Roll the dough ¼ inch (6 mm) thick. Using a 3-inch (7.5 cm) heart-shaped cookie cutter, cut out as many hearts as possible and place them on the prepared baking sheet, about 1 inch (2.5 cm) apart. Reroll and cut any scraps. If the dough is too soft, wrap it in the plastic wrap and refrigerate until firm. Place the cutout hearts in the freezer for 10 minutes before baking to ensure they keep their shape.

6 Bake for 10 minutes. Cool completely on a wire rack.

7 Frost each cookie with the chocolate-hazelnut spread and decorate with sprinkles.

PANNA COTTA WITH SOUR CHERRIES

Panna Cotta con Amarene

PREP TIME: 4 HOURS 15 MINUTES • COOK TIME: 10 MINUTES • YIELD: 4 SERVINGS

I remember my Zia Rina making this pretty pink dessert when she wanted something impressive but not too fussy. *Panna cotta* is a silky, chilled custard-like dessert. It's elegant, delicious, and comes together in 10 minutes, before chilling it in the refrigerator, so it's the perfect make-ahead dessert. She uses Amarena cherries and their syrup, which can be found in jars in many supermarkets and Italian specialty stores, to add a little more sweetness and give the panna cotta its romantic color.

2½ teaspoons unflavored gelatin

1¼ cups (300 ml) whole milk, divided

1½ cups (350 ml) heavy cream

¼ cup (50 g) sugar

½ teaspoon vanilla extract

1 jar (16 ounces, or 454 g) Amarena cherries

1 In a small bowl, dissolve the gelatin in ¼ cup (60 ml) of the milk. Let sit for 5 minutes. Have an ice bath ready.

2 In a large saucepan over medium heat, whisk together the cream, the remaining 1 cup (240 ml) milk, and the sugar. Cook, whisking, until the mixture is warm. Scald the mixture, but do not boil. Remove from the heat and whisk in the gelatin-milk mixture, whisking until the gelatin is fully dissolved and very smooth. Add the vanilla.

3 Measure ¾ cup (180 ml) of syrup from the Amarena cherries and whisk it in, creating a pretty pink hue. Put the saucepan over the prepared ice bath to cool, whisking to make sure the mixture cools evenly. After whisking for about 3 minutes the mixture should be slightly thickened and resemble heavy cream.

4 Pour it into 4 wine glasses. Cover each glass with plastic wrap and refrigerate for about 4 hours, or until the panna cotta sets.

5 Spoon a few Amarena cherries and more syrup over the top before serving.

CREAM PUFFS WITH CHOCOLATE SAUCE

Profiteroles con Crema di Cioccolato

PREP TIME: 20 MINUTES • COOK TIME: 50 MINUTES • YIELD: 6 TO 8 SERVINGS

Though the origin of the *profiterole* is French, it is quite popular in Italian cuisine. Nonna Dorotea has always loved making them with her mother-in-law's recipe and filling them with simple Pastry Cream (page 11). She began topping them with a chocolate ganache sauce to take them to the next level, because what's more romantic than chocolate?

CREAM PUFFS

1 cup (240 ml) water
10 tablespoons (140 g) unsalted butter
Pinch salt
1½ cups (180 g) all-purpose flour
5 large eggs, at room temperature
1 Pastry Cream recipe (page 11)

CHOCOLATE SAUCE

6 ounces (170 g) good-quality dark chocolate, broken up into small pieces
¾ cup (180 ml) heavy whipping cream
1 teaspoon vanilla extract
2 tablespoons (30 g) unsalted butter, softened

1   **To make the cream puffs:** Put a large saucepan over medium heat and bring the water, butter, and salt to a boil. Turn off the heat. Little by little, with a wooden spoon, stir in the flour until it is completely absorbed and a dough that pulls away from the edges of the pan forms. Remove the pan from the heat and cool to room temperature, 10 to 15 minutes.

2   Preheat the oven to 350°F (180°C). Line a baking sheet with parchment paper.

3   Stir the eggs into the dough, one at a time, until each one is fully incorporated.

4   Transfer the dough to a resealable plastic bag and snip off a lower corner. Pipe 1-inch (2.5 cm) balls, 1 inch (2.5 cm) apart, on the prepared baking sheet. Dip your finger in water and smooth any sharp points on the dough.

5   Bake until the cream puffs are golden and hollow inside, 20 to 30 minutes. Cool on a wire rack before filling.

6   Slice the cream puffs in half horizontally and spoon on the pastry cream or pipe it on with a pastry bag.

7   **To make the chocolate sauce:** Place the chopped chocolate in a small heatproof bowl. In a small saucepan over medium-high heat, bring the heavy cream and vanilla to a boil. Pour the hot cream over the chocolate. Let stand for 2 minutes. Whisk together the mixture until the chocolate is completely melted. Add the butter and whisk until the mixture is smooth and shiny.

8   **To assemble:** While the chocolate is still warm, dip the bottom of the filled cream puffs into the chocolate and arrange on a plate. Drizzle the chocolate over the top of the cream puffs.

NONNA DOROTEA CRISTINO

"I believe cooking and feeding people are the best ways to show love."

"I always wanted a big family," Nonna Dorotea says. "My father died when I was young, so we moved to a house next door to my Nonna and Zia. We shared three houses in a row, so we were like a big family then too. It was such a good feeling to be in a full house. That's why I always loved having you around, my *Rossellina*," continues Nonna Dorotea, as she and I sit on a brand-new sofa in her Bensonhurst, Brooklyn, home. She is wearing a khaki "Cooking with Nonna" apron, and her once jet-black hair shows a few strands of gray. Her makeup, however, has been consistent for as long as I can remember: soft black Kohl eyeliner, which she melts with a lighter and applies like an Egyptian princess to define her almond-shaped eyes, and a frosted pink lipstick. Her house feels like home to me because I've spent nearly three decades of my life in it. Her children have undoubtedly served as my closest friends, bordering on siblings, and Nonna Dorotea has very much been a second mother to me.

Some thirty years ago, Nonna Dorotea and my mother, Angela, struck up a conversation at a McDonald's on Bay Parkway, as they happened to be from the same small town in Italy, Mola di Bari. She is a woman that will buy you a cake pan, but never give it to you without a freshly baked cake inside of it. "I've always had a passion for

baking, ever since I was a teenager. On Sundays, I used to wake up very early to bake cakes to have for dessert after Sunday lunch." As a little girl, I remember her as the one person who would never say no if you asked her to cook you something. Her midnight frittata sandwiches, which I enjoyed on many weekend sleepovers, rank among the best things I have ever eaten. (I would learn later that it is *maleducata* to ask someone to make you a frittata sandwich at midnight, and not everyone would be so nice about it!)

When she found out her youngest daughter was expecting her first child, Nonna Dorotea was positively overjoyed. "She and her husband came over for Sunday lunch, and they brought a cake from a bakery that was inside a box. I was distracted doing something else but when I read the words 'We're having a baby' spelled across the top in icing, I couldn't stop crying. This was a moment I had been waiting for my entire life." With two grandsons and another on the way, she says the feeling never gets old. "It's more beautiful every time."

A portrait of her as a young bride hangs in the living room and shows the face of a teenage girl instead of a woman. "I got married at nineteen. We had a big wedding in Italy, and I knew it would be the last party I would have with my whole family for a long time. I looked like a baby, but I had to grow up that day." She recounts her first moments in America as not being very impressive. "On the drive home from the airport I looked around and asked myself, 'Where are the balconies?' In Italy everyone has a balcony, even poor people!" she says, smiling. "I missed my family so much at first. Talking on the phone was so expensive. It wasn't like today where you can call with the computer; then, we could only call each other once a month."

"When I got married I could bake more than I could cook, so my mother-in-law taught me the basics. She taught me how to make good sauce, pasta e fagioli, and her famous manicotti (recipe on page 177). She always taught me to make two fillings—meat and cheese—because in the end, everyone will end up eating both, and you know something? She was right!" she laughs. "But I believe cooking and feeding people are the best ways to show love. My grandsons love to cook with me. It is something very special for us to do together. They come over and look at the stand mixer and say 'vroom vroom,' " she continues. "Everything is sweeter with grandchildren, especially the holidays!"

Nonna Dorotea's holidays are impressive feats of spatial manipulation, as thirty to thirty-five people cram into her home three or four times a year. "It's a lot of work, but I do it to make memories for my children and my grandchildren, my nieces, my nephews, everybody! I want them to have memories of their Nonna like I have memories of mine," she explains. "There are still so many things I wish my Nonna was still alive to show me, like how to make her classic peach preserves. "My Nonna was named Dorotea like me, but the woman who breastfed her, her *madre di latte*, took to calling her Nenella in honor of her deceased

daughter, Caterinella. She was an incredible person, my Nonna Nenella! When my husband was courting me, he would write me letters and she would always wait for the postman to intercept them and hide them for me so no one in the house would read them first. She was my Nonna, my friend, and my confidante," she says, as a tear rolls down her cheek.

Her story strikes me like an old movie I have seen a million times, a familiar feeling one can only know if they have had this sort of Nonna-granddaughter relationship. "That's why I always loved having a big family, because every child and grandchild is a chance to teach someone and love someone. Both of my Nonne taught me that you need to give children a lot of love, because you never know what that child will become one day. They will remember your kindness." We part with a smile, and I walk home the four blocks to my house feeling grateful for the love and kindness she has shown me over the years. I carry it in my heart, knowing that having her in my life has undoubtedly made me a better person.

CARNEVALE

GOOD FRIDAY

 Home for the Holidays
Holidays growing up in Italy were usually very serious, very religious. On Good Friday you couldn't eat anything; on Holy Saturday you couldn't talk until the church bells rang. When we were little kids, it was very hard! —Nonna Annita Fallone Apruzzese

BOW TIE FRITTERS

Chiacchiere Baresi

PREP TIME: 10 MINUTES • COOK TIME: 15 MINUTES • YIELD: ABOUT 48 FRITTERS

Chiacchiere, crostoli, scorpelle, angel wings, *i uand, frappe,* twists: these are just a few names for these delicious strips of fried pastry dough coated in powdered sugar that are traditionally made for Carnevale. The recipes may vary slightly from region to region, but alcohol always makes an appearance in the dough to give the strips their signature bubbles. Using a pasta roller allows you to make a large quantity for your holiday party, and you'll need them, because these go fast!

½ cup (120 ml) dry white wine, such as Pinot Grigio

2 tablespoons (30 ml) olive oil, plus more for frying

2 tablespoons (30 ml) granulated sugar

1½ cups (180 g) all-purpose or 00 flour

Confectioners' sugar, for dusting

1   In the bowl of a stand mixer fitted with the dough hook attachment, combine the wine, olive oil, and granulated sugar. Mix on medium speed until the sugar dissolves.

2   Add the flour. Mix for 3 to 5 minutes, until a supple dough forms. Shape the dough into a ball and cover it with plastic wrap. Let rest on the counter for 20 minutes.

3   Working with a golf ball–size piece of dough at a time, flatten it between your hands and feed the dough through the widest setting of a pasta roller 2 or 3 times, folding it until you get an even rectangle and the dough no longer has any holes. Now pass the dough through a #3 setting 2 or 3 times, until you have smooth rectangular sheets. Alternatively, roll the dough with a rolling pin to ⅛-inch (3 mm) thickness.

4   Place the dough sheets on a clean work surface. Using a ravioli cutter, cut out strips of dough about 3 to 4 inches (7.5 to 10 cm) long and 1 inch (2.5 cm) wide. Twist each strip of dough once or twice and press down lightly on the centers.

5   Line a plate with paper towels and set aside. Heat about 2 inches (5 cm) of olive oil in a large heavy-bottomed skillet over high heat. Working in batches, fry the fritters until golden brown, 1 to 2 minutes per batch. Transfer to the paper towel–lined plate and dust with confectioners' sugar.

NEAPOLITAN RICOTTA AND SEMOLINA CAKE

Migliaccio Napoletano

PREP TIME: 20 MINUTES • COOK TIME: 1 HOUR 20 MINUTES • YIELD: 10 TO 12 SERVINGS

The cousin to the ricotta cheesecake is the Neapolitan *migliaccio* that Nonna Gilda prepares every Carnevale, especially on the day before Ash Wednesday. Coarse semolina is cooked in milk and added to ricotta whipped with eggs to make a light, delicious ricotta cake slightly reminiscent of *sfogliatella* filling. (See the photo for this recipe on page 32.)

2 cups (475 ml) water

2 cups (475 ml) whole milk

3 tablespoons (45 g) unsalted butter, plus more for preparing the pan

1½ cups (300 g) granulated sugar, divided

Zest of 1 lemon

Pinch salt

1 cup (170 g) semolina (not semolina flour)

All-purpose or 00 flour, for preparing the pan

4 large eggs, at room temperature

1½ cups (375 g) whole-milk ricotta

2 teaspoons vanilla extract

¼ cup (36 g) cubed (small) citron (optional)

Confectioners' sugar, for dusting

Nonna Gilda Says

If you find that the top of the cake is browning too quickly, around 40 to 50 minutes into baking, cover the top with aluminum foil and continue baking.

1. In a large saucepan over medium heat, combine the water, milk, butter, ¾ cup (150 g) of the sugar, the lemon zest, and salt. Bring to a simmer and whisk until the butter melts. Reduce the heat to low.

2. While whisking, add the semolina in a stream, continuing to whisk to prevent lumps from forming. (If any lumps should form, smooth them out with a handheld electric mixer afterward.) Continue whisking for 3 to 4 minutes, until the mixture thickens. Transfer to a shallow baking dish and spread evenly. Let cool for 15 minutes.

3. Preheat the oven to 365°F (185°C). Grease a 10-inch (25 cm) springform pan with butter and flour the pan.

4. In a large bowl, whisk together the eggs and remaining ¾ cup (150 g) of sugar. Add the ricotta and vanilla. Using a handheld electric mixer, mix on high speed until very smooth. Gradually add the cooled semolina-milk mixture and mix on high speed until smooth. Fold in the citron (if using). Pour the mixture into the prepared pan.

5. Bake for 1 hour and 10 minutes to 1 hour and 15 minutes until the center has set and the cake just begins to turn golden. Cool to room temperature.

6. Dust with confectioners' sugar before cutting.

CINNAMON AND SUGAR ZEPPOLE

Zeppole con Zucchero e Cannella

PREP TIME: 30 MINUTES • COOK TIME: 45 MINUTES • YIELD: ABOUT 30 ZEPPOLE

In Italy, Carnevale, or Mardi Gras, is celebrated the forty days before Lent, and usually includes lots of treats fried to perfection. Nonna Cecilia loves making these *zeppole* for *Martedi Grasso* (Fat Tuesday), the day that precedes Ash Wednesday and marks the beginning of Lent. Nonna Cecilia's secret when making zeppole is boiled potatoes, which make the dough pillowy and soft, just the way her mother taught her. With a quick roll in cinnamon sugar after they're fried, these are delicious enough to make year-round.

1 pound (454 g) Yukon Gold potatoes, peeled and halved

3 large eggs, at room temperature

½ cup (120 ml) vegetable oil

1 teaspoon active dry yeast

3⅓ cups (400 g) all-purpose or 00 flour, plus more for dusting

Olive oil, for frying

½ cup (100 g) sugar

1 tablespoon (15 ml) ground cinnamon

Home for the Holidays
I remember being at home with my parents in Brooklyn on cold snowy nights and my father would kindly hint at my mother to make these zeppole. *She and I would make them together, and my father would fry them for us. They would warm up the whole house, and every time we made them, it felt like a celebration.* —Nonna Cecilia DeBellis

1 In a small stockpot, combine the potatoes with enough cold water to cover completely. Bring to a boil over high heat and cook until the potatoes are fork-tender, 15 to 20 minutes. Drain the potatoes and immediately rice them into a medium bowl. Cool for 5 minutes.

2 In the bowl of a stand mixer, combine the eggs, vegetable oil, and yeast. Let stand for 3 minutes. Attach the dough hook attachment and mix on medium speed until the ingredients are combined. Add the riced potatoes and flour. Mix on medium speed until the flour is absorbed and a soft dough forms, 3 to 5 minutes. Cover the bowl with plastic wrap and let rise in a warm place for 30 minutes.

3 Flour your hands. Take a golf ball–size chunk of dough and roll it into a ½-inch-thick (13 mm) rope, 8 to 10 inches (20 to 25 cm) long. Twist the rope twice and place it on a baking sheet. Continue rolling and forming twists with the remaining dough.

4 Heat 2 inches (5 cm) of olive oil in a small stockpot over high heat. Working in batches, carefully drop the zeppole into the hot oil, 2 or 3 at a time, and fry until golden brown, 2 to 3 minutes per batch.

5 In a shallow dish, whisk the sugar and cinnamon to combine. Roll the zeppole in the sugar-cinnamon mixture while still warm and serve.

NONNA ROSA CARMELO'S

BAKED FIGS WITH ALMONDS

Fichi Mandorlati

PREP TIME: 15 MINUTES • COOK TIME: 2 HOURS • YIELD: 13 BAKED FIGS

When Nonna Romana and Zia Rosa were little girls in Mola di Bari, they looked forward to Carnevale all year long because it meant that they would be allowed sweets. These baked figs filled with almonds and lemon zest took the place of candy for many children of that generation.

14 ounces (395 g) whole dried figs (about 26 medium figs), hard stems removed

26 whole raw almonds

Peel of 1 lemon, cut into 26 (½-inch, or 13 mm) pieces

Nonna Rosa Says
To store the figs, my mother, Regina, would layer them in a big clay pot with lots of bay leaves. The aroma brings back memories, even to this day. You can store these in any container you like, but don't forget the bay leaves!

Home for the Holidays
For Carnevale, we would all dress in costume and go to parties at the homes of our friends. We would make costumes out of anything we could find then, anything to make ourselves look festive. When you went to someone's house you would hope they had some treats there for you; my friend Cenzina's mother always had fresh cookies for us. In other homes you would find chestnuts, baked figs, or even baked chickpeas. Whatever people had. —Nonna Rosa Carmelo

1 Preheat the oven to 200°F (93°C).

2 With a sharp knife, halve the figs horizontally, about three-fourths of the way through, butterflying them so each fig resembles the number 8. Arrange all the figs, cut side up.

3 On one fig half, place 1 whole almond, and 1 piece of lemon zest on the other half. Top with a butterflied fig, cut side down. Continue with the remaining figs, almonds, and lemon zest. Arrange the figs on a baking sheet.

4 Bake until the figs turn a slightly darker brown color and have hardened, about 2 hours. Cool to room temperature before eating.

OVEN-FRIED CHICKPEAS

Ceci Fritti

PREP TIME: 15 MINUTES* • COOK TIME: 35 MINUTES • YIELD: 6 TO 8 SERVINGS

*REQUIRES 12 HOURS OF SOAKING

To celebrate Carnevale in Italy, many families would throw fun costume parties in the home and serve humble treats like these oven-fried chickpeas. They are delightfully crunchy, and they double as a healthy snack.

1 pound (454 g) dried chickpeas
2 teaspoons salt
12 bay leaves

1   In a medium saucepan, combine the chickpeas, salt, and bay leaves. Cover with enough cold water to come up 3 inches (7.5 cm) above the chickpeas. Soak for 12 hours.

2   Preheat the oven to 400°F (200° C).

3   Drain and pat the chickpeas dry with a towel. Spread the chickpeas in an even layer on a baking sheet. Bake for 35 minutes, or until the chickpeas are golden brown.

SAVORY SCALLION PIE

Scalcione

PREP TIME: 10 MINUTES • COOK TIME: 1 HOUR 15 MINUTES • YIELD: 4 TO 6 SERVINGS

Every Good Friday, families from Puglia enjoy a pie crust made with white wine, oil, and flour, and stuffed with an onion filling that varies from village to village. My Zia Rosa's is by far the best in the family. We all love it so much that she makes it throughout the year.

FILLING

6 bunches scallions (35 to 40 stalks)

¼ cup (60 ml) extra-virgin olive oil

½ cup (128 g) canned crushed tomatoes or 1 cup (150 g) cherry tomatoes, halved

1 cup (192 g) pitted Gaeta or Kalamata olives

½ cup (120 ml) dry white wine, such as Pinot Grigio or Sauvignon Blanc

5 anchovy fillets, broken up into small pieces (optional)

CRUST

⅓ cup (80 ml) extra-virgin olive oil, plus more for greasing and brushing

1 cup (240 ml) dry white wine, such as Pinot Grigio or Sauvignon Blanc

1 teaspoon salt

3⅓ cups (400 g) all-purpose or 00 flour, plus more for dusting

1 **To make the filling:** Trim the green ends of the scallions. With a paring knife, split the bulbs of the scallions in half. Cut the scallions into 1½-inch (4 cm) pieces. Wash them well under cold water.

2 Heat the oil in a small stockpot over medium-high heat. Add the scallions, tomatoes, olives, and wine. Give the pot a good stir with a wooden spoon. Cover and cook until the scallions are soft, about 15 minutes. Remove from the heat and transfer to a colander with a plate underneath to drain the juice. Set aside until cool. In the meantime, make the dough for the crust.

3 **To make the crust:** Preheat the oven to 400°F (200°C). Grease a 12-inch-round (30 cm) pizza pan with olive oil.

4 In the bowl of a stand mixer fitted with the dough hook attachment, combine the olive oil, wine, and salt, and mix for 30 seconds on low speed. Add the flour and mix until a smooth dough forms, 2 to 3 minutes. Turn out the dough onto a floured surface. Cut the dough in half and roll one-half into a circle, 14 inches (36 cm) in diameter. Roll the crust around the rolling pin and unfurl it over the prepared pan. Smooth the sides and fit the crust into the corners of the pan, allowing the excess to come up the sides.

5 Add the scallion filling to the center of the crust and spread it evenly, leaving a border of about ½ inch (13 mm). Place the pieces of anchovy (if using) over the scallions.

6 Roll out the remaining dough into another circle 14 inches (36 cm) in diameter. Place it over the scallions and press the top and bottom crusts together with your fingers. Trim the excess dough from the top. Press the border of the crust with the tines of a fork to create a seal. Brush the crust with olive oil and dock all over with a fork.

7 Bake for 1 hour, or until the crust has colored. Serve warm or at room temperature.

TUNA PIE WITH TOMATOES AND PARSLEY

Pasticcio di Tonno

PREP TIME: 1 HOUR 30 MINUTES • COOK TIME: 1 HOUR 5 MINUTES • YIELD: 6 TO 8 SERVINGS

Variations of this meatless pie can be found all over the Puglia region of Italy to break the Good Friday fast. Nonna Maria's version features a light, pillowy crust that is typical of her village of Altamura. Since this pie has so few ingredients, it's imperative to use quality products. Nonna Maria loves canned tuna packed in oil and imported from Italy, which she finds at Italian specialty stores in Brooklyn. Sometimes, just opening the can makes her feel like she's back home in Italy.

DOUGH

4 cups (680 g) semolina bread flour

2 teaspoons salt

1¾ cups (425 ml) warm water

2 packets (¼ ounce, or 7 g, each) active dry yeast

FILLING

2 cans (5 ounces, or 142 g, each) yellowtail tuna, packed in olive oil, drained (if you cannot find yellowtail, use any tuna you like as long as it's packed in oil)

½ cup (120 ml) extra-virgin olive oil

6 cloves garlic, minced

2 cups (120 g) fresh parsley leaves

1½ cups (225 g) cherry tomatoes

½ teaspoon salt

ASSEMBLY

¼ cup (60 ml) extra-virgin olive oil, divided

1 **To make the dough:** Place the flour on a clean work surface and mix in the salt. Make a well in the center of the flour and add the warm water and yeast. Let the yeast sit until bubbles just begin to form, 3 to 5 minutes.

2 Using your fingers, incorporate the flour into the water. Knead for 8 to 10 minutes, until a supple dough forms. Wrap the dough in a clean kitchen towel and let sit in a warm place to rise until the dough doubles in size, about 1 hour. In the meantime, make the filling.

3 **To make the filling:** Put the tuna in a medium bowl and break it up with a fork.

4 Heat ½ cup (120 ml) of the olive oil in a medium skillet with a lid over medium heat. Add the garlic. Cook and stir for about 2 minutes, until brown.

5 Add the parsley. Cover the pan and cook for about 2 minutes, until the parsley wilts. Add the tomatoes and the salt. Reduce the heat slightly. Cover the pan and cook for 10 to 15 minutes, until the tomatoes break down. Remove from the heat and transfer to a medium bowl.

6 Mix in the tuna. Set aside.

7 **To assemble the pie:** Preheat the oven to 350°F (180°C). Drizzle a baking sheet with 2 tablespoons (30 ml) of the olive oil.

8 Turn out the dough onto a work surface and knead it for 2 to 3 minutes. Cut the dough in half. Using a rolling pin, roll out the first half into a rectangle as thin as you can get it and larger than the baking sheet. Roll the dough onto the rolling pin and transfer it to the prepared baking sheet. Let any excess dough hang over the sides.

9 Spread the tuna filling over the dough in an even layer, leaving a 1-inch (2.5 cm) border on all sides.

10 Roll out the second piece of dough to the same size and cover the filling with it. Trim any excess to the top of the pan, about 1 inch (2.5 cm). Fold the excess bottom dough over and press firmly with your fingers. Using a fork, crimp the edges to seal. Brush the top with the remaining 2 tablespoons (30 ml) olive oil and dock all over with a fork.

11 Bake for 40 to 45 minutes, or until the top of the pie is golden. Cool to room temperature, cut into slices, and serve.

EASTER DAY

LITTLE EASTER

LAMB WITH POTATOES

Tiella di Agnello e Patate

PREP TIME: 15 MINUTES • COOK TIME: 1 HOUR 15 MINUTES • YIELD: 4 TO 6 SERVINGS

If you're entertaining a big group for Easter (yes, I know this is an Italian holiday cookbook and the idea of entertaining anything but a big group is silly), and you want to make an easy but impressive entrée, then look no further than this dish, which is prepared in the true Pugliese fashion with super-simple ingredients that won't compete with the flavor of the lamb. Nonna Romana says she loves this dish because the potatoes and tomatoes are a built-in side dish of sorts and are very satisfying. If you want to be very traditional, bake this in a terra-cotta pot, which conducts heat beautifully and cooks the meat evenly; otherwise, any large baking pan will do the job.

2 pounds (907 g) lamb, mixed cuts or your preferred cut

Salt, to taste

Black pepper, to taste

5 medium russet potatoes, scrubbed, peeled, and sliced into ¼-inch-thick (6 mm) rounds

2 cups (300 g) cherry tomatoes, halved

1 medium red or white onion, cut into 1-inch (2.5 cm) dice

10 small fresh rosemary sprigs

3 or 4 bay leaves

¼ teaspoon red pepper flakes

¾ cup (180 ml) white wine, such as Pinot Grigio or Chablis

¼ cup (60 ml) extra-virgin olive oil

3 tablespoons (19 g) grated Pecorino Romano cheese

1 Preheat the oven at 400°F (200°C).

2 Season the lamb well on both sides with salt and pepper. (You might want to add a little more salt to the lamb than you think you need because lamb tends not to absorb salt as well.)

3 In a large bowl, combine the potatoes, tomatoes (reserve a few for squeezing on top), onion, rosemary, and bay leaves well.

4 Add the red pepper flakes and season with salt as desired. Pour in the wine and olive oil, and add the lamb. Mix everything until well combined.

5 Turn the contents of the bowl out onto a baking sheet or into a terra-cotta pot, spreading them into an even layer. Pour the liquids at the bottom of the bowl into the pan, too. Sprinkle the cheese over the entire surface, particularly over the potatoes. Squeeze the reserved tomatoes with your hands over the potatoes.

6 Bake until the potatoes have colored nicely and an instant-read meat thermometer inserted into the lamb reads between 145°F (63°C) for medium-rare and 160°F (71°C) for medium, 1 hour to 1 hour and 15 minutes. Remove the bay leaves before serving.

STUFFED ZUCCHINI

Zucchine Ripiene

PREP TIME: 10 MINUTES • COOK TIME: 1 HOUR 40 MINUTES • YIELD: 4 TO 6 SERVINGS

Whenever you go to Nonna Maria's house for a holiday meal, there is always something ready for you to snack on. These meat-stuffed zucchini are a lovely springtime appetizer or side dish for holiday entertaining. Nonna Maria hollows out the zucchini to make little cups and fills them with a mixture of sautéed meat and diced zucchini flesh, making them perfect for a dinner party or a buffet.

4 to 5 large zucchini (look for zucchini that are nice and wide), cut into 2-inch-thick (5 cm) rounds (about 20)

1¾ cups (425 ml) water

3 tablespoons (45 ml) extra-virgin olive oil, plus more for drizzling

1 teaspoon salt, divided

¼ teaspoon black pepper

6 tablespoons (90 ml) white wine, such as Pinot Grigio, divided

1 pound (454 g) ground beef

5 tablespoons (31 g) grated Parmigiano-Reggiano cheese

¼ cup (30 g) plain bread crumbs

1 large egg, beaten

3 tablespoons (12 g) minced fresh parsley plus 4 to 5 sprigs, divided

1 small onion, sliced

1 Preheat the oven to 400°F (200°C).

2 Using a sharp knife, hollow out the center of the zucchini rounds, leaving about ¼ inch (6 mm) on the edges. Chop the zucchini flesh into ¼-inch (6 mm) dice and transfer to a medium skillet. Set aside.

3 Stand the zucchini rounds in a 13 × 9-inch (33 × 23 cm) baking dish. Pour the water into the bottom of the dish and bake for 30 to 35 minutes, or until the flesh is easily pierced with a fork and most of the water has evaporated. Remove from the oven and set aside.

4 Put the skillet with the zucchini flesh over medium heat and add the olive oil, ½ teaspoon of the salt, and the pepper. Cook for 2 to 3 minutes, turning frequently with a wooden spoon. Add ¼ cup (60 ml) of the wine. Cook until the zucchini flesh develops some color, 12 to 15 minutes more. Using a slotted spoon, transfer the zucchini flesh to a large bowl, reserving the oil in the pan.

5 Add the ground beef, the remaining 2 tablespoons (30 ml) wine, and remaining ½ teaspoon salt to the skillet. Cook for 3 to 4 minutes, until the meat is just browned. Using a slotted spoon, transfer the meat to the bowl with the sautéed zucchini flesh. Discard the fat in the pan. Let the zucchini-meat mixture cool for 10 minutes. Once cool, stir in in the cheese, bread crumbs, egg, and minced parsley.

6 Place the onion slices and parsley sprigs between the zucchini rounds in the baking dish. Fill each zucchini cavity with 1½ to 2 tablespoons (23 to 30 g) of filling. Drizzle the zucchini with a bit of olive oil.

7 Bake for 25 to 30 minutes, or until the top of the meat is browned.

RABBIT WITH PANCETTA AND VEGETABLES

Coniglio con Pancetta e Verdure

PREP TIME: 1 HOUR 15 MINUTES • COOK TIME: 1 HOUR 15 MINUTES • YIELD: 4 SERVINGS

For Nonna Annita, rabbit is a comfort food of sorts, as it reminds her of growing up in Ciociaria, where rabbit is part of the local culinary tradition. She only began using carrots in this dish when she arrived in America because she said there were none when she was growing up in Italy.

1 rabbit (2½ pounds, or 1.1 kg), fresh or frozen and thawed (see Nonna Annita Says, below)

Cold water, as needed

1 cup (240 ml) white wine vinegar

3 tablespoons (45 ml) extra-virgin olive oil

4 ounces (113 g) pancetta, cut into ¼-inch (6 mm) dice

2 small carrots, cut into 1½-inch (4 cm) pieces

2 shallots, cut into ¼-inch (6 mm) dice

1 celery rib, cut into 1½-inch (4 cm) pieces

2 bay leaves

2 to 3 fresh rosemary sprigs

1 teaspoon salt, divided

½ teaspoon black pepper, divided

1 cup (240 ml) dry white wine, such as Pinot Grigio

❦ Nonna Annita Says
Ask your butcher to cut up the rabbit as follows: Remove and discard the kidneys, liver, and heart. Using a very sharp knife or a cleaver, cut the front legs from the backbone, cut out the hind legs, and cut the saddle into 2 pieces.

1 Place the rabbit in a large bowl and cover it with cold water. Add the vinegar and soak the rabbit for 1 hour to remove any gaminess. Drain and pat dry.

2 Put a large heavy-bottomed skillet with a lid over high heat. Add the rabbit to the dry skillet and sear for 3 to 5 minutes, turning frequently with tongs to draw out the water. Transfer to a plate or bowl. Discard the water and wash out the skillet.

3 Heat the olive oil in the cleaned skillet over medium-high heat. Add the pancetta. Cook and stir for about 5 minutes, until crisp. With a slotted spoon, transfer to a medium bowl, leaving the fat in the skillet.

4 Return the skillet to the heat and add the carrots, shallots, celery, bay leaves, and rosemary. Cook and stir for 7 to 9 minutes, until the shallots are translucent and the vegetables are soft. Season with about half the salt and pepper and transfer the vegetables to the bowl with the pancetta. Set aside.

5 Return the skillet to the heat again and add the rabbit and any juices that have collected back into the pan. Raise the heat to high. Cook for 5 to 7 minutes, turning frequently, until the rabbit develops some color. Season with the remaining salt and pepper. Add the wine to the skillet to deglaze it and scrape up any browned bits from the bottom of it. Cook for 2 to 3 minutes.

6 Add the vegetables and pancetta back into the skillet and reduce the heat to low. Cover the skillet and cook for 40 to 45 minutes, until the rabbit is tender and most of the liquid has reduced. Remove the bay leaves and rosemary sprigs before serving.

"Food brings people together. When I was young, my father demanded that we all sit at the table to eat at the same time. As Italian-Americans, we hold on to that tradition as long as we can."

"No matter what country we were in, my family's kitchen was always Italian," Nonna Annita explains as we cook together in her kitchen in Jersey City. The smell of rabbit (recipe opposite) simmering on the stove mixes with the aroma of the wine cookies (recipe on page 193), perfectly representing the traditional flavors of Nonna Annita's hometown in Italy. The scents waft through the large home she has lived in since the early fifties. The style and structure remind me of the film *Moonstruck*, where the center of the household was the kitchen. As I stand there, I can close my eyes and imagine the many holidays that Nonna Annita has hosted for her family. Nonna Annita's large gold medallion hangs over her apron and her hair is delicately styled in finger waves, making her seem like a Nonna from a different era. She strikes me as a woman who

loves to laugh, but who also takes food and family seriously. "Food brings people together. When I was young, my father demanded that we all sit at the table to eat at the same time. As Italian-Americans, we hold on to that tradition as long as we can. When you eat, you talk. No cell phones at my table." That's something I imagine Nonna Annita says often to her college-age grandchildren, whom she loves dearly. "Being a Nonna is pure joy. I'm very close with all my grandchildren. Some of them lived with me, and I've loved taking care of them and teaching them things."

Nonna Annita was born in the town of Galinaro, Frosinone. This part of Lazio is commonly called Ciociaria for the unique sandals, called *ciocie*, worn by the locals. The area was immortalized in the 1960 film *La Ciociara* (*Two Women*), starring Sophia Loren. She pulls out a photo of herself dressed in the traditional garb of the area. I glance at the photo and then glance back up at her and realize she still has the same expression.

Nonna Annita called Ciociaria home for the first twelve years of her life, even while the German army swept through Italy. "The Germans would go around to the houses looking for food. My mother was afraid, so she used to cook for them and feed them. At one time, a chicken sickness had swept the town and killed all the chickens. There was one chicken on our land who had survived the sickness, and one day, a German soldier came and tried to take it from us. My mother stood in the doorway of the chicken coop as that soldier pointed a gun at her and demanded the chicken. Somehow she talked him out of taking it. She cooked him something else and he left." Shortly after the war, Nonna Annita and her family relocated to the outskirts of Paris, where she followed her passion for sewing and dressmaking. "I always wanted to be a dressmaker," she says, beaming with pride as she shows me wedding photographs of her three children, all wearing one of her creations. Over the years, Nonna Annita lent her talents to Amsale, a top bridal designer based in New York, and eventually enjoyed a successful dressmaking business of her own. "After we had moved to France, I found a sewing *maestra*, Madame Cherier, who would teach me and other girls the basics of sewing. I loved making wedding dresses, but I didn't make my own because my mother said that it would be bad luck," she says with a giggle, as she shows me her black-and-white wedding photo.

After several years in France, Nonna Annita's father, a French citizen, decided to move the family to New York City. In America, there were no immigration limits for the French. "I wasn't too crazy about leaving France to go to America. You see, I had just learned French and I had just gotten a job. I had hoped to eventually start working for Dior or one of the big fashion houses. But I was seventeen, and I had to follow my parents. Then I had to learn a whole other language. The only things I could say in English when I got here were 'shut up' and 'I love you!' " she says with an infectious laugh.

Her family settled in New York, in an area that is now home to Lincoln Center. In those days, so many of its residents hailed from Ciociara that it was dubbed Little Ciociaria. It was there where she met her husband, who was a good friend of her brother. "My husband is from my hometown. He was in the army, and when he came back from Hawaii where he was stationed, my brother brought him to our apartment. I really wasn't interested in meeting anyone, so I went up to the roof to read. I was twenty years old and my head just wasn't there. We met again around November, and I agreed to go out with him until the holidays, so I would have someone to go out with on New Year's Eve. He asked me to marry him around Christmas, and we were married that June. It turned into fifty-four years." She and I laugh together as we reflect on how different dating is now.

Today, she is settled in Jersey City, and with the recent passing of her husband, cooking is a wellspring of solace. "I make so many holiday cookies (like her delicious Cream Cheese Knot Cookies on page 197). I make them for the Italian center, for the bishop, for my neighbors, my grandchildren. It gets a little harder every year. I ask myself, 'Am I really going to do it this year?' But I do it, because it gives me joy! This year, I had cataract surgery ten days before Christmas and I wasn't sure I could handle it. But I did it! With one good eye, I did it!"

BAKED RIGATONI WITH SPRING VEGETABLES

Rigatoni al Forno con Verdure

PREP TIME: 30 MINUTES • COOK TIME: 1 HOUR 35 MINUTES • YIELD: 6 TO 8 SERVINGS

What better way to welcome spring than with this pasta dish! This dish is perfect for holiday meals because you can fully assemble it and leave it in fridge the night before. Just let it come to room temperature before baking, and you're good to go.

SAUCE

3 tablespoons (45 ml) extra-virgin olive oil, divided

1 small onion, cut into 2-inch (5 cm) slices

4 cloves garlic, sliced

12 ounces (340 g) mini sweet peppers, cut into ¼-inch (6 mm) strips

1 medium zucchini, cut into 1-inch (2.5 cm) chunks

1 medium eggplant, skin on, cut into 2-inch (5 cm) chunks

2 teaspoons salt, divided, plus more to taste

1 can (28 ounces, or 794 g) crushed tomatoes

1 cup (240 ml) water

¼ cup (10 g) chopped fresh basil

PASTA

Salt, to taste

1 pound (454 g) dried rigatoni pasta

1 pound (454 g) mozzarella cheese, shredded, divided

⅔ cup (67 g) grated Parmigiano-Reggiano cheese, divided

1 **To make the sauce:** Heat 2 tablespoons (30 ml) of the olive oil in a large heavy-bottomed skillet over medium heat.

2 Add the onion, garlic, and peppers. Cook for 10 to 12 minutes, until the onion is translucent and the peppers soften. Add the zucchini to the skillet. Cook for 8 to 10 minutes, until soft.

3 Add the remaining 1 tablespoon (15 ml) olive oil, the eggplant, and 1 teaspoon of the salt. Cook for 5 to 7 minutes, stirring with a wooden spoon, until the eggplant softens. Stir in the tomatoes, water, basil, and remaining 1 teaspoon salt. Reduce the heat to low. Cover the skillet and cook for 10 to 12 minutes. Scoop out and reserve 2 cups (480 ml) of sauce.

4 Preheat the oven to 350°F (180°C).

5 **To make the pasta:** Bring a medium stockpot of generously salted water to a boil. Drop in the pasta and cook for half the time listed on the package instructions, about 6 minutes. You want the pasta to be very al dente. Drain and run the pasta under cold water. Add the drained pasta to the remaining vegetable sauce in the skillet. Toss well to coat the pasta in the sauce.

6 **To assemble:** Spread 1 cup (240 ml) of the reserved sauce over the bottom of a 13 × 9-inch (33 × 23 cm) baking dish. Add half the pasta and top with half the mozzarella and half the Parmigiano-Reggiano. Add the remaining pasta, spreading it into an even layer. Top with the remaining reserved sauce, mozzarella, and Parmigiano-Reggiano.

7 Bake for 35 to 45 minutes, until the cheese melts and the top pieces of pasta are slightly charred. Serve immediately.

PAPPARDELLE WITH LAMB RAGÙ AND WHIPPED RICOTTA

Pappardelle con Ragù di Agnello e Ricotta

PREP TIME: 20 MINUTES • COOK TIME: 1 HOUR • YIELD: 4 TO 6 SERVINGS

On Sundays, Italians have sauce—even on Easter Sunday. This pasta dish is the perfect first course for Easter Sunday, and the hearty meat sauce is full of flavor and comes together quickly. Try not to skip the mint leaves, which complement the lamb beautifully.

3 tablespoons (45 ml) extra-virgin olive oil

1 medium carrot, cut into ¼-inch (6 mm) dice

1 celery rib, cut into ¼-inch (6 mm) dice

1 large shallot, cut into ¼-inch (6 mm) dice

½ teaspoon red pepper flakes

1 pound (454 g) ground lamb

1 pound (454 g) lamb neck bones

2 bay leaves

2 fresh rosemary sprigs, chopped

2 fresh thyme sprigs, chopped

Salt, to taste

Black pepper, to taste

1 cup (240 ml) dry red wine, such as Merlot

3 tablespoons (48 g) tomato paste

1 can (28 ounces, or 794 g) crushed tomatoes

16 ounces (454 g) dry pappardelle pasta

1 cup (100 g) grated Pecorino Romano cheese

2 cups (500 g) whole-milk ricotta

8 to 10 fresh mint leaves, for garnish

1 Heat the olive oil in a large Dutch oven or cast-iron casserole dish over medium heat.

2 Add the carrot, celery, shallot, and red pepper flakes. Raise the heat to high and cook and stir the vegetables for 7 to 10 minutes, until soft.

3 Add the ground lamb, bones, bay leaves, rosemary, and thyme. Season with salt and pepper. Cook for 5 to 7 minutes, stirring, until the lamb is nicely browned.

4 Add the wine. Cook for about 5 minutes, until it evaporates.

5 Add the tomato paste and the tomatoes. Bring the mixture to a boil and reduce the heat to a simmer. Cover the pan and cook for 10 minutes. Uncover the pan and simmer for 20 minutes more, or until the sauce is reduced. Remove and discard the bones and bay leaves.

6 Bring a medium stockpot of salted water to a boil. Add the pasta and cook until al dente.

7 While the pasta cooks, make the whipped ricotta. In a food processor or blender, blend the ricotta for about 20 seconds. Set aside.

8 Transfer the sauce to a large bowl. Drain the pasta and add it to the sauce, tossing to combine. Add the Pecorino Romano cheese and toss again, allowing the residual heat of the pasta to melt the cheese. Serve in warm bowls topped with a dollop of whipped ricotta and garnished with the mint leaves.

HUNTER'S-STYLE QUAIL

Quaglie alla Cacciatora

PREP TIME: 15 MINUTES • COOK TIME: 45 MINUTES • YIELD: 4 TO 6 SERVINGS

"My kids loved quail growing up! They used to fight over the little legs because those always had the most meat," Nonna Teresa says of her quail cooked in a delicious hunter's-style sauce. Usually this dish is made with chicken, but quail is a wonderful alternative, because its dark flesh is well matched with the rich flavors of the sauce.

2 pounds (908 g) quail, about
    6 small birds

Salt, to taste

Black pepper, to taste

3 tablespoons (45 ml) extra-virgin
    olive oil

2 cloves garlic, halved

¼ cup (60 ml) brandy

2 tablespoons (30 ml) grappa

¼ cup (60 ml) dry white wine,
    such as Pinot Grigio

10 ounces (280 g) cremini
    mushrooms, sliced

1 medium onion, sliced into
    half-moons

2 cups (300 g) cherry tomatoes,
    halved

¼ cup (16 g) chopped fresh parsley

½ cup (120 ml) vegetable broth

Home for the Holidays

My family was always together for holidays, and I have twenty-eight first cousins alone! My cousins and I would set up the tables in the basement and my Nonna Teresa would cook. They were such simple times, but they were the best. —Nonna Teresa Petruccelli-Formato

1 Check for any little feathers still stuck to the quail and pull them off.

2 Using kitchen shears, butterfly each quail by cutting straight along the belly. Cut off any excess fat that hangs off the quail. Discard the necks and any innards, and run the quail under cold water. Pat dry with paper towels and place them on a baking sheet. Season both sides of the quail with salt and pepper.

3 Heat the olive oil in a large heavy-bottomed skillet with a lid over medium-high heat. Add the garlic. Cook for 1 to 2 minutes, until the garlic becomes golden.

4 Place the quail in the skillet, cut side down, and sear for 3 to 4 minutes per side. Remove the garlic if you like. Remove the skillet from the heat and add the brandy, grappa, and wine. Don't turn off the stove.

5 Return the skillet to the heat and reduce the heat to medium. Cook for 2 to 3 minutes, until the alcohol evaporates, scraping up any browned bits from the bottom of the pan. Transfer the quail to a plate.

6 Add the mushrooms, onion, tomatoes, and parsley. Taste and season with salt and pepper. Using a wooden spoon, smash the tomatoes. Cook for 4 to 5 minutes.

7 Add the quail back to the skillet, along with any juices that have collected. Pour in the broth and reduce the heat to low. Cover the skillet and cook for 20 minutes.

NEAPOLITAN EASTER MEAT AND CHEESE RING

Casatiello Napoletano

PREP TIME: 4 HOURS • COOK TIME: 1 HOUR • YIELD: 10 TO 12 SERVINGS

To most Neapolitans, the *casatiello* is a sacred Easter tradition. A rustic, savory, leavened bread is bathed in lard and filled with meats and cheeses; it carries great religious symbolism for the Easter holiday. The flour that makes the bread signifies the body of Christ, the eggs on top represent new life, and the strips of dough holding the eggs, Jesus' crown of thorns. Even its ring shape symbolizes infinity. Though it possesses great significance, most importantly, the casatiello is absolutely delicious, and Nonna Antoinette's is flawless. This bread is perfect when eaten hot or cold, and any leftovers can and should absolutely be eaten for *la Pasquetta* the day after Easter.

DOUGH

5 ounces (140 g) lard, plus more for greasing the pan and dotting the dough

1 packet (¼ ounce, or 7 g) active dry yeast

1 cup (240 ml) warm water, divided, plus more as needed

½ teaspoon sugar

4 cups (496 g) all-purpose or 00 flour

2 teaspoons salt

1 teaspoon coarse black pepper

1 **To make the dough:** Coat a 10-inch (25 cm) loose-bottomed tube pan with a little lard and set aside.

2 In a small bowl, combine the yeast with ½ cup (120 ml) of the warm water and the sugar. Let sit until the surface gets foamy (meaning the yeast is active).

3 On a work surface, place the flour and form a well in the center. Alternatively, make the dough in a stand mixer fitted with the dough hook attachment. Add the yeast mixture, 5 ounces (140 g) of lard, salt, and pepper. Gradually work the ingredients into the flour.

4 Add the remaining ½ cup (120 ml) warm water and mix until a soft dough ball forms. If the dough looks dry, add 1 tablespoon (15 ml) of water at a time, until it comes together. Knead until the dough is smooth and elastic.

5 Pinch off a ball of dough (about the size of a tennis ball) and save for later. With a rolling pin, roll the remaining dough into a 14 × 18-inch (36 × 46 cm) rectangle. Dot the dough all over with lard.

continued

FILLING

½ cup (50 g) grated Pecorino Romano cheese

½ cup (50 g) grated Parmigiano-Reggiano cheese

4 ounces (115 g) mortadella or ham, cut into ½-inch (13 mm) dice

4 ounces (115 g) Genoa salami, cut into ½-inch (13 mm) dice

4 ounces (115 g) pancetta, cut into ½-inch (13 mm) dice

4 ounces (115 g) semi-sharp provolone cheese, cut into ½-inch (13 mm) dice

Black pepper, to taste

TOPPING

5 large eggs, washed and dried, divided

Home for the Holidays

I've always loved cooking ever since I could walk! Both my grandmothers did so many beautiful things for all the holidays. We would make pounds and pounds of pasta together, so we could feed everyone. —Nonna Antoinette Capodicci

6 **To make the filling:** Sprinkle the dough's surface with the grated cheeses. Cover with the mortadella, salami, pancetta, and the provolone last. Sprinkle with a little pepper. Starting at the longest side closest to you, roll the dough (jellyroll style), making sure to tuck in the ends. Place it in the prepared pan, tucking the ends together to form a circle. Place little dots of lard all over the top of the bread. Cover with plastic wrap and let rise in a warm environment for 2 to 3 hours, until the bread has risen and doubled in size.

7 Preheat the oven to 375°F (190°C).

8 **To make the topping:** Place 4 of the eggs in their shells randomly on the top of the dough, pressing gently until they are halfway in. Divide the reserved piece of dough into 8 equal pieces. Roll each piece into 4-inch-long (10 cm) ropes. Use 2 pieces to make a cross over each egg, attaching the eggs to the top of the dough.

9 Bake for 45 minutes to 1 hour, or until a toothpick inserted comes out clean. When the casatiello has about 15 minutes to go, beat the remaining egg and brush the surface of the dough with it. This will give it a shiny golden-brown color. If the top is getting too dark, loosely cover it with aluminum foil to prevent overbrowning while continuing to cook the center.

10 When the bread is done, remove it from the oven and transfer to a wire rack to cool. Run a knife along the inside edges of the pan, loosen the bottom, and remove it from the pan. Cut into slices and serve warm.

SWEET AND SOUR LAMB

Agnello Agrodolce

PREP TIME: 10 MINUTES • COOK TIME: 55 MINUTES • YIELD: 6 TO 8 SERVINGS

You will absolutely want to make Nonna Angelina's sweet and sour lamb for your next Easter dinner. This dish is bursting with exuberant flavors and textures that represent Sicily: sweet, sour, and crunchy. She sears the lamb to perfection in a pan with plenty of onion, and then cooks it in a wine and vinegar emulsion before topping it with sugared almonds for some delicious crunch.

½ cup (72 g) whole raw almonds

2 pounds (907 g) lamb, any cut,
    as long as the pieces are about
    1 inch (2.5 cm) thick

Salt, to taste

Black pepper, to taste

½ cup (120 ml) extra-virgin olive oil

1 large onion, sliced

1 cup (240 ml) dry white wine,
    such as Pinot Grigio

¼ cup (50 g) plus 1 teaspoon
    sugar, divided

¼ cup (60 ml) red wine vinegar

1   Preheat the oven to 400°F (200°C).

2   Spread the almonds on a baking sheet and toast them in the oven for 10 minutes. Remove, coarsely chop, and set aside.

3   Season the lamb well with salt and pepper. (You might want to add a little more salt to the lamb than you think you need because lamb tends not to absorb salt as well.)

4   Heat the olive oil in a large skillet over medium-high heat. Add the lamb. Sear for 2 to 3 minutes per side. Transfer to a plate and set aside.

5   Add the onion to the skillet. Cook for 2 to 3 minutes, until soft and slightly golden. Return the lamb to the pan, along with any juices that have collected on the plate. Cook for 2 to 3 minutes.

6   Add the wine to deglaze the skillet and scrape up any browned bits from the bottom of it with a wooden spoon. Reduce the heat to medium-low. Cover the pan and cook for 20 to 25 minutes.

7   In a small bowl, toss together the chopped toasted almonds and 1 teaspoon of the sugar. Set aside.

8   In another small bowl, stir together the vinegar and remaining ¼ cup (50 g) sugar. Add the vinegar and sugar mixture to the skillet and cook, uncovered, for 5 minutes, stirring occasionally.

9   Transfer the lamb to a serving plate and sprinkle with the sugared almonds. Ideally, serve at room temperature.

PIZZA RUSTICA

PREP TIME: 50 MINUTES • COOK TIME: 1 HOUR 15 MINUTES • YIELD: 6 TO 8 SERVINGS

Nonna Romana's *pizza rustica*, also known as *pizza chiena* (stuffed pizza), quickly became one of the most popular recipes on *Cooking with Nonna*. This rich, decadent recipe is the perfect mix of cheeses and meats baked together in a flaky pastry dough that Italians usually serve to break the Lenten fast for the Easter holidays.

CRUST

3⅓ cups (400 g) all-purpose or 00 flour, plus more for dusting and preparing the pan

Dash salt

1 cup (2 sticks, or 240 g) cold unsalted butter, cubed, plus more for preparing the pan

2 eggs plus 1 egg for egg wash, divided

¼ cup (60 ml) whole milk

1 tablespoon (15 ml) water

FILLING

4 ounces (113 g) prosciutto, cut into ½-inch (13 mm) cubes

4 ounces (113 g) sopressata, cut into ½-inch (13 mm) cubes

4 ounces (113 g) mortadella, cut into ½-inch (13 mm) cubes

4 ounces (113 g) fresh mozzarella, cut into ½-inch (13 mm) cubes

4 ounces (113 g) sharp provolone, cut into ½-inch (13 mm) cubes

¼ cup (25 g) grated Pecorino Romano cheese

3 eggs

16 ounces (454 g) basket cheese, cut into ½-inch (13 mm) cubes

Black pepper, to taste

1 **To make the crust:** In the bowl of a stand mixer fitted with the dough hook attachment, combine the flour, salt, and butter. Start on low speed first and then switch to high speed and mix until all the flour is absorbed.

2 Add the 2 eggs, one at a time, until they are fully incorporated. Add the milk and mix until a ball of dough forms. (If the dough seems a bit dry, add another tablespoon, or 15 ml, of milk.) Continue to mix on medium speed for about 10 minutes, or until the dough is supple.

3 Wrap the dough in plastic wrap and let rest in the refrigerator for 30 minutes. Meanwhile, prepare the filling.

4 **To make the filling:** In a large mixing bowl, combine the prosciutto, sopressata, mortadella, mozzarella, provolone, and Pecorino Romana, and mix well.

5 Add the 3 eggs and mix well, making sure the eggs evenly coat everything.

6 Add the basket cheese and mix gently so as not to break it apart too much. Season with fresh black pepper. Set aside.

7 **To assemble the pizza rustica:** Preheat the oven to 350°F (175°C). Butter and flour a 9-inch (23 cm) springform pan.

8 Take two-thirds of the crust dough and put it on a floured work surface. Wrap the other third of dough in plastic wrap and refrigerate until ready to use. Roll it out to a ¼-inch-thick (6 mm) circle at least 16 inches (41 cm) in diameter. You want the crust to come up the sides of the springform pan and hang over.

Nonna Romana Says

You can replace all the meats and some of the cheeses with any that you prefer, but do not replace the sharp provolone. It is the cheese that makes the difference.

9   Roll the dough onto your rolling pin and unfurl it over the pan and up the sides. Leave some excess dough hanging over the sides.

10 Add the filling and spread it evenly. With a sharp knife, cut the excess dough from around the border of the pan.

11 Add the scraps to the remaining one-third of dough and roll it out to a ¼-inch-thick (6 mm) circle. With a ravioli cutter, cut 1½-inch (4 cm) strips to create the lattice top.

12 Beat the remaining 1 egg in a small bowl with the tablespoon (15 ml) of water and brush the lattice with the egg wash.

13 Bake for 1 hour and 15 minutes, or until the center is set and the crust is nicely colored. Cool completely before serving.

NONNA CARMELA D'ANGELO'S

BACCALÀ PIE

Crostata di Baccalà

PREP TIME: 20 MINUTES* • COOK TIME: 40 MINUTES • YIELD: 6 TO 8 SERVINGS

*REQUIRES 1 TO 3 DAYS OF SOAKING

Once regarded as a fish for the poor, *baccalà*, or salt cod, is making a comeback on the food scene. Nonna Carmela's baccalà pie uses the traditional Pugliese dough and has a filling that is the perfect blend of sweet and savory. Her grandchildren have taken on the tradition of making these pies every year for Easter.

FILLING

1 pound (454 g) baccalà (salt cod)

2 tablespoons (30 ml) extra-virgin olive oil

1 medium onion, sliced

½ cup (75 g) raisins

½ cup (96 g) pitted green olives, coarsely chopped

¼ cup (36 g) capers

2 anchovy fillets, packed in olive oil

½ teaspoon black pepper

CRUST

⅓ cup (180 ml) extra-virgin olive oil, plus more for greasing and brushing

1 cup (240 ml) dry white wine, such as Pinot Grigio or Sauvignon Blanc

1 teaspoon salt

3⅓ cups (400 g) all-purpose or 00 flour, plus more for dusting

1 egg beaten with 1 tablespoon (15 ml) water (for egg wash)

1 **To make the filling:** Put the baccalà in a large bowl and cover with cold water. Place the bowl in the refrigerator and change the water 3 times a day. Soak for 1 to 3 days, depending on saltiness. Drain the baccalà and shred by hand into bite-size pieces.

2 Heat the olive oil in a large skillet over medium heat. Add the onion and cook and stir until soft and transparent, 8 to 10 minutes.

3 Add the shredded baccalà to the pan along with the raisins, olives, capers, anchovies, and black pepper. Cook, stirring with a wooden spoon, for 3 to 5 minutes. Remove from the heat and set aside to cool to room temperature. In the meantime, make the dough for the crust.

4 **To make the crust:** In the bowl of a stand mixer fitted with the dough hook attachment, combine the olive oil, wine, and salt, and mix for 30 seconds on low speed.

5 Add the flour and mix until a smooth dough forms, 2 to 3 minutes.

6 **To assemble the pie:** Preheat the oven to 425°F (220°C). Grease a 9-inch-round (23 cm) pie pan with olive oil.

7 Turn out the dough onto a floured work surface and cut the dough in half. Roll out half of the dough into a ¼-inch-thick (6 mm) circle about 12 inches (30 cm) in diameter. Roll the dough up onto the rolling pin and unfurl it into the prepared pie pan.

8 Add the cooled filling to the crust and spread into an even layer.

9 Roll out the other half of the dough to 10 inches (25 cm) and transfer to the top of the pie. Press the edges with your fingers to seal. Trim any excess dough and then press with the tines of a fork. Brush the top with the egg wash and dock all over with a fork.

10 Bake for 35 to 40 minutes, or until the crust is nicely colored.

❦

NONNA ANTOINETTE CAPODICCI'S

SOFT EASTER BREAD

Pane di Pasqua

PREP TIME: 2 HOURS 40 MINUTES • COOK TIME: 25 MINUTES • YIELD: ONE 1-POUND (454 G) EASTER BREAD

Every year, Nonna Antoinette's *nipotini* (grandchildren) look forward to her soft Easter bread, which bakes up fluffy with a wonderfully tender crumb every time. And I'm not sure what it is, but even though I'm all grown up, there's just something about seeing those pastel-colored Easter eggs in the bread that fills me with wonder. You can make this recipe in a stand mixer, but Nonna Antoinette urges that mixing it by hand on a board the old-fashioned way is the way to go, and Nonna knows best!

BREAD

⅔ cup (160 ml) whole milk

1 packet (¼ ounce, or 7 g) active dry yeast

½ cup (100 g) granulated sugar, divided

2¾ cups (330 g) all-purpose or 00 flour, plus more for dusting

1 teaspoon salt

2 large eggs, at room temperature

3 tablespoons (45 g) unsalted butter, at room temperature

1 teaspoon lemon extract

1 teaspoon orange extract

Olive oil, for coating the bowl

TOPPING

4 large eggs, dyed (not hard-boiled eggs)

2 large egg yolks, beaten

½ cup (60 g) confectioners' sugar

¼ cup (60 ml) whole milk

1 teaspoon anise extract

Rainbow nonpareils, for decorating

1 **To make the bread:** Line a baking sheet with parchment paper. Set aside.

2 In a small saucepan over low heat, warm the milk until it is lukewarm. Pour it into a small bowl and stir in the yeast and 1 teaspoon of the granulated sugar. Let stand until the mixture bubbles, about 10 minutes.

3 In a large bowl, combine the flour, remaining granulated sugar, and salt. Whisk to combine. Make a well in the dry ingredients and slowly pour the milk mixture into it, gently stirring.

4 Add the eggs, butter, and extracts. Mix with your hands until a dough begins to come together. Generously flour a work surface and turn the dough out onto it. Knead the dough by hand until it is smooth and elastic. The dough should be soft and a little sticky. Shape the dough into a ball. Lightly coat a bowl with olive oil and place the dough ball in it. Cover the bowl with plastic wrap and let rise in a warm place until doubled in size, about 1 hour and 30 minutes.

5 Generously flour a work surface and transfer the risen dough to it, dividing it in half. Cover the dough with a clean kitchen towel and let rest for 15 minutes. Roll each piece of dough into a 2-inch-thick (5 cm) log about 30 inches long (75 cm). Intertwine the 2 logs loosely and shape into a ring, pressing the ends together firmly.

continued

6 **To make the topping:** Spreading them out equally, gently position the 4 dyed eggs in the folds of the Easter bread, making sure they are secured in the dough folds. Place the bread on the prepared baking sheet. Cover with a clean kitchen towel and let rise for 45 minutes.

7 After 30 minutes, preheat the oven to 350°F (180°C).

8 Just before baking, brush the top of bread with the beaten egg yolks. Do not brush the dyed eggs. Bake for 20 to 25 minutes, until the bread is golden brown. Cool completely on a wire rack before glazing.

9 In a small bowl, whisk together the confectioners' sugar, milk, and anise extract. (You can make your glaze as thin or as thick as you like; for a thicker glaze, add more confectioners' sugar, and for a thinner glaze, add more milk.)

10 Spoon the glaze over the Easter bread. Decorate with rainbow nonpareils. Let dry on a wire rack.

NONNA CARMELA TORNATORE'S

RICOTTA-FILLED SICILIAN PASTRIES

Sciauni

PREP TIME: 45 MINUTES • COOK TIME: 15 MINUTES • YIELD: ABOUT 17 PASTRIES

Sciauni are sweet, fried calzones, typical of eastern Sicily. Every year, Nonna Carmela and her daughter fill them with a sheep's milk ricotta mixed with a little sugar, cinnamon, and a few semisweet chocolate chips to keep the flavors of Sicily alive in their home.

DOUGH

1 cup (240 ml) white wine, such
    as Chablis
¼ cup (60 ml) water
3 cups (360 g) all-purpose or
    00 flour, plus more for dusting
½ cup (100 g) shortening

FILLING

16 ounces (454 g) ricotta impastata
¼ cup (50 g) sugar
¾ teaspoon ground cinnamon
6 tablespoons (68 g) mini
    semisweet chocolate chips

ASSEMBLY

1 large egg white
1 tablespoon (15 ml) water
Oil, for frying (use any oil you like)
Sugar, for sprinkling

Nonna Carmela Says
I like to use a 5-inch (13 cm) plate to make the circles uniform. I brought back a set of plates from my honeymoon and this is the last one left from the whole set. I use it every time I make sciauni. If I ever lose it, I don't know what I will do!

1 **To make the dough:** In a small bowl, whisk together the wine and water. Set aside.

2 In a medium bowl, combine the flour and shortening. With a pastry cutter or a fork, cut the shortening into the flour. Add the wine-water mixture, mixing with a fork until absorbed.

3 Flour a work surface and turn the dough out onto it. Knead the dough with your hands until smooth and elastic. The dough should be humid to the touch but not sticky. Cover with a clean kitchen towel and let rest for 10 minutes.

4 **To make the filling:** In a medium bowl, combine the ricotta, sugar, and cinnamon. Stir until combined. Fold in the chocolate chips. Set aside.

5 **To assemble:** Divide the dough into 4 pieces. Using a rolling pin, roll out 1 piece of dough at a time, ⅛ inch (3 mm) thick. Using a 5-inch-round (13 cm) cookie cutter or plate, cut out circles of dough. Reroll and cut any scraps.

6 In a small bowl, beat the egg white and water together with a fork.

7 Place about 2 tablespoons (30 g) of filling in the center of each circle. Brush the dough edges with the egg wash and fold the dough over. With your fingers, firmly press the dough together surrounding the filling and seal the edges with a fork. Trim any edges with a ravioli cutter, if you like.

8 Heat about 2½ inches (6 cm) of oil in a small stockpot over high heat. Working in batches, fry the pastries until golden brown, 2 to 3 minutes per batch. With a slotted spoon, transfer to a serving dish and immediately sprinkle with sugar. Serve at room temperature.

"Food in an Italian family not only feeds your family, but it also feeds your soul and your heart."

It's a chilly winter Sunday afternoon when Nonna Carmela and I settle down for a chat in her formal living room on the first floor of her Connecticut home, where she lives with her husband and one of her four children. Like many Italian families, much of the everyday cooking and living takes place in the basement, which is outfitted with a full kitchen and living area, leaving the first floor pristine—you know, in case the Pope or royalty drops by for espresso. She sits comfortably next to me on a beautifully upholstered antique sofa, still wearing her apron from a few minutes earlier, when she had been teaching me all her secrets of the kitchen. Her lovely black hair is cut into a bob, and her soft face hides behind dark-rimmed glasses. Upon meeting her, I notice she bears a striking resemblance to the ubiquitous *Barefoot Contessa* of Food Network fame . . . well, the Sicilian version. Nonna Carmela has only recently become a Nonna to her first granddaughter, Emma, a moment she's been anticipating for many years now. "My Nonna's name was Carmela. I was named after her and we were best friends. When my granddaughter was born, the first thought that came to mind was that I am finally Nonna Carmela myself," she says in a soft voice.

Nonna Carmela's life began in Sicily, in a little town called Mojo Alcantara on the Alcantara river, not far from the port of Messina that runs from north to south along the eastern part of Sicily. While she seems perfectly content with her life here in America, she has fond memories of growing up. "Our house in Sicily was small, with just a little balcony, but we were so happy. I wish my children could go back and taste that. A time with no cell phones, when life was easy and slow-paced. We weren't the wealthiest or the poorest people in the village. We had clean clothes, food on the table, and a roof over our heads. We had enough to be happy," she says smiling.

A twist of fate would bring Nonna Carmela's family to America. Her grandmother's status as a US-born citizen meant that she could return and petition for her eleven children. Nonna Carmela's father's family would be the last of the siblings to immigrate, and she admits the news didn't sit well with her at first. "I was so sad when they told us we were going to America, because I loved my Nonna Carmela. She lived two houses down from us, and every day as soon as I would finish eating, I would walk over there where she would be waiting for me to sleep over. She had a huge bed that I needed a stepstool to get onto that would envelop me. After saying my prayers, I would fall asleep laughing as she told me little jokes. Leaving her made me very sad. She passed away six months after we came to America. I think she died of a broken heart. We didn't even know she had died until a month later." She pauses for a moment and wipes some tears away behind her glasses.

Today, in an age where communication is instantaneous and defies distances, her story moves me greatly. She collects herself and tells me about her fateful first day in America. "I'll never forget the day our ship, the *Christopher Columbus*, came to port in New York after an eleven-day journey. It was very early in the morning, and they had made an announcement that anyone who wanted to see the Statue of Liberty should come up on deck.

I'll never forget that misty morning with everyone looking at Lady Liberty. You could hear a pin drop. Once in a while, you could hear a sob from some of the people. Maybe they were crying because we had finally crossed the Atlantic Ocean. Maybe it was because they realized that they left their country, and this would be a whole new world. I just held onto my little sister and looked up at my mother's face and saw tears were rolling down her cheeks. I was barely five years old, but I knew everything would be different now."

With the passing of years, Nonna Carmela's family found their footing in a new world. Her mother supported their family, sometimes working three jobs when her father couldn't find employment. These very struggles would make her into the fabulous cook she is today. "I started cooking at a very young age because my mother worked several jobs. She would often bring work home. She would leave me a piece of paper with instructions on exactly what to do and at what time, so when she would return home from a long day at work, food would be ready. Even if they were very simple recipes, they excited me." Today, Nonna Carmela relishes cooking large meals for her growing family. "Food in an Italian family not only feeds your family, but it also feeds your soul and your heart. A meal is a time to reconnect with your family. When kids grow up and move out, a family dinner brings everyone back together."

When she was barely nineteen, Carmela married her Sicilian sweetheart Sebastian, whom she met at a mutual friend's wedding. She describes their meeting as a "bolt of lightning," which brings a huge smile to her face. "You know, it's funny," Nonna Carmela begins, "I didn't think about marrying someone who was Sicilian, but my husband's family came from a town only ten minutes from my family's town in Sicily. His father was a furniture maker, and he actually made my mother's bedroom set for her. His uncle was a baker, and made all the cookies for my baptism. Sometimes my husband would go along with him to make deliveries as a little boy. I like to think that we actually met when I was an infant, but we had to cross the seas and meet here in America."

Nonna Carmela's love of cooking is especially apparent during the holidays. Something inside her makes her feel the need to recreate the holidays she had growing up. "Holidays were always very special growing up. My father was from a big family, and even though my mother had no family in this country, she always wanted to keep the family together. All holidays were at my parents' house. We would prep for days in advance and we would set up extra tables and there would be dishes everywhere. We would all play bingo until midnight and tell stories. It was the best time ever." It always amazes me how all the work of putting the big holiday meals together never fazes a Nonna; it's as if being a good host is in their DNA.

Today, Carmela has parlayed her passion for cooking into a food truck concept, Carmela's Kitchen, which serves the Norwalk area of Connecticut. "I love to cook. Cooking is my therapy, because when I cook or bake, I give 100 percent concentration on what I'm doing and it relaxes me." Even though her life has gotten busier, her most important role of all is being a Nonna. "Being a Nonna is your second chance to raise a child. A new, young mother is so busy. There is so much going on. With grandchildren, you really enjoy them without all the stress of raising a family." She looks at me and smiles as she says, "And I'm finally Nonna Carmela!"

WHEAT PIE

Pastiera Napoletana

PREP TIME: 1 HOUR • COOK TIME: 1 HOUR 55 MINUTES • YIELD: 8 TO 10 SERVINGS

Nonna Gilda makes these classic grain pies two at a time for the Easter holidays. An old Neapolitan tradition mandates that the *pastiera* be made a few days before the Easter holidays—but no later than the Thursday or Good Friday of Holy Week—so that all the flavors have a chance to meld.

CRUST

2½ cups (300 g) all-purpose or 00 flour, plus more for dusting

½ cup (100 g) sugar

3 large eggs

2½ tablespoons (36 g) vegetable shortening, plus more for greasing

Dash salt

Zest of 1 lemon

FILLING

2 ounces (44 g) hulled wheat (spelt)

2 cups (475 ml) cold water

2 eggs, separated

12 ounces (340 g) whole milk ricotta

1 cup (200 g) sugar

2 teaspoons vanilla extract

½ teaspoon orange extract

¼ cup (36 g) citron or candied fruit (optional)

1 **To make the crust:** In a large mixing bowl, combine the flour, sugar, eggs, shortening, salt, and lemon zest. Mix with your hands until a firm dough forms. Flatten the dough into a disk. Wrap in plastic wrap and refrigerate for at least 1 hour or overnight.

2 **To make the filling:** Rinse the hulled wheat under cold water. Pour the water into a small saucepan over low heat. Add the rinsed wheat and cook until tender, stirring occasionally with a wooden spoon, 30 to 40 minutes. Drain and set aside until cool.

3 In the bowl of a stand mixer fitted with the paddle attachment, beat the egg yolks on medium speed until fluffy and lemon-colored, about 5 minutes. Add the ricotta, wheat, and sugar, and mix until combined. Add the extracts and citron (if using), and mix until incorporated.

4 In a separate medium bowl, beat the egg whites with a handheld electric mixer until soft peaks form. Gently fold the egg whites into the ricotta mixture. Set aside.

5 **To assemble the pie:** Preheat the oven to 350°F (175°C). Grease a 9-inch-round (23 cm) pie pan with vegetable shortening.

6 Roll out the dough on a lightly floured surface into a 12-inch (30 cm) circle about ¼ inch (6 mm) thick. Roll the dough up onto the rolling pin and unfurl it over the pie pan, allowing the excess to hang off the sides. Pour the filling into the crust and trim the excess dough. On a lightly floured surface, roll out the excess dough into a ⅛-inch-thick (3 mm) circle. With a ravioli cutter, cut out 1-inch (2.5 cm) strips and place them in a lattice pattern over the filling, pressing the edges slightly to adhere. Trim the excess dough.

7 Bake for 1 hour and 15 minutes, until the crust has colored and the filling has set. Let cool before serving.

ITALIAN PEACH PASTRIES

Pesche con Alkermes

PREP TIME: 30 MINUTES • COOK TIME: 28 MINUTES • YIELD: 6 PASTRIES

If you peer into the windows of many bakeries in Italy, you will see these gorgeous peaches staring back at you. Italian-Americans have taken to naming them peach cookies, and while some of them are indeed cookies, here, they are little half spheres of cake with velvety Pastry Cream (page 11) sandwiched between them. These peaches are soaked in a sweet, bitter, red liqueur called Alkermes, which is used in many desserts. A final coating of granulated sugar gives them the look of real peaches, making them perfect for a spring holiday such as Easter.

CAKES

Nonstick baking spray, for
preparing the pan
2 cups (240 g) all-purpose or
00 flour
1½ teaspoons baking powder
5 large eggs, at room temperature
1 cup (200 g) sugar

ASSEMBLY

1 cup (240 ml) Alkermes liqueur
(or Aperol or grenadine)
Sugar, for rolling the pastries
1 Pastry Cream recipe (page 11)
Fresh mint leaves, for decorating

1 Preheat the oven to 350°F (180°C). Spray an oven-safe 6-cavity silicone half-sphere pan with baking spray. Set aside.

2 **To make the cakes:** In a small bowl, whisk together the flour and baking powder. Set aside.

3 In the bowl of a stand mixer fitted with the paddle attachment, combine the eggs and sugar. Beat on medium speed for 30 seconds. Increase the speed to high and beat until the mixture is pale yellow, doubles in volume, and ribbons form, 15 to 20 minutes.

4 Reduce the speed to low. Spoon in the dry ingredients, a little at a time, mixing until fully absorbed. Pour ¼ cup (60 ml) of batter into each cavity of the prepared pan and place the pan on a baking sheet. (Note: For a total of 12 cakes, you will need to fill and bake the pan twice.)

5 Bake until the cakes are golden and springy in the middle, about 20 minutes. Cool to room temperature.

6 **To assemble:** Pour the Alkermes into a small bowl. Put some sugar into a shallow dish.

7 Using a very sharp knife, slice the domes off the tops of the cakes so they have a straight edge. Either with a knife or your fingers, slightly hollow out each cake, removing about 1 tablespoon (15 g) of cake crumb from the center.

continued

8 Place about 3 tablespoons (45 g) of pastry cream in the hollow of each cake. Place another half of cake over the cream to form a sphere. Some cream should peak out of the edges; smooth the cream with a knife so it's flush with the cake.

9 Dip the spheres into the Alchermes, just until the sponge is completely colored. Do not immerse too long.

10 Roll the spheres in the sugar, making sure they're completely coated. Place each pastry into a jumbo paper cupcake liner. Decorate with fresh mint leaves.

HOUSEWIVES' CASSATA CAKE

Cassata Casalinga

PREP TIME: 9 HOURS • COOK TIME: 40 MINUTES • YIELD: ONE 12-INCH (30 CM) CAKE

A *cassata* cake is synonymous with Sicily. In this slightly simplified version, delicate layers of Italian sponge cake are soaked in rum, topped with decadent ricotta frosting, and decorated with colorful candied fruits, providing a feast of textures and colors for the senses. Usually, a decorative layer of marzipan is placed around the cake, but Nonna Lilliana prefers to leave it out, cutting down on the sweetness and the time it takes to make. Since their retirement, she and her husband, Sal, have taken to making this cake together, which is super sweet in and of itself. "I love to make this cake for my *pupiddo* (my love)," she says with a knowing smile.

RICOTTA FILLING

2½ pounds (1.1 kg) ricotta impastata

1¼ cups (250 g) granulated sugar

1 teaspoon vanilla extract

½ cup (90 g) mini semisweet chocolate chips

2½ ounces (70 g) zuccata (candied pumpkin) or candied orange peel, lemon peel, or citron, cut into ¼-inch (6 mm) dice

RICOTTA FROSTING

16 ounces (454 g) ricotta impastata

¼ cup (50 g) granulated sugar

1 **To make the ricotta filling:** In a large bowl, combine the ricotta, granulated sugar, and vanilla. Fold in the chocolate chips and zuccata, mixing until fully incorporated. Cover the bowl with plastic wrap and refrigerate for at least 4 hours or overnight.

2 **To make the ricotta frosting:** In a medium bowl, combine the ricotta and granulated sugar until smooth. Cover the bowl with plastic wrap and refrigerate for at least 4 hours or overnight.

3 **To make the sponge cake:** Preheat the oven to 375°F (190°C). Grease a 10-inch (25 cm) springform pan with butter and dust with flour and a sprinkle of confectioners' sugar.

4 In a large bowl, using a handheld electric mixer, beat the egg whites on high speed until soft peaks form. Set aside.

5 In another large bowl, combine the vanilla, granulated sugar, and egg yolks. With clean beaters, beat on high speed until pale yellow, about 5 minutes. Add the egg whites to the yolk mixture. Mix on medium speed to incorporate.

6 Add the flour, a little at a time, mixing on medium speed until fully incorporated. Pour the batter into the prepared pan.

7 Bake for about 40 minutes, until the top of the cake is golden brown and springy. Cool to room temperature.

continued

SPONGE CAKE

Butter, for preparing the pan
1½ cups (173 g) self-rising flour,
    plus more for dusting the pan
Confectioners' sugar, for dusting
    the pan
8 large eggs, separated
1 teaspoon vanilla extract
1 cup (200 g) granulated sugar

SOAK

¼ cup (60 ml) white rum
¼ cup (60 ml) warm water

DECORATION

Candied fruits and nuts, such as
    orange peels, cherries, citron,
    and pistachios

Home for the Holidays
*Usually for Lent, everyone gives
up sweets, so the* cassata, *and all
its sumptuousness, is eaten to break
the Lenten fast. In Palermo, we
love ornate desserts that are full of
sweetness. It's a part of our culture.*
—Nonna Liliana Barone

8 **To make the soak:** In a small bowl, combine the rum and water.

9 **To assemble the cassata:** Line the bottom of a 10-inch (25 cm) springform pan with plastic wrap. Dust the sides of the pan with a bit of flour.

10 Slice off the very top of the sponge cake dome and discard. Slice the cake horizontally into 3 even layers about 1 inch (2.5 cm) thick. Set aside the top layer of the cake, as this will become the bottom of the cake once inverted.

11 Slice the 2 remaining layers into strips about 2½ inches (6 cm) wide; the strips should be the same width as the height of the springform pan. Reserve the rounded edges for the bottom layer of the cake. Trim off the crust from the edges of the cake strips, making the edges straight.

12 Line the sides of the prepared pan with the cake strips. Line the bottom of the pan with the remaining pieces of cake, using the rounded edge pieces from the sides. Brush the cake with half of the soak.

13 Pour the ricotta filling into the pan and evenly spread it.

14 Trim off the crust from the edges of the remaining cake layer. Place the trimmed layer on top of the filling. Brush it with the remaining soak. Cover the cake with plastic wrap and refrigerate for at least 4 hours or overnight.

15 Release the springform pan and invert the cake onto a serving platter. Spread the ricotta frosting over the cake and decorate with candied fruits and nuts as desired. Serve chilled.

PUGLIESE EASTER BREAD

Scarcella di Pasqua

PREP TIME: 20 MINUTES • COOK TIME: 20 MINUTES • YIELD: 5 BRAIDED SCARCELLE

Nonna Romana's classic Easter bread from Puglia is my absolute favorite thing about Easter. A classic Pugliese *scarcella*, or *gurrugulo*, as they are called in Nonna's hometown of Mola di Bari, are traditionally given to children for Easter. Usually, they are shaped into a braided ring and an egg is placed on top with a cross over it to symbolize fertility. The dough of the scarcella is more like a cookie than bread, and it has the most wonderful lemon scent. The olive oil–based dough is super easy to work with, and once you get the hang of it, you can expand into making much more intricate shapes, like a purse or doll.

DOUGH

4¼ cups (510 g) all-purpose or 00 flour, plus more for working the dough
2 teaspoons baking powder
4 large eggs
1 cup (200 g) sugar
¾ cup (180 ml) olive oil
Zest of 1 lemon or 1 tablespoon (15 ml) Nonna Laura's Sweet Lemon Zest (page 13)

DECORATION

5 large eggs, dyed (not hard-boiled eggs)
1 large egg, beaten
Rainbow nonpareils, for decorating

Nonna Romana Says
If you have leftover dough, don't throw it away! Instead, make a little cookie or two by braiding it or twisting it. Get creative! I don't throw away anything!

1 Preheat the oven to 400°F (200°C). Line 2 baking sheets with parchment paper. Set aside.

2 **To make the dough:** In a large bowl, whisk together the flour and baking powder. Set aside.

3 In the bowl of a stand mixer fitted with the paddle attachment, combine the eggs, sugar, olive oil, and lemon zest. Mix on medium speed until combined. Add the flour–baking powder mixture. Mix on medium speed until the dry ingredients are absorbed.

4 Generously flour a work surface and turn the dough out onto it. Flour your hands. To make a braid, divide the dough into 15 equal pieces, reserving enough dough to secure the eggs in step 7. With your floured hands, roll one piece of dough into a rope about ¾ inch (2 cm) thick and 14 inches (35 cm) long. Repeat with 2 more dough pieces (you'll have 3 ropes at this point). Pinch the 3 ropes together at one end. Slowly and carefully, braid the 3 pieces to the very end. Pinch the end of the braid closed and trim any unevenness with a knife. Bring the ends of the braid together, overlapping them slightly, to form a ring.

5 Repeat, making the logs and braided rings, until you have 5 rings total. Quickly transfer the braided rings to the prepared baking sheets.

6 **To decorate:** Press the dough together where the ends overlap. Place 1 egg on top of the seam of each ring.

continued

7 Divide the reserved dough into 10 pieces. Roll each piece into a small rope about ¼ inch (6 mm) thick. Place 2 strips over each egg, forming a cross, pressing each end into the braid to secure it. Gently press the dough together where it overlaps on top of the egg.

8 Brush all the dough with the beaten egg, including the cross on top of the egg. Take care not to get any egg on the whole eggs themselves. Sprinkle the braids with nonpareils.

9 Bake for 15 to 18 minutes, or until the tops of the braids are lightly golden and shiny, and the bottoms are nicely browned. Serve at room temperature.

Home for the Holidays

Every year for Easter, since I was little, Nonna Romana would give me and all the children in my family a scarcella *in a clear plastic sandwich bag closed with a metal twist tie and say, 'Buona Pasqua, bella di Nonna! (Happy Easter, Nonna's darling!)' I'm a bit embarrassed to admit it now, but I didn't always appreciate this meaningful tradition. I wanted one of those beautifully wrapped chocolate eggs that I would see at the store, and not a braided cookie with an egg in it. Believe it or not, I wasn't always the perfect child! But one year, Nonna Romana turned to me and said, 'Chocolate! Do you think there was always chocolate, my love? Mamma had seven children and a chocolate egg for everyone wasn't possible then; it was just too expensive. But there were always eggs, a little flour, a little oil, a little bit of sugar. That's what we had and we were all happy!'*

Today, I've taken over making the scarcelle for all the children in the family. To me, it's a tradition no chocolate egg could ever live up to. —Rossella Rago

LEMON DROP COOKIES

Anginetti

PREP TIME: 15 MINUTES • COOK TIME: 15 MINUTES • YIELD: ABOUT 30 COOKIES

These lovely lemon drops are made in honor of many occasions in southern Italian families. Nonna Romana always makes these delightful cookies, in a variety of shapes, around Easter because their vibrant lemon flavor pairs perfectly with the onset of spring.

COOKIES

3 cups (360 g) all-purpose or
    00 flour, plus more for dusting
2 teaspoons baking powder
Pinch salt
¾ cup (150 g) granulated sugar
½ cup (1 stick, or 120 g) butter, at
    room temperature
Zest of 2 lemons or 2 tablespoons
    (30 ml) Nonna Laura's Sweet
    Lemon Zest (page 13)
1½ teaspoons lemon extract
1 packet (½ ounce, or 15 g) Italian
    vanilla powder or 1 teaspoon
    vanilla extract
2 large eggs, at room temperature
2 tablespoons (30 ml) heavy cream,
    at room temperature

GLAZE

1 cup (120 g) confectioners' sugar
Zest of 1 lemon
Juice of 1 lemon or 1 tablespoon
    (15 ml) Nonna Laura's Sweet
    Lemon Zest (page 13)
1 teaspoon vanilla extract
3 tablespoons (45 ml) whole milk
White nonpareils, for decorating

1   Preheat the oven to 350°F (180°C). Line 2 baking sheets with parchment paper. Set aside.

2   **To make the cookies:** In a medium bowl, whisk together the flour, baking powder, and salt. Set aside.

3   In the bowl of a stand mixer fitted with the paddle attachment, combine the sugar, butter, lemon zest, lemon extract, and vanilla. Mix on medium speed until fluffy, about 5 minutes. Add the eggs, one at a time, mixing on medium speed until fully incorporated.

4   Reduce the speed to low and add the flour mixture. Mix until almost fully absorbed. Add the heavy cream. Mix until just combined.

5   Lightly flour a work surface and turn the dough out onto it. Divide the dough in half. With one half of the dough, make twists, and the other half, make knots. To make twists: Flour your hands. Grab a chunk of dough and roll it into a ½-inch-thick (13 mm) rope. Cut pieces from the rope, each about 8 inches (20 cm) long. Fold each piece in half and twist it 3 times, pressing the ends together. To make knots: Flour your hands. Grab a chunk of dough and roll it into a ¾-inch-thick (2 cm) rope about 6 inches (15 cm) long. Shape the rope into a knot by bringing one end over the other, then through the middle. Continue making twists and knots with the remaining dough.

6   Arrange the cookies on the prepared baking sheets, 2 inches (5 cm) apart. Bake for 12 to 15 minutes, until the bottoms are golden brown. Cool completely before icing.

7   **To make the glaze:** In a small bowl, whisk together the confectioners' sugar, lemon zest, lemon juice, vanilla, and milk. Sprinkle the icing with white nonpareils. Dip the cookies into the glaze and place them on a wire rack to dry.

GENOVESE-STYLE FOCACCIA WITH ONIONS

Focaccia Genovese con Cipolle

PREP TIME: 2 HOURS • COOK TIME: 30 MINUTES • YIELD: 8 TO 10 SERVINGS

If you've ever had a piece of warm, freshly baked *focaccia* in Italy, you'll understand why it's such an important part of Italian cuisine. Romans would give pieces of focaccia as an offering to their gods, and ever since, every region has its own specialty focaccia. This version is topped simply with white onions. What sets it apart is the water and oil emulsion that fills tiny indentations made by hand in the dough.

DOUGH

½ cup (120 ml) extra-virgin olive oil, divided, plus more for brushing

2 packets (¼ ounce, or 7 g, each) active dry yeast

1½ cups (350 ml) warm water

4 cups (480 g) all-purpose or 00 flour

2 teaspoons salt

FOCACCIA

¼ cup (60 ml) water

6 tablespoons (90 ml) extra-virgin olive oil, divided

1½ teaspoons coarse salt

2 large onions, halved, with halves sliced into thin half-moons

1 **To make the dough:** In the bowl of a stand mixer fitted with the dough hook attachment, combine ¼ cup (60 ml) of the olive oil, the yeast, and warm water. Let stand for 5 to 8 minutes, until the yeast dissolves.

2 In a medium bowl, whisk together the flour and salt. With the mixer running on low speed, gradually add the flour. Mix for 8 to 10 minutes, until a smooth, supple dough forms.

3 Brush a large bowl with olive oil and transfer the dough to it. Brush the dough ball with olive oil too. Cover the bowl with plastic wrap and set aside in a warm place to rise for 1 hour, or until the dough doubles in size. Punch down the dough.

4 Preheat the oven to 475°F (240°C).

5 Add the remaining ¼ cup (60 ml) olive oil to an 18 × 13-inch (46 × 33 cm) baking sheet and spread it evenly, making sure to coat the bottom and sides of the pan. With your fingers, spread the dough to the edges of the pan, starting from the center and working outward. Cover the dough with plastic wrap and set aside to rise in a warm place for 1 hour. Remove the plastic wrap, and using your fingertips, lightly make indentations all over the dough.

6 **To assemble the focaccia:** In a small bowl, whisk the water and ¼ cup (60 ml) of the olive oil. Pour the mixture over the dough, making sure to fill all the indentations. Sprinkle the dough with the salt.

7 In a medium bowl, drizzle the onions with the remaining 2 tablespoons (30 ml) olive oil. Toss to coat. Scatter the onions over the focaccia. Bake for about 30 minutes, or until the top of the focaccia is golden and the onions have completely softened.

BROCCOLI RABE AND SAUSAGE FRITTATA

Frittata di Cime di Rapa e Salsiccia

PREP TIME: 10 MINUTES • COOK TIME: 55 MINUTES • YIELD: 6 TO 8 SERVINGS

Nonna Romana likes to recall when she and her seven brothers and sisters would go into *la campagna* (the countryside) of Mola di Bari to celebrate *la Pasquetta*. Such an occasion would require a frittata fit for an army! Today, our family celebrates *la Pasquetta* in Nonna's Brooklyn basement apartment, but this frittata, which is baked instead of fried, keeps filling our stomachs and our souls, year after year.

1 teaspoon salt, plus more to taste

8 ounces (227 g) broccoli rabe, washed, ends trimmed, and chopped into bite-size pieces

½ cup (120 ml) plus 3 tablespoons (45 ml) extra-virgin olive oil, divided

8 ounces (227 g) sweet Italian sausage, casings removed

8 large eggs

3 cloves garlic, minced

¾ cup (90 g) plain bread crumbs

¼ cup (60 ml) whole milk

1½ cups (150 g) grated Pecorino Romano cheese

¼ teaspoon black pepper

Nonna Romana Says
This frittata is ideally made in a cast-iron skillet, but if you must use another pan, make sure to add a bit more olive oil to the bottom.

1 Bring a medium stockpot of lightly salted water to a boil. Drop in the broccoli rabe and blanch just until the stems are tender, about 5 minutes. Drain and run under cold water. Squeeze out the excess moisture with your hands. Set aside.

2 Heat 1 tablespoon (15 ml) of the olive oil in a medium cast-iron skillet (see Nonna Romana Says) over medium-high heat. Add the sausage to the skillet. Cook for 7 to 9 minutes, breaking it up with a wooden spoon, until the sausage has browned nicely. Transfer to a plate and set aside.

3 In a medium bowl, add the eggs, garlic, bread crumbs, milk, cheese, 1 teaspoon salt, pepper, and 2 tablespoons (30 ml) of the olive oil. Combine until smooth.

4 Mix in the broccoli rabe and sausage. Set aside.

5 Preheat the oven to 400°F (200°C).

6 Heat the remaining ½ cup (120 ml) olive oil in a medium cast-iron or oven-safe skillet over high heat. Add the egg mixture to the skillet and spread it evenly in the pan using a spoon or a rubber scraper. Cook for 2 to 3 minutes, until the eggs have just set around the edges. Transfer the skillet to the middle rack of the oven.

7 Bake for 30 to 35 minutes, until the middle of the frittata is set and golden brown. Serve warm or at room temperature.

BATTERED CAULIFLOWER AND BABY ARTICHOKES

Cavolfiori e Carciofini Fritti in Pastella

PREP TIME: 10 MINUTES • COOK TIME: 25 MINUTES • YIELD: 8 TO 10 SERVINGS

Nonna Romana's classic Puglia-style batter, bursting with garlic, cheese, and mint, creates a light, crispy coating on your favorite vegetables. Artichokes and cauliflower are a wonderful pairing of flavors and have contrasting textures that pack a ton of flavor in every bite.

2 pounds (907 g) fresh baby artichokes

2 lemons, halved

1¼ cups (125 g) grated Parmigiano-Reggiano cheese

½ cup (32 g) minced fresh mint

6 cloves garlic, minced

1 teaspoon salt

2 large eggs, beaten

1½ cups (350 ml) plus 2 tablespoons (30 ml) water

10 ounces (280 g) fresh cauliflower florets

Oil, for frying

1 Fill a large bowl with cold water and set aside.

2 Clean the artichokes by removing the outer leaves until you reach the yellow or light green part of the artichokes. Remove and discard the artichokes' stems. Quarter the artichokes and place them in the bowl filled with cold water. Add the halved lemons to prevent browing.

3 In another large bowl, add the cheese, mint, garlic, salt, eggs, and water. Whisk until you have a smooth batter.

4 Pat the artichokes dry with a paper towel and add them to the batter. Add the cauliflower florets and mix well so the vegetables are coated.

5 Line a plate with paper towels and set aside.

6 Heat about 1½ inches (4 cm) of oil in a large heavy-bottomed skillet over medium-high heat. Working in batches, fry the battered vegetables until golden brown, 5 to 6 minutes per batch. Transfer to the paper towel–lined plate. Serve hot.

PUGLIA-STYLE STUFFED ARTICHOKES

Carciofi Ripieni alla Pugliese

PREP TIME: 15 MINUTES • COOK TIME: 30 MINUTES • YIELD: 4 SERVINGS

Nonna Romana's stuffed-artichoke recipe from Mola di Bari has been made in my family for generations. The beautiful spring peas and savory pancetta cook up some serious flavor and make for a vibrant side dish. Traditionally, these would be made for Easter, and any leftovers would have been taken into the country to celebrate *la Pasquetta* picnic.

4 medium fresh artichokes

2 lemons, halved

1 cup (100 g) grated Pecorino Romano cheese

½ cup (60 g) plain bread crumbs

2 large eggs

3 cloves garlic, minced

1 tablespoon (4 g) minced fresh parsley

½ teaspoon salt, plus more to taste

¼ teaspoon black pepper, plus more to taste

6 tablespoons (90 ml) extra-virgin olive oil, divided

2 tablespoons (30 ml) whole milk, as needed

12 ounces (340 g) frozen peas, thawed

1 medium onion, cut into ¼-inch (6 mm) dice

4 ounces (113 g) pancetta, cut into ½-inch (13 mm) cubes

2 cups (475 ml) water

❚ Nonna Romana Says
I usually like to make these the night before I serve them, so the filling has a chance to rest and absorb all the flavors.

1 Clean the artichokes by removing the outer leaves until you reach the light green part of the artichokes. Remove and discard the tough outer skin from the stems. Cut off the top parts of the leaves, about ¾ inch (2 cm); trim ¼ inch (6 mm) off the bottom of the stems and peel the stems. Halve the artichokes vertically through the stem. With a small spoon, scoop out and discard the fuzzy choke. Place the artichoke halves in a bowl filled with cold water and add the halved lemons to prevent browning.

2 In another large bowl, combine the cheese, bread crumbs, eggs, garlic, parsley, salt, pepper, and 3 tablespoons (45 ml) of the olive oil. Stir to combine. If the mixture is dry, add 1 tablespoon (15 ml) of milk at a time until you achieve a soft consistency. The mixture should be soft, not runny.

3 Preheat the oven to 350°F (180°C).

4 In the bottom of a 13 × 9-inch (33 × 23 cm) stovetop-safe baking dish, combine the peas, onion, pancetta, and the remaining 3 tablespoons (45 ml) olive oil. Season with salt and pepper. Mix well so everything is coated in the oil.

5 Spread 2 tablespoons (30 g) of filling over each artichoke half. Place the stuffed artichoke, filling side up, over the bed of peas.

6 Pour the water into the bottom of the pan. Put the pan on the stovetop over high heat and bring to a boil.

7 Transfer the pan to the oven and bake for about 30 minutes, until the peas are cooked and the artichokes are tender.

NEAPOLITAN SPAGHETTI PIE

Frittata di Spaghetti alla Napoletana

PREP TIME: 10 MINUTES • COOK TIME: 20 MINUTES • YIELD: 6 TO 8 SERVINGS

This traditional spaghetti pie is a post-Easter favorite at Nonna Lorella's house. It's the perfect thing to make if you're going on a picnic, because it tastes divine at room temperature, and it easily can be served by cutting it into wedges. It's also a great way to utilize any leftover pasta you have, even if it has sauce on it. The secret to flipping it without making a mess is not to rush and to let the bottom cook enough to get the pasta nice and brown. "You want to make sure you have crispy edges all over," says Nonna Lorella. I totally agree—that's the best part!

1 cup (250 g) whole-milk ricotta

5 ounces (142 g) dry sausage, cut into ¼-inch (6 mm) dice (you can also use prosciutto, pancetta, or ham)

5 large eggs, beaten

¾ cup (75 g) grated Pecorino Romano cheese

4 ounces (113 g) fresh mozzarella cheese, shredded

1 teaspoon salt

½ teaspoon black pepper

1 tablespoon (15 g) unsalted butter, at room temperature

8 ounces (227 g) dried spaghetti, cooked al dente (you can also use leftover spaghetti, even if it has sauce on it)

2 tablespoons (30 ml) extra-virgin olive oil

1 In a large bowl, whisk together the ricotta, sausage, eggs, Pecorino Romano, mozzarella, salt, pepper, and butter.

2 Add the spaghetti to the bowl and mix well until the pasta is coated in the egg mixture.

3 Heat the olive oil in a large nonstick skillet over medium-high heat. Pour the pasta mixture into the skillet and spread it into an even layer. Reduce the heat to medium-low. Cover the skillet and cook for 10 to 12 minutes, until the bottom and sides of the frittata are set.

4 Wearing oven mitts on both hands, uncover the skillet and place a large plate or large, flat lid over the pan. Quickly flip the pan over so the frittata rests on the plate. Quickly slide the frittata back into the skillet. Cook for 5 to 7 minutes more, until set.

THANKSGIVING

Home for the Holidays

I remember my first Thanksgiving so well. It brought tears to my eyes. My mother was still back in Italy and only my father and my brother were here in America. My father worked in a factory and his boss gifted us a big turkey, which I had never really seen before. It was so big! I had no idea how to cook it. In Italy, we would have a capon once in a while for holidays, but never a turkey. I was so nervous, but I asked a few of my new American neighbors what to do and they showed me. —Nonna Maria Fiore

NONNA MARIA PESCE'S

BUTTERNUT SQUASH LASAGNA

Lasagne di Zucca

PREP TIME: 35 MINUTES • COOK TIME: 1 HOUR 40 MINUTES • YIELD: 6 SERVINGS

Italian-Americans can't seem to celebrate Thanksgiving without a pasta course preceding the turkey. You know, just in case a twelve-pound (5.4 kg) turkey with all the trimmings isn't enough food. *Lasagne* or some other kind of *pasta al forno* is a classic choice. I first tasted Nonna Maria's yummy, autumn-inspired lasagna three years ago when my boyfriend Nick invited me over for our first Thanksgiving together. When I told her it was fantastic, I'm sure she thought that I was just being polite (after all, I was her son's new girlfriend and she is a quintessential Italian Mamma), but my reaction was totally genuine. She starts by cooking chunks of butternut squash with aromatics and purees it into a velvety sauce, which adds a delightful sweetness to the dish. She then layers it with delicious mortadella and bakes it to perfection. It even tastes great the next day, reheated after a marathon of Black Friday shopping.

SAUCE

2 tablespoons (30 ml) extra-virgin olive oil

3 celery ribs, cut into ¼-inch (6 mm) dice

1 small carrot, cut into ¼-inch (6 mm) dice

1 small onion, cut into ¼-inch (6 mm) dice

¾ cup (182 g) canned crushed tomatoes

¼ cup (60 ml) cold water

1 teaspoon salt, plus more to taste

Black pepper, to taste

2½ pounds (1.3 kg) butternut squash, cut into 1-inch (2.5 cm) dice

1 **To make the sauce:** Put a skillet over medium heat and add the olive oil, celery, carrot, and onion. Cook for 7 to 10 minutes, until soft.

2 Stir in the tomatoes, cold water, salt, and pepper. Cook for 15 minutes.

3 In a large saucepan over high heat, bring 4 cups (960 ml) of water to a boil. Stir in the butternut squash and season with salt. Cook for 25 to 30 minutes, until soft. Remove from the heat, drain, and let cool for 15 minutes.

4 Transfer the cooled butternut squash to a blender with the sauce and puree until smooth. Transfer to a medium bowl. Set aside.

5 **To make the lasagna:** Preheat the oven to 400°F (200°C). Butter a 13 × 9-inch (33 × 23 cm) baking pan. Set aside.

6 Bring a medium stockpot of salted water to a boil. Drop in the lasagna noodles and cook until very al dente, about 10 minutes. Drain and run the noodles under cold running water. Fold all the noodles over the edge of the pot to dry.

continued

LASAGNA

Unsalted butter, for greasing

Salt, to taste

17 or 18 dried lasagna pasta
noodles

2 large eggs, beaten

16 ounces (454 g) fresh mozzarella
cheese, cut into ¼-inch (6 mm)
cubes

12 ounces (340 g) mortadella or
ham, about 12 slices (optional)

½ cup (50 g) grated Parmigiano-
Reggiano cheese, divided

7   Spread 1¼ cups (300 ml) of sauce over the bottom of the prepared
pan and lay about 4 lasagna noodles to cover the sauce completely.
Spread another ½ cup (120 ml) of sauce over the noodles and drizzle
with 2 to 3 teaspoons of the beaten egg.

8   Top with one-quarter of the mozzarella, one-third of the
mortadella (if using), and 2 tablespoons (13 g) of the Parmigiano-
Reggiano. Repeat the layering twice more. Add the final layer
of noodles to cover the entire surface. Spread 1 cup (240 ml)
of the sauce over the noodles and top with the remaining
beaten egg, mozzarella, and remaining 2 tablespoons (13 g)
Parmigiano-Reggiano.

9   Bake for 30 to 40 minutes, or until the pasta is very easily
pierced with a fork. Let rest for 15 to 20 minutes before cutting
and serving with any leftover sauce on the side.

RICE AND MEAT STUFFING

Ripieno di Riso e Carne

PREP TIME: 15 MINUTES • COOK TIME: 1 HOUR 15 MINUTES • YIELD: 8 TO 10 SERVINGS

The concept of stuffing has always been a bit strange for Italian-Americans to grasp, especially for the immigrant generation. So, when Nonna Liliana was coming up with a way to make stuffing, she immediately thought about the foods Italians *do* stuff: peppers, eggplant, etc. This stuffing is full of Italian flavors and is reminiscent of classic stuffed peppers; at the same time, it is satisfying and goes well with classic American roasted turkey.

3½ cups (840 ml) water

½ teaspoon salt, plus a pinch and more to taste

1 cup (185 g) long-grain rice, rinsed

2 celery ribs, minced

1 small carrot, minced

1 pound (454 g) sweet Italian sausage, casings removed

1 pound (454 g) ground beef

2 bay leaves

5 tablespoons (75 ml) extra-virgin olive oil

6 bunches scallions, green stalks removed and white bulbs cut into ¼-inch (6 mm) dice

Black pepper, to taste

¼ cup (34 g) pinoli (pine nuts)

10 ounces (280 g) cremini mushrooms, sliced

1½ teaspoons fennel seeds

1 cup (240 ml) beef broth

1 In a large saucepan, combine the water and ½ teaspoon of salt, and bring to a boil. Add the rice. Boil, uncovered, for about 15 minutes, until the rice is halfway cooked. Drain and spread the rice in a thin layer on a large plate to cool. Set aside.

2 In a small saucepan, combine the celery and carrot with enough water to cover. Bring to a boil. Cook, uncovered, for 5 minutes. Drain and set aside.

3 Put a large skillet over medium-high heat and add the sausage, ground beef, a pinch of salt, and the bay leaves. Cook and stir for 7 to 10 minutes, until the meat is nicely browned. Drain the fat and set aside.

4 Heat the olive oil in another large heavy-bottomed skillet over medium heat. Add the scallions. Season with salt and pepper. Cook and stir for 10 to 12 minutes, until the scallions are soft. Add the pinoli and cook for 2 to 3 minutes more.

5 Add the mushrooms and cook for 4 to 6 minutes. Add the meat mixture to the scallion-mushroom mixture, along with the fennel seeds and the carrot-celery mixture. Cook for 2 to 3 minutes.

6 Stir in the broth and the cooled rice. Cook for about 5 minutes, until the rice is tender. Transfer to a serving dish. Serve warm.

Home for the Holidays
I still cook for the holidays because I enjoy it. You have to enjoy it; if you don't, the food doesn't taste the same. —Nonna Liliana Barone

PARMIGIANO ROASTED VEGETABLES

Verdure al Forno con Parmigiano

PREP TIME: 10 MINUTES • COOK TIME: 35 MINUTES • YIELD: 6 TO 8 SERVINGS

Nonna and I love this easy vegetable dish because it's a breeze to prep. Toss everything in the bread crumb and cheese mixture and roast until the veggies are beautifully charred. Feel free to swap out the veggies for your seasonal favourites.

10 cloves garlic, peeled

1 pound (454 g) small red potatoes, quartered

9 ounces (255 g) Brussels sprouts, ends trimmed and halved

8 ounces (227 g) baby carrots

1 large sweet potato, peeled and cut into 1½-inch (4 cm) chunks

¾ cup (180 ml) extra-virgin olive oil

½ cup (50 g) grated Parmigiano-Reggiano cheese

¼ cup (30 g) plain bread crumbs

1½ teaspoons salt

½ teaspoon black pepper

5 fresh rosemary sprigs

5 fresh thyme sprigs

1 Preheat the oven to 450°F (230°C).

2 Spread out all the vegetables on a baking sheet. Pour the olive oil over the vegetables and sprinkle with the cheese, bread crumbs, salt, and pepper. Add the rosemary and thyme.

3 Either with your hands or a large spoon, stir the vegetables until they are coated in the mixture.

4 Roast for 30 to 35 minutes, turning the vegetables halfway through the cooking time. Serve immediately.

THANKSGIVING CITRUS TURKEY

Tacchino agli Agrumi

PREP TIME: 15 MINUTES • COOK TIME: 3 HOURS 10 MINUTES • YIELD: 8 TO 10 SERVINGS

No Thanksgiving holiday would be complete without a turkey. Nonna Maria confesses that she was a bit lost her first Thanksgiving in America when faced with the unfamiliar bird. (In Italy, turkey is rarely eaten; capon, if anything, is prepared in its place.) But over the years she learned to love the American-style tradition. She did add her own Italian flair to the preparation, of course!

TURKEY

13-pound (5.9 kg) turkey, thawed if frozen
½ cup (1 stick, or 120 g) salted butter, at room temperature
⅓ cup (80 ml) extra-virgin olive oil
¼ cup (8 g) minced fresh rosemary
Salt, to taste
Black pepper, taste

STUFFING

1 navel orange, halved
1 lemon, halved
1 apple, halved
5 cloves garlic, peeled
4 to 5 fresh rosemary sprigs
4 to 5 fresh thyme sprigs
6 to 7 fresh sage leaves
2 tablespoons (30 ml) dry white wine, such as Pinot Grigio

TRIMMINGS

3 lemons, halved
1 orange, quartered
15 cloves garlic, peeled
1 cup (240 ml) dry white wine, such as Pinot Grigio
1 cup (240 ml) water

1 **To make the turkey:** Preheat the oven to 350°F (180°C).

2 Pull the neck and giblets out of the turkey's cavity and discard. Using kitchen shears or a sharp knife, trim the skin from the neck of the turkey and discard. Pat the turkey dry with paper towels, making sure to dry the inside of the cavity as well.

3 Lift the skin over the turkey breast (on the side closest to the legs) and slide your hand under the skin, separating it from the breast meat. Do this on both sides of the breast. With your hands, spread the butter underneath the loosened turkey skin, spreading it evenly on both sides of the breast.

4 In a small bowl, stir together the olive oil and rosemary. Rub the mixture over the entire surface of the turkey. Season the turkey well with salt and pepper, seasoning the inside of the cavity as well.

5 **To make the stuffing:** Fill the cavity with the halved orange, lemon, and apple. Insert the garlic, rosemary, thyme, and sage, and pour in the wine.

6 **To make the trimmings:** Place the turkey, breast side up, inside the rack of a roasting pan. Place the halved lemons, orange quarters, and garlic around the turkey. Pour the wine and water into the bottom of the pan.

7 Tent the turkey with aluminum foil and roast for 2 hours and 30 minutes. Remove the foil and roast for 30 to 40 minutes more, or until an instant-read meat thermometer reads 175° to 180°F (79° to 82°C). Let stand for 15 to 20 minutes before slicing and serving.

BROCCOLI RABE AND SAUSAGE STUFFING

Ripieno di Cime di Rapa e Salsiccia

PREP TIME: 15 MINUTES • COOK TIME: 1 HOUR 20 MINUTES • YIELD: 8 SERVINGS

Growing up as a first-generation Italian-American, I would sometimes long for classic American fare in an attempt to assimilate with the kids at school. My brother and I would take trips to the supermarket in secret to buy boxed stuffing (don't judge), cook it while no one was in the kitchen, and pray no one else noticed it on the table. The secrecy eventually became too much, and I realized I needed to come up with a stuffing recipe the rest of my family would want to eat. Nonna Romana actually looks forward to this stuffing every year!

½ cup (1 stick, or 120 g) unsalted butter, melted, plus more for greasing

1 large loaf Italian bread, torn into bite-size pieces (about 8 cups, or 280 g)

¼ cup (60 ml) extra-virgin olive oil, divided

1 pound (454 g) sweet Italian sausage, casings removed

3 celery ribs, minced

2 medium carrots, minced

10 cloves fresh garlic, sliced

1 bunch broccoli rabe, washed, ends trimmed, and cut into bite-size pieces

Salt, to taste

2½ cups (600 ml) chicken broth, divided

2 large eggs

1 cup (100 g) grated Pecorino Romano cheese

Black pepper, to taste

1 Preheat the oven to 400°F (200°C). Grease a large casserole dish and a sheet of aluminum foil with butter. Set aside.

2 Spread out the bread on 2 baking sheets. Bake the bread until dry, about 10 minutes. Remove from the oven and transfer to a large bowl. Set aside.

3 Heat 2 tablespoons (30 ml) of the olive oil in a large skillet with a lid over medium heat. Add the sausage and cook and stir while breaking it up into small pieces with a wooden spoon. Cook until the sausage has browned, 7 to 10 minutes. Transfer to a plate using a slotted spoon. Set aside.

4 Add the remaining 2 tablespoons (30 ml) olive oil to the pan, along with the celery, carrots, and garlic. Cook until the celery and carrots are slightly softened, about 5 minutes. Add the broccoli rabe and a generous sprinkle of salt. Cook until the broccoli rabe begins to wilt, 3 to 4 minutes. Add the sausage back to the pan. Add ½ cup (120 ml) of the chicken broth to the pan. Cover and cook until the broccoli rabe has softened considerably and the liquid has evaporated, 8 to 10 minutes. Remove from the heat and add to the bowl with the bread.

5 In a medium bowl, whisk together the remaining 2 cups (480 ml) broth, the eggs, melted butter, cheese, salt, and pepper. Pour the mixture over the bread, little by little, while mixing with a spoon. It may appear dry at first, but just keep mixing. Transfer the mixture to the prepared casserole dish and cover with the foil, butter side down.

6 Bake for 20 minutes. Uncover and bake for an additional 20 minutes, or until the top is golden brown.

MARSALA PEAS AND MUSHROOMS

Funghi e Piselli con Marsala

PREP TIME: 5 MINUTES • COOK TIME: 30 MINUTES • YIELD: 4 TO 6 SERVINGS

It's amazing how just a splash of Marsala wine can add so much flavor to a dish. Nonna Maria loves dressing up simple peas and mushrooms, which soak up the wine beautifully, as an elegant holiday side dish that is anything but boring.

1 large onion, cut into ½-inch (13 mm) dice

2 tablespoons (30 ml) extra-virgin olive oil

Salt, to taste

Black pepper, to taste

10 ounces (280 g) frozen peas, thawed

10 ounces (280 g) cremini mushrooms, sliced

¼ cup (60 ml) sweet Marsala wine

2 tablespoons (30 ml) water

1 Put a medium skillet over medium heat and add the onion and olive oil. Season with salt and pepper as desired. Cook and stir for 10 to 12 minutes, until the onion is very soft.

2 Stir in the peas, mushrooms, and a bit more salt. Cook and stir for 5 to 7 minutes, or until some water has been drawn out of the mushrooms.

3 Stir in the Marsala and water. Cook for 7 to 10 minutes, or until no alcohol can be tasted and the liquid has reduced by half.

"I wouldn't feel right if I didn't make the baccalà or the seafood salad myself. It's a part of our culture as Molesi, a piece of who we are."

"I have always been a person who lived for her family, *tutto per i figli*, (all for my children)" Nonna Maria Pesce says resolutely as I help her make a second lasagna for Sunday dinner. We're testing the recipe for her famous Butternut Squash Lasagna (see recipe on page 95), but her husband prefers her classic red version with pieces of mortadella in it. She's the type of Nonna who will cook something different to accommodate each of her three grandchildren if they ask her to, always with a smile. "I give my three children and my grandchildren everything I have. I live for them. All the grandchildren are different from each other. It's beautiful to see all their different characters, and how much they like the food I make for them."

Nonna Maria is especially important to me, as she isn't just any Nonna, she's the mother of the man I love. I still remember nervously anticipating the day of our first meeting and wondering if she would like me. I had already seen her at a few cultural events in the neighborhood, always impeccably dressed and beautifully coiffed; she seemed more like Queen Maria than Nonna Maria. We met about six months into my relationship with her son, Nick, and she was finally glad to get to know the person who had been sending him home with so many cakes. Over the years, we've built a relationship full of great respect, and I can say we genuinely enjoy each other's company.

After we finish cooking, she sits before me in the sunroom of her impressive home in Dyker Heights, Brooklyn, an area made famous for its Christmas-light displays and a long way from her hometown. I ask her about her memories growing up in Mola di Bari. "It was a happy life there. My mother, Giovanna, was very strong. She raised five children and had a store in town that she fed us from." Maria's father, like many men at that time, had gone abroad to Venezuela to work and help support the family by sending money back home. It was something my very own Nonno Nino had done. "We missed him very much, but you did what you had to then. When he came back, we were so happy to finally be together."

But it was from her mother that Maria inherited her passion for cooking. "My mother was a brilliant cook. When people were getting married, they would call my mother to come and help them with the catered food, because she really knew what she was doing. They were all friends who lived on the same street as us. They would call out from the balconies *"Giovanna! Devi venire?* (Giovanna! Are you coming?)" And she would go. It was so beautiful because everyone helped each other," she continues. "She always stressed how important it is to learn how to make the traditional food. For my first daughter's baptism, my mother made all the traditional almond cookies for the party. She looked at me and said, 'Make sure you watch because I won't live forever.' "

It's clear that Nonna Maria took those beautiful words to heart. Anyone who has been lucky enough to be her guest for Christmas Eve dinner knows just how much *amore* she puts into tradition. "I wake up at 5 a.m. on Christmas Eve and start cooking. I still feel good, so I still do it. I'm used to it and the cooking adds to the energy of the holiday. I wouldn't feel right if I didn't make the baccalà or the seafood salad myself. It's a part of our culture as Molesi, a piece of who we are."

"Growing up, we had a very simple life. Saturdays in *piazza*, mass every Sunday, and summers at the beach." She shows me a portrait of her and her husband taken shortly after their marriage: a beautiful couple who look in love despite their modest grins. "I met my husband for the first time when I was thirteen and he was sixteen. He went into the merchant marines, and then to America with his family, but he always thought about me. When I was twenty-two, he came back to town, and within nine months, we were married."

Their wedding and all its preparations were steeped in great tradition. "At the time, there were no bridal showers, so your *corredo* (bridal trousseau) was displayed all over the house and people would come and visit you to congratulate you in the days leading up to your wedding. I had *panna dieci*, which meant that I had ten pairs of everything. Ten bedsheets, ten tablecloths, ten linens, etc. At the time it meant great sacrifice to have all those things. People would come and you would have coffee and cookies," she smiles, remembering those happy times.

Shortly after the wedding, Maria knew she would leave for America to begin a new life. "I remember my very first day in America. It was very chilly and my cousin who had come to pick us up from the port had a cup of coffee for me, and she told me don't expect it to be espresso from Italy! It's American coffee! I had never tasted it before." She and her husband spent their days as newlyweds living with her mother-in-law, who was the undisputed matriarch of the family. "My mother-in-law was a little tough, but she was a good woman. I'm lucky that when I got married, I already knew how to cook well, so I even taught her a thing or two!" she says giggling.

While Maria stayed home with the children, her husband risked their savings by buying a local supermarket with his two brothers, a business move that would later become the genesis of the family businesses: La Bella Marketplace, a chain of Italian markets, and Bella Mia Foods, an importer of fine Italian foodstuffs. "At the time, we were either going to buy a house or buy the store, and it was a scary thought, but *grazie a Dio*! (thank God!) Everything was okay," she says as she gazes toward the corner shrine in gratitude. "It wasn't easy. People see a picture of success but don't see the sacrifices that go into it. There were so many days my husband brought home the produce that wasn't perfect, and it was my job to make a meal out of it and feed our kids. We both worked hard. Him outside and me inside, but we did it so our community could have the food they remembered from our home."

NONNA ANTOINETTE CAPODICCI'S

PUMPKIN RISOTTO

Risotto alla Zucca

PREP TIME: 10 MINUTES • COOK TIME: 30 MINUTES • YIELD: 10 TO 12 SERVINGS

This incredibly rich risotto will leave all your guests satisfied. It gets its lovely color from the pumpkin puree and its unique flavor from the Fontina cheese, which takes the place of butter in the *mantecare* process, when the ingredients are creamed together. This recipe makes a large batch that Nonna Antoinette usually serves buffet-style for her big Italian-American Thanksgiving, which never has fewer than a dozen people.

2 quarts (1.9 L) chicken broth

3 tablespoons (45 ml) extra-virgin olive oil

6 ounces (170 g) pancetta, cut into ¼-inch (6 mm) dice

1 large red onion, cut into ¼-inch (6 mm) dice

2 cloves garlic, minced

24 ounces (679 g) Arborio rice, rinsed

1 pound (454 g) butternut squash, fresh or frozen, cut into ½-inch (13 mm) dice

1 can (15 ounces, or 425 g) pure pumpkin (not pumpkin pie filling)

6 ounces (170 g) Parmigiano-Reggiano cheese, coarsely grated

6 ounces (170 g) Fontina cheese, cut into ½-inch (13 mm) dice

2 teaspoons salt

Black pepper, to taste

Dash ground nutmeg

1 In a small stockpot over medium-high heat, bring the chicken broth to a simmer, keeping it at a simmer.

2 Heat the olive oil in a large heavy-bottomed skillet with a lid over medium heat. Add the pancetta and cook and stir for 5 to 7 minutes, until crispy. Add the onion and garlic, and cook and stir for 2 to 3 minutes, until the garlic is golden.

3 Add the rice to the skillet and toast for 2 to 3 minutes. Add the butternut squash and cook for 5 minutes, stirring with a wooden spoon.

4 Reduce the heat under the skillet to low. Stir in 1 cup (240 ml) of simmering broth and cover the skillet. Every minute or so, or when you see the broth has been absorbed, stir in more broth. Stir frequently to prevent sticking. Continue this process until all the broth is absorbed and the rice is al dente, 20 to 25 minutes.

5 Add the pumpkin and cheeses, stirring until the cheeses are melted and everything is fully incorporated.

6 Taste and season with salt, pepper, and a dash of nutmeg. Let rest for 10 minutes before serving.

SICILIAN POTATO PIE

Gattò di Patate

PREP TIME: 15 MINUTES • COOK TIME: 1 HOUR 30 MINUTES • YIELD: 10 SERVINGS

A *gattò* is a savory potato pie layered with different meats and cheeses typical of the regions of Sicily and Campania. Nonna Liliana fills her gattò with savory *prosciutto cotto* and provolone, and makes it every Thanksgiving in place of mashed potatoes as a way of melding cultures.

Salt, to taste

5 pounds (2.3 kg) Idaho potatoes, washed and peeled

3 tablespoons (45 ml) extra-virgin olive oil, plus more for greasing the pan and drizzling

¾ cup (180 ml) whole milk

½ cup (1 stick, or 120 g) unsalted butter, melted

¾ cup (75 g) grated Pecorino Romano cheese

3 large eggs, at room temperature

3 tablespoons (12 g) chopped fresh parsley (optional)

¼ cup (30 g) plain bread crumbs, plus more for sprinkling

4 ounces (113 g) provolone cheese, sliced

4 ounces (113 g) sliced ham

8 ounces (227 g) fresh mozzarella, sliced

1 Bring a large stockpot of generously salted water to a boil. Drop the potatoes in, whole, and cook until a fork can easily pierce a potato, about 30 minutes.

2 Preheat the oven to 375°F (190°C). Grease a 13 × 9-inch (33 × 23 cm) pan with olive oil. Set aside

3 Drain the potatoes and transfer them to a large bowl. While the potatoes are still warm, push the potatoes through a ricer and mix well with a spatula until smooth.

4 Add the milk, butter, and Pecorino Romano to the potatoes. Taste for seasoning and add salt as needed. Add the eggs to the mixture and combine well.

5 Sprinkle ¼ cup (30 g) bread crumbs over the bottom and sides of the prepared pan.

6 Evenly spread half of the potato mixture into the pan. Over the potatoes, place a layer of the provolone, followed by a layer of the ham and then a layer of the mozzarella.

7 Spread the remaining half of the potato mixture into the pan. Using a fork, refine the surface and create some grooves.

8 Drizzle some olive oil over the potatoes and sprinkle a thin coat of bread crumbs over the top.

9 Bake for 45 to 60 minutes. Place the gattò under the broiler to give it a little color.

Home for the Holidays
When I first came to America, we would have Thanksgiving at my sister-in-law's house. It was one day a year when we tried our hardest to eat only American Thanksgiving food, but over the years, I snuck my gattó in there!
—Nonna Liliana Barone

NONNA ROSA CARMELO'S

HONEY SWEET POTATOES

Patate Dolci con Miele

PREP TIME: 5 MINUTES • COOK TIME: 45 MINUTES • YIELD: 4 TO 6 SERVINGS

Every Thanksgiving we must have Zia Rosa's honey sweet potatoes. In this super-easy recipe, Zia boils sliced sweet potatoes until "al dente," as she says, and then coats them with a honey and water emulsion before baking them until tender. Simple and delicious.

3 pounds (1.3 kg) sweet potatoes (about 3 medium potatoes), unpeeled and scrubbed

¾ cup (255 g) honey

¾ cup (180 ml) water

Home for the Holidays
I remember the years when I would look at my mother and wonder how we were going to fit everyone in the house for the holidays. Our family was so many, and the house was so small. But my mother, Regina, always made us fit. Being together was so important to her. —Nonna Rosa Carmelo

1 In a large stockpot, combine the sweet potatoes and enough cold water to cover completely. Cover the pot and bring to a boil. Cook for about 25 minutes, until a fork only pierces the first inch (2.5 cm) or so of the potatoes. Drain and cool.

2 Once the sweet potatoes are cool enough to handle, peel and slice them into ½-inch-thick (13 mm) slices. Transfer the sweet potatoes to a 13 × 9-inch (33 × 23 cm) baking dish in an even layer. Set aside.

3 Preheat the oven to 500°F (250°C).

4 Combine the honey and water in a small saucepan and bring to a boil over high heat. Pour the mixture over the potatoes.

5 Bake for 20 minutes, flipping the sweet potatoes halfway through the baking time.

6 Transfer the sweet potatoes to a serving dish and pour the liquid from the pan over them.

CRANBERRY SAUCE WITH LIMONCELLO

Salsa di Mirtilli Rossi al Limoncello

PREP TIME: 5 MINUTES • COOK TIME: 16 MINUTES • YIELD: 6 TO 8 SERVINGS

Cranberry sauce is one of Nonna Romana's favorite things. "I love too much," she says every year as we pass the sauce around the table. While there's something incredibly nostalgic for me about opening canned cranberry sauce, it is very easy to make your own. Seriously, just throw everything in a saucepan and simmer. It is also a great way to be able to control the sugar content and add flavors, such as limoncello, which gives this American classic a bit of Italian flair.

12 ounces (340 g) fresh
   cranberries
1 cup (200 g) sugar
Zest and juice of 1 orange
¼ teaspoon ground cinnamon
¼ cup (60 ml) limoncello liqueur

1 In a large saucepan, combine the cranberries, sugar, orange zest and juice, and cinnamon. Cover the pan and bring the mixture to a boil over high heat. Reduce the heat to low. Cook for 15 minutes, stirring occasionally with a wooden spoon.

2 Stir in the limoncello. Cook for 30 seconds to 1 minute, stirring constantly. Remove from the heat and let cool to room temperature. The sauce will thicken slightly as it cools.

Home for the Holidays

I remember the first time we had it [cranberry sauce] at my first Thanksgiving in America. My brother, Vito, brought it home and I wasn't too sure about it because I had never seen it before. It was fruit, but it was meant to go on the turkey, which I had also barely ever eaten in my life. It was so confusing, but as soon as I tasted it, I said, 'God bless America!'
—Nonna Romana Sciddurlo

PUMPKIN TIRAMISU

Tiramisù alla Zucca

PREP TIME: 4 HOURS 20 MINUTES • YIELD: 8 TO 10 SERVINGS

Tiramisu is a beloved Italian dessert. It's smooth, creamy, and caffeinated, so what's not to like? Nonna Romana and I love making this pumpkin version for the holidays, primarily because it's no-bake. Let's be honest, we're all trying to find an easy and delicious way to make something special for big gatherings. You can leave out the amaretto or substitute it with a touch of almond extract to make it alcohol-free.

FILLING

2 cups (475 ml) heavy whipping cream

2 tablespoons (15 g) confectioners' sugar

16 ounces (454 g) mascarpone cheese, at room temperature

1 can (15 ounces, or 425 g) pure pumpkin (not pumpkin pie filling)

½ cup (120 g) packed brown sugar

2 teaspoons pumpkin pie spice

CRUST

2¼ cups (540 ml) brewed espresso coffee

¾ cup (180 ml) amaretto liqueur or almond extract to taste

¼ cup (60 ml) whole milk

48 to 50 ladyfinger cookies or savoiardi (I use about 16 per layer and make 3 layers in a 13 × 9-inch, or 33 × 23 cm, pan)

TOPPING

1 tablespoon (15 ml) granulated sugar

1 tablespoon (15 ml) ground cinnamon

1 **To make the filling:** In a large bowl, combine the heavy whipping cream and confectioners' sugar and beat with a handheld electric mixer until stiff peaks form. Set aside.

2 In another large bowl, combine the mascarpone, pumpkin, brown sugar, and pumpkin pie spice. Gently fold together the ingredients with a rubber spatula until smooth and well combined. (Be gentle while mixing the mascarpone because it has a tendency to curdle and become a bit grainy if it's overworked.) Gently fold the whipped cream into the pumpkin mixture until smooth and airy. Set aside.

3 **To make the crust:** In a shallow dish, mix together the espresso, amaretto, and milk. Dip each ladyfinger cookie into the coffee mixture and place in a 13 × 9-inch (33 × 23 cm) pan. Break the cookies to fit, if necessary. Spoon one-third of the filling over the first layer of cookies and repeat the cookie layer and the filling layer 2 more times.

4 **To make the topping:** In a small bowl, whisk together the granulated sugar and cinnamon. Sprinkle it over the top layer. Refrigerate for at least 4 hours or overnight. Serve chilled.

NO-BAKE CRANBERRY AND MASCARPONE TART

Crostata con Mirtilli Rossi e Mascarpone

PREP TIME: 2 HOURS • COOK TIME: 20 MINUTES • YIELD: ONE 11-INCH (28 CM) TART

Fun fact: Nonna Romana absolutely loves cranberry sauce (page 111)! She loves it so much that, together, we made it into this dessert. The topping for this effortlessly beautiful no-bake tart is super simple, and I'll let you in on a little secret: it's a great way to repurpose leftover cranberry sauce from Thanksgiving.

TOPPING

12 ounces (340 g) cranberries, fresh or frozen

⅔ cup (150 g) packed brown sugar

½ cup (120 ml) freshly squeezed orange juice

¼ cup (60 ml) Cointreau or another orange-flavored liqueur

Zest of 1 orange, plus more for garnishing (optional)

1 cinnamon stick

¼ cup (36 g) toasted almonds, coarsely chopped

CRUST

12 ounces (340 g) Stella D'oro Margherite Vanilla cookies or vanilla wafers or graham crackers

½ cup (1 stick, or 120 g) unsalted butter, melted

FILLING

1½ cups (350 ml) heavy whipping cream

¾ cup (90 g) confectioners' sugar

16 ounces (454 g) mascarpone cheese, at room temperature

1 **To make the topping:** In a small saucepan over medium heat, combine the cranberries, brown sugar, orange juice, Cointreau, orange zest, and cinnamon stick. Bring the mixture to a boil, stirring occasionally with a wooden spoon. Cook for 15 to 20 minutes as the cranberries pop and become smooth. Set aside to cool.

2 **To make the crust:** Add the cookies to a food processor and process until fine. Add the melted butter. Process until the mixture resembles sand. Press the crumbs into an 11-inch (28 cm) loose-bottomed tart pan and refrigerate. In the meantime, make the filling.

3 **To make the filling:** In a large bowl, add the heavy whipping cream and confectioners' sugar and mix with a handheld electric mixer until stiff peaks form.

4 In another large bowl, place the mascarpone. Using a rubber spatula, gently fold in the whipped cream. Transfer the mixture to the crust and smooth with the spatula. Refrigerate until the filling is firm, 1 to 2 hours.

5 Spoon the cranberry topping over the tart before serving. Sprinkle with the toasted almonds and orange zest, if desired.

PUMPKIN RICOTTA COOKIES

Biscotti di Ricotta e Zucca

PREP TIME: 10 MINUTES • COOK TIME: 15 MINUTES • YIELD: ABOUT 40 COOKIES

There is an unwritten rule that cookies must be made for every Italian-American holiday. Okay, I just made that up, but who's to say there isn't? It's unwritten! These pumpkin ricotta cookies are a spiced-up version of Nonna Romana's classic ricotta cookies and are melt-in-your-mouth deliciousness. Nonna Romana will sometimes serve these without the cinnamon-sugar glaze, as they're perfect for dipping in her morning coffee!

COOKIES

2 cups (240 g) all-purpose or 00 flour

2 teaspoons pumpkin pie spice

1 teaspoon baking powder

½ teaspoon salt

1 cup (225 g) packed brown sugar

½ cup (1 stick, or 120 g) unsalted butter, at room temperature

8 ounces (227 g) ricotta

4 ounces (113 g) canned pure pumpkin (not pumpkin pie filling)

1 teaspoon vanilla extract

1 large egg

GLAZE

2 cups (240 g) confectioners' sugar

2 tablespoons (30 ml) milk

¼ teaspoon ground cinnamon

1 Preheat the oven to 350°F (180°C). Line 2 baking sheets with parchment paper or aluminum foil. Set aside.

2 **To make the cookies:** In a large bowl, whisk together the flour, pumpkin pie spice, baking powder, and salt. Set aside.

3 In the bowl of a stand mixer fitted with the paddle attachment, combine the brown sugar and butter. Mix on medium speed until fluffy, about 5 minutes.

4 Add the ricotta, pumpkin, vanilla, and egg. Beat on medium-high speed until well combined. Turn the speed to low. Add the dry ingredients and continue beating on low speed until the flour is absorbed and a dough forms.

5 Roll the dough into rounded tablespoons (15 g each) and place them about 2 inches (5 cm) apart on the prepared baking sheets. Bake for 15 minutes, or until the cookies are very lightly golden. Transfer the cookies to a wire rack to cool. Cool completely before icing.

6 **To make the glaze:** In a small bowl, mix together the confectioners' sugar, milk, and cinnamon until smooth.

7 Dip each cookie into the glaze and place it on a wire rack to allow the icing to dry completely.

APPLE CINNAMON RICOTTA CAKE

Torta di Mele e Ricotta

PREP TIME: 10 MINUTES • COOK TIME: 1 HOUR • YIELD: ONE 9-INCH (23 CM) CAKE

When it comes to Thanksgiving desserts, Nonna Romana likes to jazz up the classic recipes in her repertoire. She has made so many versions of this humble olive oil and ricotta cake, but this one really brings out the essence of the holiday. The aroma of sweet apple-cinnamon goodness will fill your home from top to bottom. Should there be any leftovers (which isn't likely), this cake works beautifully as a breakfast cake with coffee in the morning.

Nonstick baking spray, for preparing the pan

4 large eggs

1½ cups (375 g) whole-milk ricotta

1 cup (200 g) granulated sugar

1 teaspoon vanilla extract

¾ cup (180 ml) olive oil

Zest of 1 orange

2 teaspoons ground cinnamon

2 cups (240 g) all-purpose or 00 flour

1 tablespoon (15 ml) baking powder

3 Gala apples, 2 cut into 1-inch (2.5 cm) chunks and 1 thinly sliced

Confectioners' sugar, for dusting

1 Preheat the oven to 350°F (180°C). Coat a 9-inch (23 cm) springform pan with baking spray. Set aside.

2 In a large bowl, add the eggs, ricotta, granulated sugar, and vanilla. Mix well with a spoon.

3 Add the olive oil, orange zest, and cinnamon. Stir to combine.

4 Stir in the flour and baking powder, little by little, mixing until fully combined. Fold in the apple chunks.

5 Pour the batter into the prepared pan. Arrange the sliced apples on top and sprinkle with confectioners' sugar.

6 Bake for 1 hour, or until the apples are golden. Serve at room temperature.

AMARETTO PUMPKIN PIE

Crostata di Zucca all'Amaretto

PREP TIME: 10 MINUTES • COOK TIME: 1 HOUR 30 MINUTES • YIELD: ONE 9-INCH (23 CM) PIE

No Thanksgiving would be complete without a delicious pumpkin pie. My Zia Rosa was introduced to this iconic American dessert in 1966, when her American-born sister-in-law brought it over for Thanksgiving dinner. Over the years, Zia Rosa "Italianized" the classic filling with the addition of a splash of the amaretto liqueur that Zio Domenico loves too much. The plain crust has evolved as well, with the addition of almonds for crunch and sweet amaretto cookies replacing the graham crackers. The final touch is a dollop of amaretto-spiked whipped cream spread generously over the top to create the perfect Italian-American confection.

CRUST

Butter, for preparing the pie plate

4 ounces (113 g) amaretti cookies, plus more for garnishing

¼ cup (30 g) all-purpose or 00 flour

2 tablespoons (14 g) slivered almonds

1 tablespoon (15 g) packed brown sugar

1 teaspoon ground cinnamon

Pinch salt

½ cup (1 stick, or 120 g) salted butter, melted

FILLING

1 can (15 ounces, or 425 g) pure pumpkin (not pumpkin pie filling)

8 ounces (225 g) almond paste

1 cup (240 ml) heavy cream

½ cup (120 g) packed brown sugar

3 tablespoons (45 ml) amaretto liqueur

1 Preheat the oven to 350°F (180°C). Butter a 9-inch (23 cm) pie plate and set aside.

2 **To make the crust:** Add the amaretti cookies, flour, almonds, brown sugar, cinnamon, and salt to a food processor, and process for about 20 seconds, until finely ground.

3 Drizzle in the melted butter and process until the mixture resembles wet sand. Press the crumbs into the prepared pie plate using the bottom of a glass to create a smooth crust. Bake for 10 to 12 minutes, or until the edges begin to color.

4 Remove the crust from the oven and, while it's still hot, use the back of a spoon to further smooth out the crust and push it up the sides of the pie plate. Set aside to cool while you make the filling

5 **To make the filling:** Put the pumpkin in a large bowl. Using a large cheese grater, grate the almond paste over the pumpkin. With a handheld electric mixer, mix on high speed until the almond paste is fully incorporated and there are no lumps.

6 Add the heavy cream, brown sugar, amaretto, eggs, vanilla, and pumpkin pie spice. Mix again on high speed until well combined. Pour the filling into the prepared crust. Bake for about 1 hour to 1 hour and 15 minutes, until the edges are fully set but the center is still wobbly.

7 Turn off the oven and let the pie cool completely in the oven, with the oven door open, to prevent cracks.

2 large eggs

1 packet (½ ounce, or 15 g) Italian vanilla powder or 1 teaspoon vanilla extract

2 teaspoons pumpkin pie spice

AMARETTO WHIPPED CREAM

1 cup (240 ml) heavy whipping cream

1 tablespoon (15 ml) amaretto liqueur

1 tablespoon (8 g) confectioners' sugar

Splash vanilla extract

8 **To make the amaretto whipped cream:** In a large bowl, combine the heavy whipping cream, amaretto, confectioners' sugar, and vanilla. Beat with a handheld electric mixer until soft peaks form.

9 Spread the whipped cream over the cooled pie and garnish with amaretti cookie crumbs.

CHRISTMAS EVE

Home for the Holidays

Oh, how my sisters and I would look forward to the Christmas holidays. We would always have this deep red-colored tissue paper in the house that we would wet with water and press onto our lips and cheeks. We would be overjoyed to see that deep red pigment on our faces to give us nu poco di colore *(a bit of color)! Today, we have lipstick and rouge, but back then, the paper was all we had to make ourselves look a little festive.*
—Nonna Michelina Gagliardo

LIVORNESE SEAFOOD RICE

Riso alla Marinara

PREP TIME: 20 MINUTES • COOK TIME: 1 HOUR 15 MINUTES • YIELD: 6 SERVINGS

Christmas Eve at Nonna Rosa's house isn't complete without this seafood rice on the table. This specialty from Livorno is very similar to its Neapolitan cousin, the famous *risotto alla pescatora* (seafood risotto), with a few differences. The rice is baked in the oven instead of cooked on the stovetop, and the blend of seafood is cooked separately. Both components are then added together with butter in a process called *mantecare*, which is used in classic risotto preparation to cream the ingredients together.

24 mussels, scrubbed, rinsed, and beards removed

2 pounds (907 g) cockles or 24 littleneck clams, scrubbed and rinsed

2 pounds (907 g) large shrimp, peeled, deveined, and cut into 1-inch (2.5 cm) pieces

2 pounds (907 g) calamari, cleaned, cut into 1-inch (2.5 cm) rings, and tentacles cut into 1-inch (2.5 cm) pieces

3½ cups (28 ounces, or 840 ml) beef broth

3½ cups (28 ounces, or 840 ml) chicken broth

5 tablespoons (75 ml) extra-virgin olive oil

10 cloves garlic, minced

½ teaspoon red pepper flakes

½ cup (30 g) chopped fresh parsley

16 ounces (454 g) long-grain white rice, rinsed

½ cup (1 stick, or 120 g) salted butter

1 Put a large skillet with a lid over medium-high heat. Add the mussels. Cover and steam for 5 to 7 minutes, until the mussels open. Discard any mussels that do not open. Remove the meat from the shells and transfer to a large bowl. Discard the shells. Strain the juice from the pan through a fine-mesh strainer lined with cheesecloth into a medium bowl. Set aside.

2 Return the skillet to medium heat and add the cockles. Cover the pan and steam for 3 to 5 minutes, until they open. Discard any cockles that do not open. Remove the meat from the shells and transfer to the bowl with the mussels. Discard the shells. Strain the juice from the pan through a fine-mesh strainer lined with cheesecloth into the bowl with the mussel juice.

3 In a large saucepan, combine the shrimp with cold running water, until the shrimp are just covered. Bring the saucepan to a boil. Cook for 10 minutes. Reserve 1 cup (240 ml) of the cooking water. Drain the shrimp and add them to the bowl with the mussels and clams.

4 In the same saucepan, combine the calamari with enough cold running water just to cover. Bring the saucepan to a boil. Cook for 10 minutes. Reserve 1 cup (240 ml) of the cooking water. Drain the calamari and add them to the bowl with the rest of the seafood. Set aside.

continued

5 Preheat the oven to 400°F (200°C).

6 In a small stockpot, bring the beef and chicken broths to a boil. Remove from the heat and set aside.

7 Heat the olive oil in a large skillet over medium heat. Add the garlic, red pepper flakes, and parsley. Cook for 1 minute. Reduce the heat to low. Add the rice and toast for 2 to 3 minutes. Add two-thirds of the warmed broth, about $4\frac{1}{2}$ cups (1 L), and stir it in, reserving the remaining broth in case the rice gets too dry in the oven. Keep the broth warm on the stove while the rice bakes.

8 Spread the rice in a 13 × 9-inch (33 × 23 cm) oven-safe baking dish. Cover with aluminum foil and bake for 20 minutes. Check on the rice halfway through: If it looks too dry, add some of the reserved broth; the rice should be tender but still have some bite to it. Remove from the oven and cool for 5 minutes.

9 Put the same 12-inch (30 cm) skillet used for the rice over medium heat and melt the butter. Add the rice to the pan and stir, coating it in the butter.

10 Add the mussels, clams, shrimp, and calamari and the reserved juices and cooking water to the pan. Cook for 10 to 12 minutes, stirring constantly with a wooden spoon to prevent sticking. The rice is done when half the liquid is absorbed and the rice is perfectly tender. Serve immediately.

NONNA ROSA VELLA

"It's the nicest thing when people enjoy your food."

"My mother's name was Modesta and she had ten children: eight girls and two boys. Thank God her name wasn't Maria, or she might have had twenty!" Nonna Rosa says to me, laughing, as we gaze at a family photo in the living room of her cozy home in Roseto, Pennsylvania. She makes her way back into the kitchen, where the sweet smell of rice fritters still lingers in the air. She begins to chop some garlic with her prized *mezzaluna*. "Cooking has always helped me relax. I love garlic. When a recipe says to put two cloves of garlic, I put ten! Those people who say they don't like too much garlic, they don't know nothing!" Nonna Rosa says with a serious expression. Already I'm in love with her slightly sarcastic, tell-it-like-it-is attitude. As we keep talking, she makes it very clear that she's at a point in her life where she is totally content. "I'm very happy. I have the beautiful grandchildren. I have my little garden here where I grow whatever I like. I am a happy woman."

Nonna Rosa's journey began in Livorno, Italy, and has brought her here to Roseto, which was once regarded as an Italian enclave, where residents purportedly lived forever. She lives along Garibaldi Avenue, where all the homes look alike, and you can see remnants of old storefronts with faded signs written in Italian. Though the neighborhood outside has changed, inside Nonna

Rosa's home, I feel as though I am in Italy. Her quaint kitchen is adorned with murals of grape vines and photos of her beloved Livorno. An Italian game show blares on the television. She turns it down so I can hear her better. "My life was full of sacrifices. Growing up, my father was a railroad worker. He would have to stay by the railroad crossing twenty-four hours a day. Sometimes I would keep watch for him while he snuck back home to have an espresso or to get some sleep. Even as small children, we would all work together as a family," she says smiling. I'm amazed at how she recalls these events with such happiness.

Even when she speaks about her memories of World War II, it is with a sense of pride of having survived and endured. "The war was very difficult for everyone. Our coffee was made of orzo. At home we would get rations of bread and my mother would distribute it to each of us, and it would have to last us for breakfast, lunch, and dinner. We were to take the bread and put it in our *cassetto* with our clothes, and we knew not to ask for any more, because there was none." But being hungry wasn't the gravest challenge Nonna Rosa had to face during the war. "When the Germans arrived in our area, everyone was afraid. Someone in town told my mother she had better get my sisters and me to safety. Surely someone would have told the soldiers that there was a house in town with eight young women. My father couldn't stay with us. If a man was found in the house and not at work, he would be killed. My mother never panicked, though. She sent us to an aunt's house that was a cable car ride away. Sure enough, the soldiers came knocking that night. My mother was shaken, but she knew she had saved us. These are things I can never forget," she says as she closes her eyes behind her gold-rimmed glasses.

With the end of the war, Nonna Rosa met and married her Sicilian husband, whom she credits with giving her the confidence to be a truly great cook. "My husband was a hairdresser by trade, but at one point, we decided to open a restaurant together. I helped out at first, but one day, I got behind the burners, and from that day on, I was a chef! That's how it happens sometimes. You never know in life." Shortly after that, Nonna Rosa, her husband, and their three children decided to join one of her sisters in America. "I love America because anything is possible. My husband and I came here to work, and it was so much easier for us. He found work as a waiter, and I found work in a clothing factory, although I was nervous at first. I trained in sewing at *la sarta*, but who had ever used a big sewing machine to add a zipper? In Italy, everything was by hand, but I got used to it all."

Imagining Nonna Rosa's new world makes me feel so inspired by how much she has overcome. "We felt as if we left our worst struggles behind. Everything was different, especially holidays. In America we have so much food that we take it for granted. I relish cooking for my family for the holidays now because there's so much more to work with. When I was growing up, you can just imagine how our holidays were. We would all sit at one long table with benches on either side and one chair at each head of the table for Mamma and Papa. If we were lucky, there would be a chicken for dinner. One chicken to feed ten people!" she says, laughing. "You could imagine the fights between my siblings over who had the bigger piece. My father would stand up at the table and yell that if we kept at it, there would be no chicken for anyone and just he and my mother would eat it themselves!"

Her holidays have come a long way from fighting over a single chicken; now, her family is fighting over second helpings of her delicious dishes, such as her Livornese Seafood Rice (see recipe on page 123). "I make that every Christmas and my son-in-law, who isn't Italian, loves it so much. One year, I didn't make it and he was so sad, I had to make it for him the very next day. That's how I am, what do you want from me? It's the nicest thing when people enjoy your food."

NONNA ROMANA SCIDDURLO'S

FRIED BACCALÀ

Baccalà Fritto

PREP TIME: 15 MINUTES* • COOK TIME: 20 MINUTES • YIELD: 4 TO 6 SERVINGS

*REQUIRES 1 TO 3 DAYS OF SOAKING

If you visit Nonna Romana in her Brooklyn basement apartment anytime between the day after Thanksgiving and Christmas Eve, there's a good chance you'll be met with the warm and intoxicating aroma of fried baccalà. It's no secret that baccalà, or salt cod fish, is an integral part of Christmas in an Italian household. Though it requires a bit of preparation, many Italians view it as a ritual or tradition. Nonna Romana's favorite way to prepare it is to batter it in a traditional Pugliese *pastella* (batter) full of garlic, mint, and cheese, and fry it until it's golden brown and crispy on the outside.

1½ pounds (680 g) baccalà
 (salt cod)
2 large eggs
½ cup (50 g) grated Pecorino
 Romano cheese
4 cloves garlic, minced
1 tablespoon (4 g) minced
 fresh parsley
1 teaspoon salt
1 cup (124 g) all-purpose or
 00 flour
1 cup (240 ml) water
Oil, for frying

1 Put the baccalà in a large bowl with enough cold water to cover it. Place the bowl in the refrigerator and change the water 3 times a day. Soak for 1 to 3 days, depending on the saltiness. Drain. Cut the baccalà into 3- to 4-inch (7.5 to 10 cm) pieces and pat dry with a paper towel.

2 In a medium bowl, whisk together the eggs, cheese, garlic, parsley, and salt. Add the flour and whisk until absorbed. Whisk in the water until smooth. The batter should fall in ribbons.

3 Heat about 1½ inches (4 cm) of oil in a medium heavy-bottomed skillet over high heat. Working one at a time, dip the baccalà into the batter, letting the excess fall back into the bowl. Carefully add it to the hot oil and fry, working in batches, for 3 to 5 minutes per side, until golden. Fry any leftover batter to make fritters. Serve immediately.

NONNA MICHELINA GAGLIARDO'S

SALT COD WITH POTATOES

Baccalà Ghiotta

PREP TIME: 15 MINUTES* • COOK TIME: 55 MINUTES • YIELD: 4 TO 6 SERVINGS

*REQUIRES 1 TO 3 DAYS OF SOAKING

At Zia Michelina's house in the Bronx, *baccalà* is floured and fried to lock in the flavor, and then cooked in a hearty tomato sauce full of olives, potatoes, and capers, until the fried baccalà pieces are beautifully tender, or as Zia Michelina would say, "*Molto* beautiful, baby!" The leftover sauce is tossed with pasta, because "you no waste nothing!"

BACCALÀ

1½ pounds (680 g) baccalà (salt cod)

Oil, for frying

All-purpose or 00 flour, for dredging

SAUCE

¼ cup (60 ml) extra-virgin olive oil

1 medium onion, cut into ¼-inch (6 mm) dice

3 celery ribs, cut into ½-inch (13 mm) dice

1 cup (155 g) Kalamata or Gaeta olives, pitted

1 can (28 ounces, or 794 g) crushed tomatoes

3 small russet potatoes, peeled and cut into 1-inch (2.5 cm) cubes

2 tablespoons (18 g) capers, rinsed

Salt, to taste

16 ounces (454 g) dried mezzi rigatoni

🥄 **Nonna Michelina Says**
This dish can also be made with any leftover fried baccalà pieces you may have.

1. **To make the baccalà:** Put the baccalà in a large bowl with enough cold water to cover it. Place the bowl in the refrigerator and change the water 3 times a day. Soak for 1 to 3 days, depending on the saltiness. Drain.

2. Heat 1 inch (2.5 cm) of oil in a medium heavy-bottomed skillet over high heat.

3. Line a plate with paper towels and set aside. Place the flour in a shallow dish and dredge the baccalà pieces in the flour. Carefully add them to the hot oil and, working in batches, fry for 3 to 5 minutes per side, until golden. Transfer to the paper towel–lined plate.

4. **To make the sauce:** Heat the olive oil in a large saucepan with a lid over medium heat. Add the onion, celery, and olives. Cook for 5 to 7 minutes, until the onion is translucent and the celery is soft.

5. Add the tomatoes. Fill the empty crushed tomatoes can three-fourths full of water, swish it around, and add the tomato water to the pan as well. Add the potatoes and bring the mixture to a boil. Cook for 5 minutes. Reduce the heat to low. Cover the pan and let the sauce simmer for 15 to 20 minutes.

6. Add the capers and fried baccalà to the sauce. Cook, covered, for 5 minutes more. Transfer the baccalà to a plate, leaving the sauce in the pan.

7. Bring a medium stockpot of generously salted water to a boil. Drop in the pasta and cook until al dente. Drain and add the pasta to the sauce. Cook, tossing, over medium-high heat for 1 to 2 minutes. Serve in warm bowls with pieces of the baccalà broken up on top of the pasta, or as a first course with the baccalà served as a second course.

OCTOPUS SALAD

Insalata di Polpo

PREP TIME: 4 HOURS • COOK TIME: 45 MINUTES • YIELD: 4 SERVINGS

Nonna Lorella dresses her salad with super-simple, clean flavors, so the octopus can be the star of the show. Some people may be intimidated by the prospect of cooking an octopus, but it's much easier than you think. Try and buy octopi that are smaller in size, which will be much more tender than larger ones.

OCTOPUS

3 pounds (1.3 kg) octopus, use one 1- to 3-pound (454 g to 1.3 kg) octopus or several smaller ones that add up to 3 pounds (1.3 kg) total (see Nonna Lorella Says)

1 medium Idaho potato, washed and unpeeled

2 celery ribs, cut into ½-inch (13 mm) dice

DRESSING

3 cloves garlic, minced

⅔ cup (160 ml) extra-virgin olive oil

Juice of 3 lemons

1 tablespoon (15 ml) white wine

Salt, to taste

Black pepper, to taste

1 **To cook the octopus:** Wash the octopus under cold running water. Bring a large stockpot filled with about 14 cups (3.3 L) of water to a boil. You want enough water to cover the octopus completely. Add the potato to the pot. (According to Nonna lore, if you boil a potato with octopus, when the potato is tender, the octopus will also be tender.)

2 Hold the octopus by the head and plunge it, tentacles first, 3 times into the boiling water. Drop the octopus into the pot and return the water to a boil. Cook for 30 to 45 minutes, until both the octopus and the potato are fork-tender. Drain and transfer to a bowl. Discard the potato. Cool to room temperature.

3 Cut the cooled octopus into 1-inch (2.5 cm) pieces and place them in a large bowl. Add the diced celery to the bowl.

4 **To make the dressing:** In a small bowl, whisk together the garlic, olive oil, lemon juice, and wine. Pour the dressing over the octopus and celery and toss to coat. Taste and season with salt and pepper as desired.

5 Refrigerate for at least 4 hours or overnight before serving. This can be made up to 2 days in advance.

Nonna Lorella Says

I recommend using frozen octopus because the octopus becomes more tender during the freezing process, and the eyes and beak will most likely have been removed. If using fresh octopus, you will need to clean the inside of the head thoroughly and remove the eyes and beak.

SPAGHETTI WITH NUTS, RAISINS, AND ANCHOVIES

Spaghetti di Natale

PREP TIME: 5 MINUTES • COOK TIME: 25 MINUTES • YIELD: 4 TO 6 SERVINGS

A dinner at Nonna Lorella's house is always an event. Everyone is always singing Neapolitan love songs, telling stories, and sipping bottomless glasses of wine, and that's just on a Tuesday! Christmas Eve is even livelier, and usually goes well into the early morning hours. Their feast tends to begin a little later in the evening, because most of her family is in the restaurant business. So this super-quick and flavorful pasta dish is a no-brainer. The spaghetti spends most of the time cooking directly in a sauce chock-full of raisins, pinoli, olives, and walnuts, which allows it to perfectly absorb the sweet and savory flavors. As Nonna Lorella says, *"Na cosa sciue sciue, ma buona!* (Something super quick, but good!)"

Salt, to taste

¾ cup (180 ml) extra-virgin olive oil

3 cloves garlic, sliced

⅓ cup (33 g) walnuts

⅓ cup (45 g) pinoli (pine nuts)

7 or 8 anchovy fillets

½ cup (121 g) canned crushed tomatoes

16 ounces (454 g) dried spaghetti

⅓ cup (50 g) currants or raisins

1 cup (155 g) Kalamata or Gaeta olives, pitted

1 Bring a medium stockpot of generously salted water to a boil.

2 Put a large skillet over medium heat and add the olive oil, garlic, walnuts, pinoli, and anchovies. Cook for 3 to 4 minutes, stirring with a wooden spoon, until the anchovies melt and the garlic is golden. Stir in the currants and olives, and cook for 1 to 2 minutes.

3 Add the tomatoes and reduce the heat to low. Cook for 5 minutes, stirring occasionally with a wooden spoon.

4 While the tomatoes cook, drop the pasta into the boiling water. Cook for half the time indicated on the package, 5 to 6 minutes. The pasta will still be quite hard. Scoop out 2½ cups (600 ml) of pasta water and add it to the sauce. Drain the spaghetti and add it to the sauce as well.

5 Increase the heat to medium-high. Cook, tossing the pasta, for 7 to 10 minutes, until the sauce reduces and no longer pools at the bottom of the pan, and the pasta is al dente. Taste and season with salt as desired.

NONNA GIUSEPPA VALENTI COCCIOLA'S

SEVEN FISHES SEAFOOD SALAD

Insalata di Mare

PREP TIME: 3 HOURS* • COOK TIME: 1 HOUR 50 MINUTES • YIELD: 8 TO 10 SERVINGS

*REQUIRES AT LEAST 1 TO 3 DAYS OF SOAKING

Okay, so this recipe can be a labor of love, but every single bite will be absolutely worth it (if you manage to get some on your plate)! No matter how much seafood salad Nonna Giuseppa makes, there never seems to be enough to go around. Traditionally, she makes it every Christmas Eve as part of her legendary Feast of the Seven Fishes, but it's so light and refreshing that it works beautifully as a summer antipasto as well.

SEAFOOD

1 pound (454 g) baccalà (salt cod)

½ cup (120 ml) dry white wine

3 pounds (1.3 kg) mussels, rinsed, scrubbed, and beards removed

1 pound (454 g) calamari, cleaned, bodies cut into ½-inch (13 mm) rings, and tentacles left whole

1 pound (454 g) small scallops, washed

1 pound (454 g) shrimp, washed, peeled, and deveined

1 pound (454 g) scungilli (whelk)

1 pound (454 g) tenderized octopus

BROTH

3 cloves garlic, left whole

3 bay leaves

12 black peppercorns

1 teaspoon fennel seeds

1 tablespoon (4 g) minced fresh parsley

Peel of ½ lemon

½ cup (120 ml) dry white wine

1 tablespoon (15 ml) salt

1 **To make the seafood:** Put the baccalà in a large bowl and cover it with cold water. Place the bowl in the refrigerator and change the water 3 times a day. Soak for 1 to 3 days, depending on saltiness. Drain.

2 Put a large heavy-bottomed saucepan with a lid over medium heat. Add the wine and mussels, and cover. Cook the mussels until they have all opened and the meat is detached from the shell, about 10 minutes. Discard any mussels that haven't opened. Remove the meat from the shells of the mussels and set aside. Discard the shells. Strain the juice from the pan through a fine-mesh strainer lined with cheesecloth into a medium bowl and set aside.

3 **To make the broth and cook the seafood:** Fill a small double boiler halfway with water. (If you don't have a double boiler, a regular stockpot can be used with a large strainer or colander to scoop out the fish.) Add all the broth ingredients to the pot and bring the water to a boil.

4 Add the baccalà and cook it for 6 to 7 minutes. Remove it from the water and set aside. Bring the water back to a boil.

5 Add the calamari to the pot and cook them for 4 to 5 minutes. Remove them from the water and set aside. Bring the water back to a boil.

continued

VEGETABLES

2 celery ribs, cut into ½-inch
(13 mm) dice

½ cup (30 g) chopped fresh
parsley

2 medium carrots, grated

1 cup (192 g) green olives with
pimento

SALAD DRESSING

1 cup (240 ml) freshly squeezed
lemon juice

¾ cup (180 ml) extra-virgin
olive oil

12 cloves garlic, minced

1 tablespoon (15 ml) white
wine vinegar

Dash dried oregano

Salt, to taste

Red pepper flakes, to taste
(optional)

Nonna Giuseppa Says

*Feel free to change up the
seafood depending on your taste.
Lobster is a special and delicious
addition. When I'm making this
for Christmas, I always make the
salad a day or two before so the
flavors intensify.*

6   Add the scallops to the pot and cook them for 4 to 5 minutes. Remove them from the water and set aside. Bring the water back to a boil.

7   Add the shrimp to the pot and cook them until pink and tender, 6 to 7 minutes (depending on the size). Remove them from the water and set aside. Bring the water back to a boil.

8   Add the scungilli to the pot and cook them until firm but tender, about 50 minutes. Remove them from the pot and set aside. Bring the water back to a boil.

9   Finally, add the octopus to the pot, dip the colander in and out 2 times, and then let the octopus cook for about 20 minutes, or until the octopus is tender and the tentacles have curled. Remove from the pot and set aside.

10 In a large mixing bowl, combine the mussels, calamari, scallops, and shrimp.

11 Slice the scungilli into ½-inch (13 mm) pieces and add to the bowl. Cut the octopus into ½-inch (13 mm) pieces and add to the bowl as well. Finally, shred the baccalà by hand into bite-size pieces and add to the bowl.

12 **To make the vegetables:** Add the celery, parsley, carrots, and olives to the bowl, and toss well.

13 **To make the dressing:** Add all the dressing ingredients and the reserved mussel juice to a medium bowl, mix well, and then drizzle the mixture over the seafood and vegetables. Toss well.

14 Cover the bowl and let it marinate in the refrigerator for at least 3 hours or overnight. The salad can be chilled for up to 2 days.

Home for the Holidays

*I remember my first Christmas [in America], in 1958, when I was
thirteen years old. I saw snow for the first time! I had never seen
snow in my life in Sicily! That Christmas Eve, we went over to my
Zia's house, and it was a night I would never forget—the lights, the
food, the welcome feeling, all the signs that said 'Merry Christmas.'
I thought these things were only in the movies. We ate so much that
night, and seeing the way my Zia put everything together inspired
me to have my Christmas dinners the same way. —Nonna Giuseppa
Valenti Cocciola*

FRIED CARDOONS

Cardoni Fritti

PREP TIME: 15 MINUTES • COOK TIME: 45 MINUTES • YIELD: 8 TO 10 SERVINGS

Every holiday season, Nonna Carmela and her grandson John take a trip to Arthur Avenue in the Bronx to shop for ingredients for Christmas. One of their first stops is for fresh produce at Boiano Foods Inc. in the Arthur Avenue Retail Market. A cardoon is the thistle part of the artichoke plant, and it tends to resemble large claws of celery filled with strings that need to be peeled. "These are a lot of work," Nonna Carmela says, "but every year they all ask for them, so as long as I'm here I'll do it." Nonna Carmela saw her first cardoon when she married her Sicilian husband and wanted to keep his traditions alive. When prepared Nonna Carmela's way, the whole plate is in danger before they're even served. "I have to hide them!" she says with a wink and a smile. I believe you, Nonna Carmela.

1½ pounds (680 g) cardoons

All-purpose or 00 flour, for dredging

4 large eggs

2 tablespoons (30 ml) whole milk

1 cup (115 g) plain bread crumbs

1 tablespoon (4 g) chopped fresh parsley

¼ cup (25 g) grated Parmigiano-Reggiano cheese

2 cloves garlic, minced

1 teaspoon salt

¼ teaspoon black pepper

Olive oil, for frying

1 Discard any brown or discolored leaves and smaller stalks from the cardoons. Trim the bottoms of the cardoons to make individual stalks. Using either a vegetable peeler or your fingernail, peel the outer fibrous strings off each rib as you would with celery. This step is paramount.

2 Cut the cardoon stalks crosswise into 4- to 5-inch (10 to 13 cm) pieces and place in a bowl of water to prevent oxidation. Drain the water and wash the cardoons well under cold running water. Transfer the cardoons to a small stockpot and cover them with cold water.

3 Bring the pot to a boil, then reduce the heat to a simmer. Cook the cardoons for 20 to 30 minutes, until tender and easily pierced with a knife. Drain and transfer to a plate.

4 Place the flour in a shallow dish. In another shallow dish, beat the eggs and milk together with a fork. In a third shallow dish, mix together the bread crumbs, parsley, cheese, garlic, salt, and pepper.

5 Heat about 1½ inches (4 cm) of olive oil in a large skillet over medium-high heat. Line a plate with paper towels and set aside.

6 Dredge each cardoon first in the flour, then in the beaten egg, and finally in the bread-crumb mixture. Working in batches, place the coated cardoons in the hot oil and fry for 2 to 3 minutes per batch, turning frequently, until golden brown. Transfer to the paper towel–lined plate. Serve warm.

ESCAROLE PIE

Pizza di Scarola

PREP TIME: 35 MINUTES • COOK TIME: 1 HOUR 25 MINUTES • YIELD: 6 TO 8 SERVINGS

There is a saying according to a Neapolitan Christmas tradition, *"la vigilia è di magro* (the eve must be light)."* There is usually no meat consumed on Christmas Eve at Nonna Lorella's house. Just a "light" snack, if you will, of several courses of seafood and vegetables. And, of course, her classic pizza, which in this case refers to her exquisite escarole pie bursting with olives, raisins, and nuts. She rolls out her crust with a pasta roller to get it super thin, allowing it to virtually "fry" in the oven.

FILLING

3 teaspoons salt, divided

3 heads escarole, ends trimmed, washed, and cut into 1-inch (2.5 cm) strips

4 cloves garlic, minced

½ cup (50 g) walnuts, coarsely chopped

½ cup (78 g) Kalamata olives, pitted and coarsely chopped

¼ cup (35 g) raisins

¼ cup (34 g) pinoli (pine nuts)

5 tablespoons (75 ml) extra-virgin olive oil

3 or 4 anchovy fillets

DOUGH

3 cups (360 g) all-purpose or 00 flour

½ teaspoon baking soda

½ teaspoon baking powder

½ teaspoon salt

Dash black pepper

1 cup (240 ml) warm water

1 tablespoon (15 ml) apple cider vinegar

1 cup (240 ml) extra-virgin olive oil, divided, plus more for brushing

1 **To make the filling:** Bring a large stockpot of water with 2 teaspoons of the salt to a boil. Add the escarole, cover the pot, and cook for 30 minutes.

2 Drain the escarole and run it under cold water. Squeeze out the excess water and transfer the escarole to a large bowl. Add the garlic, walnuts, olives, raisins, pinoli, olive oil, the remaining 1 teaspoon salt, and the anchovies. Combine well. Set aside.

3 **To make the dough:** In a medium bowl, whisk together the flour, baking soda, baking powder, salt, and pepper. Set aside.

4 In the bowl of a stand mixer fitted with the dough hook attachment, combine the warm water, vinegar, and ½ cup (120 ml) of the olive oil. Mix on medium speed for 1 minute. Add the flour mixture and mix on medium speed until a smooth ball of dough begins to form, 3 to 5 minutes. Form the dough into a log about 12 inches (30 cm) long and cut it into 6 equal pieces.

5 Preheat the oven to 400°F (200°C).

6 Take 4 pieces of the dough and, using a pasta press stand mixer attachment set on the #1 setting, begin passing each piece of dough through the pasta press 2 or 3 times. Change to the #2 setting and pass the dough through the press 2 or 3 more times, until you have smooth sheets at least 12 inches (30 cm) long.

7 Lay the sheets on the bottom of a 12-inch (30 cm) aluminum oven-safe skillet, overlapping one another by at least 1 inch (2.5 cm). Let any excess hang over the sides of the pan. Spread the filling over the bottom of the dough in an even layer, leaving about a 1-inch (2.5 cm) border.

8 Prepare the remaining 2 dough pieces like the pieces in step 6. Place them over the filling in the center of the pan, overlapping each other by at least 1 inch (2.5 cm). Fold the excess dough over the filling so it just meets the top 2 pieces of dough. Trim any excess. Patch any holes with the trimmed pieces. This will end up being the bottom of the pizza, so it doesn't have to be perfect.

9 Dock the pie with a fork and pour the remaining ½ cup (120 ml) olive oil over the pizza. Brush it to coat properly.

10 Bake for 35 minutes. Wearing oven mitts on both hands, remove the skillet from the oven. Place a large dinner plate over the pizza. Place your hand over the plate and quickly flip the pizza onto the plate. Slide the pizza back into the skillet and brush with a bit of extra olive oil. Bake for 20 minutes more, or until the crust is firm and golden brown. Let the pizza cool in the pan for about 15 minutes before sliding it onto a plate.

11 Cool to room temperature before cutting into slices and serving.

NONNA LORELLA COLANDREA

"I'm guilty of being that Italian woman who pushes people to eat. I made it, so why do we have to let it go to waste?"

"My granddaughter is my favorite person to be with. The feeling I get when she holds her arms out for me to pick her up is indescribable. It's so special when your daughter has a daughter," the stunning Nonna Lorella tells me as she holds her very first granddaughter, Victoria, in her arms. Her own daughter, Maryla, is a longtime friend of mine. She joins us in the office of her beautiful Connecticut home, where she and Nonna Lorella run their Italian-destination wedding business, Art of Perfection Designs.

I arrived at her home to an impeccably set table with candles and flowers. Everything from the china to the napkins to the beautifully wrapped bundles of herbs at each place setting match perfectly. Such an extravagant reception might seem out of place anywhere else, but at Nonna Lorella's house, any occasion, even a Tuesday night, is an excuse to celebrate. "I always loved entertaining. I guess I passed it onto my daughter. Maybe she will pass it onto the baby?" Nonna

Lorella says as she glances at her granddaughter who is voraciously eating a piece of bread.

The resemblance among the three of them is astounding. The high cheekbones, olive complexions, and delicate cat eyes make them look like three generations of Sophia Loren. When I mention this to Nonna Lorella, she laughs. "You know, a lot of people actually call me that! They don't know my name, so they yell, 'Hey, Sophia!' " she says with the inflection of a true *Napoletana*.

In many ways, Nonna Lorella is the modern Nonna, always impeccably dressed, with a Neapolitan flair for glamour. "When I was younger, I really cared about dressing. I was always to the letter, but then you get older and you don't care as much," she says, smiling ironically as she pulls up the beaded edge of her dress sleeve to brush away a strand of perfectly highlighted hair from her face. She pulls out a faded photograph of herself posing by the beach in her hometown of Monte di Procida along the Neapolitan coast in Italy; it reminds me of a vintage ad from *Vogue*. "Can you believe that when I was little I wanted to be a nun?" I am definitely surprised, but glamour aside, Nonna Lorella is a traditional Nonna at heart.

"Being a Nonna has made me into a different kind of chef. I make all my granddaughter's baby food for her, but I don't like to make it plain. When my kids were little I put a little oil, salt, and cheese, because the doctor said it was okay. Both my kids are healthy, and I do the same for my granddaughter." It's hard to argue with a woman with her sense of confidence, especially when baby Victoria looks like the picture of health and happiness, leading me to believe that Nonna knows best.

Being the youngest of six children forced Lorella to grow up quickly. "I only had one doll growing up! My brother took it apart because it could talk, so he could see how it worked. Girls were treated differently then. I remember when it was a holiday or a birthday the only gifts people would give you were linens to embroider. I wanted clothes or jewelry; I didn't understand at the time. But when I got older I had a chest full of these hand-embroidered linens, which became my *corredo* (bridal trousseau). You can't replace those things."

Thinking back to those different times, she recalls some of her first memories in the kitchen. "One day I went to my sister's house, who had a cast on her broken leg. She asked me to cook something. At first, I was afraid to turn the stove on because my mother never wanted me to cook, but all of a sudden, I started cooking. I don't know where it came from, but I made *involtini*, *tortellini* with cream sauce, a bunch of things I was surprised I even knew how to make! I guess it's in my blood." After she was married and living in America, her own personal culinary evolution began. "I was always looking at cookbooks and trying recipes on my own. My kids still remember my very first risotto with champagne that was a disaster," she laughs. "They tasted it and asked for some *pasta pomodoro* instead," she recounts with a big smile. "But I'm guilty of being that Italian woman who pushes people to eat. I made it, so why do we have to let it go to waste?"

Love brought Nonna Lorella to America when she was barely out of her teens. "I met my husband, Massimo, when I was ten, because my brother was going out with his sister. It was all so innocent and he lived in America already. A few years later he came back to town on vacation and just to see him I would pretend to sweep outside the house." We all laugh at how it used to be to flirt Italian-style. "I wanted to go to America with him, but everyone thought I was too young and I had to get married first. So we did, and I found myself in a little apartment in Brooklyn. I was happy because my sisters were living here

already. I learned English by playing bingo, and then I had my two kids." While Lorella raised the children, her husband ran their family restaurant, Massimo's, which has become an Italian-American institution in the town of Bridgeport, Connecticut. "When we bought the restaurant, we made our tagline *fatto con amore*, made with love, because our clients were all like our friends. The restaurant is like our home, and I think people feel at home there."

Nonna Lorella admits that restaurant life wasn't always easy for her family. "At least once a week, both our children have to come over to eat. It's not easy in the restaurant business to find that time, but we make it happen because it's important. The restaurant is the restaurant, but home is home," she continues.

"Holidays are a big deal at my house. My family is very big, so now when I get together with all my siblings, it's a lot of fun. We start with this long dining room table, and as the night goes on, we keep adding pieces to it to make the table even longer, because more and more people keep dropping by." It's the Italian way. On Christmas, Nonna Lorella and her family try to keep things simple by attending midnight Mass to watch Nonna Lorella sing in the church choir, something she has been doing since her youth. Everyone then reunites at her house for a little nibble of her famous Pizza di Scarola (recipe on page 36), which is an old Neapolitan Christmas tradition. The night is filled with singing and storytelling. "I love people. I love making them feel welcome. Some people, you go to their house and they make you feel funny if you stay for dinner, but my house is always open for my friends," she says with a big smile, as she pours me a second limoncello, not seeming to care that it is well past midnight. "My friends are my family."

SEAFOOD CAVATELLI

Cavatelli ai Frutti di Mare

PREP TIME: 15 MINUTES • COOK TIME: 35 MINUTES • YIELD: 4 TO 6 SERVINGS

This incredibly versatile seafood pasta packs in all the flavor. *Frutti di mare* literally translates to "fruits of the sea," so feel free to mix up the combination of seafood for your Feast of the Seven Fishes. Nonna Romana loves to serve this with cavatelli, as the little "cave" shape of the pasta perfectly absorbs the sauce.

1½ pounds (680 g) live lobster

¼ cup (60 ml) extra-virgin olive oil, divided

Salt, to taste

16 ounces (454 g) cavatelli pasta, preferably homemade

4 cloves garlic, sliced

Red pepper flakes, to taste

10 cherry tomatoes, halved

½ cup (120 ml) white wine

18 littleneck clams, meat removed and juice separated and filtered

2 tablespoons (8 g) minced fresh parsley, divided

½ pound (227 g) large shrimp, washed and deveined

1   Place the lobster on a cutting board, belly side up with the tail closest to you. With a large chef's knife or cleaver, halve the lobster lengthwise, beginning at the head and splitting down the tail. Separate the two claws from the arms. Chop the arms in pieces and set aside. Roughly chop the lobster halves into 2-inch (5 cm) pieces and set aside.

2   Heat 2 tablespoons (30 ml) of the olive oil in a large skillet over medium-high heat. Add all the lobster pieces to the pan, meat side down, and sear for about 5 minutes, until the meat is firm. Transfer the lobster to a plate and set aside.

3   Bring a medium stockpot of salted water to a boil. Drop the cavatelli into the boiling water. Cook until al dente. Drain.

4   In the same pan you cooked the lobster, add the remaining 2 tablespoons (30 ml) olive oil, the garlic, and red pepper flakes. Cook the garlic for about 30 seconds, until it just begins to turn golden. Add the cherry tomatoes. Cook for 2 to 3 minutes.

5   Stir in the wine. Cook for 2 to 3 minutes, until the alcohol evaporates. Add the juice from the clams and let the mixture come to a boil. Add 1 tablespoon (4 g) of the parsley and return all the lobster pieces to the pan. Cook for 2 minutes.

6   Add the clams and shrimp to the pan. Cook for 6 to 7 minutes, until the shrimp are pink and the clams are firm. Taste for and season with salt as desired.

7   Add the cavatelli to the pan. Cook, tossing, for 2 minutes. Sprinkle with the remaining 1 tablespoon (4 g) parsley and serve.

LIVORNESE FISH STEW

Cacciucco Livornese

PREP TIME: 20 MINUTES • COOK TIME: 2 HOURS • YIELD: 6 TO 8 SERVINGS

This Tuscan seafood stew used to be made by poor fishermen as a way to utilize fish that didn't sell. Nonna Rosa remembers her trips as a girl to the *mercato centrale* in Livorno, where her mother would send her and her sisters to buy fish for a *cacciucco* that would feed their family of ten. "They were all fishes you don't see too much today. *Palombo, gallinella, pesce prete, cicale.* Maybe we didn't appreciate them then because they were all we had, but the flavors were so good!"

3 tablespoons (45 ml) extra-virgin olive oil, plus more for drizzling

9 cloves garlic, divided

½ teaspoon red pepper flakes

5 fresh sage leaves

2 pounds (907 g) octopus, cleaned, tentacles cut into 3 pieces, and heads halved

1 cup (240 ml) water, plus more for the octopus as needed

1½ pounds (680 g) cuttlefish, cleaned

2½ cups (625 g) passata or tomato puree

1 pound (454 g) monkfish, cut into 3-inch (7.5 cm) pieces

2 pounds (907 g) mussels

1 pound (454 g) shrimp, heads on if possible

Salt, to taste

1 loaf semolina bread, sliced

❙ Nonna Rosa Says
Leaving the heads on the shrimp and the shells of the mussels in the stew while it cooks is very important, because they add much more complexity in flavor.

1   Heat 3 tablespoons (45 ml) olive oil in a large skillet with a lid over medium-high heat. Add 8 of the garlic cloves, the red pepper flakes, and sage. Cook for 1 minute. Add the octopus to the pan. Cook for 3 to 5 minutes, tossing with a wooden spoon until the purple liquid is drawn out.

2   Reduce the heat to low, cover the pan, and cook for 40 to 45 minutes, until the octopus is tender. Check on the octopus occasionally; if it looks dry, add a few tablespoons (45 ml) of water. Add the cuttlefish to the pan. Cook, tossing with a wooden spoon, for 1 minute.

3   Add the passata and 1 cup (240 ml) water. Increase the heat to medium-high and bring the mixture to a boil. Reduce the heat to low, cover the pan, and cook for 20 minutes, until the sauce reduces some. Add the monkfish to the pan, cover, and cook for 20 minutes.

4   Add the mussels and shrimp. Increase the heat to medium-high. Cook for 10 to 15 minutes, until the shrimp are firm and the mussels have opened (discard any that do not open). Taste and season with salt as desired. Let rest for 15 minutes before serving. In the meantime, toast the garlic bread.

5   Preheat the oven to 400°F (200°C).

6   Rub each slice of bread with the remaining garlic clove and drizzle with olive oil. Arrange the bread slices in a single layer on a baking sheet. Toast for 10 minutes, or until the bread develops some color.

7   Ladle the stew into bowls and serve with the bread.

BAKED CLAMS

Vongole Gratinate

PREP TIME: 15 MINUTES • COOK TIME: 10 MINUTES • YIELD: 12 SERVINGS

On Christmas Eve, there never seems to be enough baked clams, and a good baked clam is a thing of beauty. You will find them on most Italian-American restaurant menus, and everyone—and I do mean everyone—has their own secret to the bread-crumb topping, which can make or break this dish. Nonna Romana's secret is to keep it incredibly simple. She says no to crazy spices and wine, which can really overpower the delicate flavor of the clams. But she says a resounding yes to a bit of cheese—Pecorino Romano, to be precise—which is the only cheese she dares mix with any shellfish (but never on a pasta dish). You want to make sure to use a smaller variety of clams, which are more flavorful than the larger ones. Littlenecks are ideal.

24 littleneck clams, washed and scrubbed

1 cup (115 g) plain bread crumbs

1 tablespoon (6 g) grated Pecorino Romano cheese

4 cloves garlic, minced

2 tablespoons (8 g) minced fresh parsley

¼ cup (60 ml) extra-virgin olive oil, plus more for drizzling

¼ teaspoon salt

Dash black pepper

Lemon wedges, for serving

1 Preheat the oven to 500°F (250°C).

2 Shuck the clams with a bowl underneath to catch the juice and leave the meat on the half shell. Reserve the juice from the clams. Alternatively, put a medium stockpot with a lid over medium heat and add the clams. Cover and cook the clams for about 2 minutes, just until they begin to open. You don't want to cook the clams, just open the shells. Using a sturdy knife, pry open the shells and position the meat on the half shell. Place all the clams on a baking sheet.

3 In a medium bowl, add the bread crumbs, cheese, garlic, parsley, and olive oil. Mix until the olive oil is fully absorbed by the bread crumbs and the mixture looks uniformly wet. Season with the salt and pepper.

4 Place 1 heaping tablespoon (15 g) of the bread-crumb mixture over each clam until the clam is completely covered. Do not pack it down. Drizzle the clams with olive oil. Pour the reserved clam juice into the bottom of the baking sheet.

5 Bake for 5 to 7 minutes. Turn the oven to broil and broil the clams for 1 minute to brown, watching closely to prevent burning. Serve with the lemon wedges.

BAKED CALAMARI WITH BREAD CRUMBS

Calamari alla Graffiu'

PREP TIME: 15 MINUTES • COOK TIME: 18 MINUTES • YIELD: 4 TO 6 SERVINGS

My Zia Rosa may kill me for letting you guys in on this little secret, but I have to tell the truth: this particular recipe actually belongs to my Zio Domenico. Variations of this super-simple baked calamari dish, known as *calamari alla graffiu'* in Puglia, can be found throughout southern Italy. My Zio Domenico spent nearly half a century working at the Italian-American institution that is Gargiulo's restaurant in Coney Island, and in between waiting tables, he wandered into the kitchen to learn a few things. One day years ago, he came home and tried to replicate their famous baked calamari, which are tossed in a delicious savory bread crumb and cheese mixture that becomes beautifully charred in a hot oven. The secret is giving the pan a good scrape every few minutes, so they char evenly on all sides.

2 pounds (907 g) cleaned calamari, bodies cut into 1½-inch (4 cm) rings and tentacles left whole

1 cup (240 ml) extra-virgin olive oil

2 cups (230 g) plain bread crumbs

¾ cup (75 g) grated Pecorino Romano cheese

¼ cup (15 g) minced fresh parsley

10 cloves garlic, minced

½ teaspoon salt

¼ teaspoon black pepper

Lemon wedges, for serving

1 Preheat the oven to 500°F (250°C).

2 Wash the calamari under cold running water and pat dry with a paper towel. Make sure the calamari are as dry as possible.

3 Place the olive oil in a small bowl. Set aside.

4 In a medium bowl, add the bread crumbs, cheese, parsley, garlic, salt, and pepper. Mix well.

5 Dip the calamari in the oil and then in the bread-crumb mixture. Shake off the excess and spread the calamari onto 2 baking sheets. Make sure not to crowd the calamari too much.

6 Bake for 15 to 18 minutes, until the calamari are very golden brown and almost charred. Using a metal spatula, scrape and turn the calamari halfway through the baking time. Serve with the lemon wedges.

FRITTERS WITH BACCALÀ AND ANCHOVIES

Pizze Fritte con Baccalà e Acciughe

PREP TIME: 2 HOURS 30 MINUTES* • COOK TIME: 30 MINUTES • YIELD: ABOUT 60 FRITTERS

*REQUIRES 1 TO 3 DAYS OF SOAKING

"On Christmas we gotta have the *pizze fritt' e baccalà*," Nonna Antoinette says to me. Even when she speaks English, it's with a little Neapolitan flair! Pizze fritte are a classic savory variety of *zeppole* from the Naples area that are filled with steamed baccalà or salty anchovies and fried to perfection.

1 pound (454 g) baccalà (salt cod)

½ teaspoon sugar

2 cups (480 ml) warm water, divided

1 packet (¼ ounce, or 7 g) active dry yeast

4 cups (480 g) all-purpose or 00 flour

2 teaspoons salt

1 teaspoon black pepper

Oil, for frying

Oil-packed anchovy fillets, as desired, broken into small pieces

Home for the Holidays

If there's one tradition I hope my children continue after I'm gone, it's making pizze fritte. *Because it's not like you can go buy them at a bakery if you want to; they're the kind of things you have to make fresh yourself. So personal to our family.*
—Nonna Antoinette Capodicci

1   Put the baccalà in a large bowl with enough cold water to cover it. Place the bowl in the refrigerator and change the water 3 times a day. Soak for 1 to 3 days, depending on the saltiness. Drain.

2   Put the baccalà in a small stockpot and cover with cold water. Bring to a boil over high heat. Reduce the heat to a simmer and cook the baccalà for 15 to 20 minutes, or until it flakes easily. Transfer to a plate and let cool. Once the baccalà is cool enough to handle, shred it by hand into small pieces. Set aside.

3   In a small bowl, dissolve the sugar in 1 cup (240 ml) of the warm water. Add the yeast and let sit until the mixture begins to bubble, 3 to 5 minutes.

4   In a large bowl, combine the flour, salt, and pepper. Whisk in the yeast mixture and the remaining 1 cup (240 ml) warm water until you have a very soft batter. Continue whisking until the mixture is very smooth, 3 to 5 minutes. Cover the bowl with plastic wrap and let rise in a very warm place for 2 hours, or until the batter doubles in size.

5   Heat about 2 inches (5 cm) of oil in a small stockpot over high heat. Line a plate with paper towels and set aside.

6   Take a full tablespoon (15 g) of dough and add some pieces of baccalà or bits of anchovy as desired and enclose it with more dough. Repeat with the remaining dough, baccalà, and anchovy as desired.

7   Working in batches, carefully drop the filled dough into the hot oil and fry until golden, 2 to 3 minutes per batch. Transfer to the paper towel–lined plate. Serve hot.

LINGUINE WITH EEL

Linguine con Capitone

PREP TIME: 2 HOURS • COOK TIME: 45 MINUTES • YIELD: 4 TO 6 SERVINGS

Of all the dishes served on *la Vigilia*, eel has the longest-standing place in Italian Christmas tradition. I still know many families who make their way to remote fish stores, hours away, to purchase an eel and let it live rent-free in their bathtub until Christmas Eve. The tradition of eating *capitone*, a female eel, has been going on for centuries in southern Italy, and is rooted deep in superstition. It is said that the eel symbolizes the snake that tempted Eve in the garden of Eden, and by eating it on Christmas Eve, it is possible to conquer it and ward off evil spirits. Many peasant families also appreciated the eel for its rich, fatty flesh, which provided great sustenance for the holiday. Most families who still carry on the tradition prefer to have their fishmonger prep the eel for them.

1½ pounds (680 g) fresh eel, cut into 3- to 4-inch-long (7.5 to 10 cm) pieces (ask your fishmonger to clean and skin it for you)

½ cup (120 ml) red wine vinegar

2 tablespoons (30 ml) extra-virgin olive oil

4 cloves garlic

4 bay leaves

½ cup (120 ml) dry white wine, such as Pinot Grigio

14 ounces (395 g) crushed tomatoes

1½ cups (350 ml) water

¼ teaspoon red pepper flakes

2 tablespoons (8 g) minced fresh parsley, divided

Salt, to taste

16 ounces (454 g) dried linguine

1. In a large bowl, combine the eel pieces and enough cold running water to cover. Add the vinegar. Soak for 2 hours. Drain and rinse the eel under cold running water.

2. Heat the olive oil in a large skillet with a lid over medium heat. Add the garlic and bay leaves. Cook for 1 to 2 minutes, until the garlic has colored and is fragrant.

3. Add the eel to the pan and sear for 5 to 7 minutes, turning occasionally with tongs.

4. Add the wine. Cook for about 2 minutes, until the alcohol evaporates.

5. Stir in the tomatoes, water, red pepper flakes, and 1 tablespoon (4 g) of the parsley. Reduce the heat to a simmer. Cover the pan and cook for 30 minutes. Taste and season with salt as desired.

6. Bring a medium stockpot of generously salted water to a boil. Drop in the linguine. Cook 1 to 2 minutes shy of al dente. Drain the pasta and add it to the sauce along with the remaining 1 tablespoon (4 g) parsley. Cook, tossing, for 1 to 2 minutes over medium-high heat.

7. Serve immediately in warm bowls.

Home for the Holidays
We would keep it [the eel] in a tub in the kitchen until Christmas Eve, and my mother, Regina, would go out back and kill it. My sisters and I were so scared at first, but my mother was tough!
—Nonna Rina Pesce

MUSSELS IN RED SAUCE

Zuppa di Cozze con Pomodoro

PREP TIME: 10 MINUTES • COOK TIME: 20 MINUTES • YIELD: 6 SERVINGS

Mussels were always plentiful and inexpensive in southern Italy, especially in Puglia, where my family has roots. Back in Italy, my Zia Rosa would have classically prepared these *in bianco*, in a simple white wine sauce. She learned to make them in this delightfully spicy red sauce from a Neapolitan neighbor in Brooklyn. We look forward to them every Christmas Eve, with crusty bread for dipping!

¼ cup (60 ml) extra-virgin olive oil, divided

6 cloves garlic, divided

2 pounds (907 g) mussels, scrubbed, rinsed, and beards removed

½ cup (120 ml) white wine

2 tablespoons (8 g) minced fresh parsley, divided

¼ teaspoon red pepper flakes, or to taste

14 ounces (395 g) crushed tomatoes

Salt, to taste

Italian bread, for serving (optional)

1 Put a small stockpot over medium heat and add 2 tablespoons (30 ml) of the olive oil. Once hot, add 3 of the garlic cloves. Cook for about 2 minutes, until golden and fragrant.

2 Add the mussels to the pot and cover the pot with a lid. Cook for 2 to 3 minutes, stirring the mussels occasionally with a wooden spoon, until the mussels have partially opened. Add the wine and 1 tablespoon (4 g) of the parsley. Cook, uncovered, for 2 to 3 more minutes, until the alcohol evaporates and the mussels have fully opened. Discard any mussels that do not open and set the rest aside. Strain the juice from the mussels through a fine-mesh strainer lined with a cheesecloth. Set aside.

3 Heat the remaining 2 tablespoons (30 ml) olive oil in a large skillet over medium-high heat. Add the red pepper flakes and the remaining 3 garlic cloves. Cook for 1 to 2 minutes, until the garlic is golden. Stir in the crushed tomatoes and remaining 1 tablespoon (4 g) parsley. Cook for about 5 minutes and then stir in the strained mussel juice. Bring to a boil and cook for 3 to 4 minutes. Taste and season with salt as desired.

4 Add the mussels to the sauce. Cover the pan and cook for 4 to 5 minutes. Serve with crusty Italian bread, if desired.

FRITTERS WITH BLACK OLIVES

Pettole con Olive

PREP TIME: 1 HOUR • COOK TIME: 20 MINUTES • YIELD: ABOUT 48 FRITTERS

Pettole are a type of yeast *zeppole* from southern Italy, usually eaten on Christmas Eve. Many villages also have pettole recipes that correspond with different saint days and holidays. Nonna Maria's pettole, with salt-cured olives, are a savory treat that works beautifully as an appetizer or even as a great addition to a holiday bread basket.

1¼ cups (150 g) all-purpose or 00 flour

1 teaspoon salt

1 packet (¼ ounce, or 7 g) active dry yeast

1 cup (240 ml) warm water

2 large eggs, at room temperature

1 cup (155 g) salt-cured olives, pitted and finely chopped

Olive oil, for dipping and frying

1 In a small bowl, whisk together the flour and salt. Set aside.

2 In another small bowl, dissolve the yeast in the warm water until it bubbles, about 3 minutes.

3 Add the eggs to the yeast and stir with a spoon until incorporated. Little by little, add the flour-salt mixture, stirring until fully incorporated and a smooth dough forms. Fold in the olives. Cover the bowl with plastic wrap and let rise in a warm place for 45 minutes to 1 hour, or until the dough doubles in size.

4 Heat about 1½ inches (4 cm) of olive oil in a small stockpot over high heat.

5 Fill a cup with some olive oil. Line a plate with paper towels and set aside.

6 Using a small ice cream scoop, dip the scoop into the olive oil and then into the dough. Working in batches, carefully drop the dough into the hot oil. Fry the fritters until golden brown, about 2 minutes per batch. Transfer to the paper towel–lined plate. Serve hot or warm.

FRIED WHITING

Merluzzi Fritti

PREP TIME: 4 HOURS 20 MINUTES • COOK TIME: 25 MINUTES • YIELD: 8 TO 10 SERVINGS

Whiting, or *merluzzi*, is a small fish that is often fried whole and then marinated in garlic, mint, and vinegar. While this dish can be a bit of an acquired taste, you just have to have some fried whiting to have a proper old-school Italian Christmas Eve. Nonna Romana and her sisters used to chase me around the house on Christmas Eve with a big plate trying to get me to eat it because the fish is considered "brain food," but today, I don't need too much convincing. I love how this fish is cooked with all the bones in, making its flesh super succulent.

WHITING

2 pounds (907 g) whiting, cleaned
   and gutted
Olive oil, for frying
All-purpose or 00 flour, for dredging

VINAIGRETTE MARINADE

2 tablespoons (12 g) minced
   fresh mint
5 cloves garlic, minced
½ cup (120 ml) red wine vinegar

1 **To make the whiting:** Rinse the whiting under cold running water and pat dry with paper towels. Try to get the fish as dry as possible to prevent the flour from caking on it.

2 Heat about 1½ inches (4 cm) of olive oil in a medium skillet over high heat.

3 Line a plate with paper towels and set aside. Place the flour in a shallow dish and dredge each whiting in the flour.

4 Carefully add 2 or 3 pieces at a time to the hot oil and fry until golden brown, 4 to 5 minutes per batch. Transfer to the paper towel–lined plate. Cool to room temperature.

5 **To make the vinaigrette marinade:** In a small bowl, whisk together the mint, garlic, and vinegar. Arrange the fried whiting in a 13 × 9-inch (33 × 23 cm) pan, in a single layer if possible. Pour the marinade over the cooled whiting and refrigerate for at least 4 hours or overnight. This can be made up to 2 days in advance.

BAKED SHRIMP WITH BREAD CRUMBS

Gamberi al Forno

PREP TIME: 5 MINUTES • COOK TIME: 30 MINUTES • YIELD: 6 TO 8 SERVINGS

This shrimp recipe is fast, easy, and super flavorful. Nonna Maria usually has the shrimp ready to go on a baking sheet and pops them in the oven as soon as guests arrive, so they're cooked to perfection by the time everyone is ready to eat. They're great for holiday entertaining because they can be served hot, but they're just as delicious at room temperature.

½ cup (120 ml) extra-virgin olive oil, plus more for greasing the pan and drizzling

2 tablespoons (8 g) minced fresh parsley

1 teaspoon dried oregano

¼ cup (30 g) plain bread crumbs

¼ cup (25 g) grated Pecorino Romano cheese

Salt, to taste

Black pepper, to taste

2 pounds (907 g) jumbo shrimp, peeled and deveined, tails on

1 Preheat the oven to 370°F (188°C). Grease a baking sheet with olive oil.

2 In a medium bowl, mix together the parsley, oregano, bread crumbs, cheese, salt, and pepper. Set aside.

3 In a large bowl, toss the shrimp with ½ cup (120 ml) olive oil, until the shrimp are evenly coated. Add the oiled shrimp to the bread-crumb mixture and toss until the shrimp are evenly coated. Arrange the shrimp on the prepared baking sheet and drizzle with a bit more olive oil.

4 Bake for 30 minutes, or until the shrimp are golden. For a bit more color, turn the oven to broil and broil for 1 to 2 minutes, if desired.

Home for the Holidays
On Christmas Eve at midnight, I always ask the youngest grandchild to hold the baby Jesus from the presepe *(nativity) and lead a little procession around the house as we sing the song 'Tu scendi dalle stelle.' It's a song that celebrates the birth of* Gesu' bambino *(baby Jesus). Then we pass the little doll around because everyone must kiss it before we open presents. This is my favorite Christmas tradition.* —Nonna Maria Pesce

SAVORY FRITTERS WITH CINNAMON AND CLOVES

Piccialetiegli

PREP TIME: 1 HOUR 15 MINUTES • COOK TIME: 15 MINUTES • YIELD: ABOUT 12 FRITTERS

The shape of *piccialatiegli* resembles a pretzel, and once the dough hits the hot oil, its unmistakable aroma fills Nonna Teresa's kitchen in Queens, New York. Nonna Teresa adopted her Neapolitan mother-in-law's tradition of making these savory fritters on Christmas Eve when she married over forty years ago. "When my mother-in-law was alive, she would be rolling the dough and someone else would fry them, and we could never make enough because everyone would eat them as we made them. She would always want to drop the last one into the oil herself, and she would proudly declare, '*E quest' é cento!* (And this makes one hundred!)'"

3 cups (360 g) all-purpose or
    00 flour, plus more for dusting
1 teaspoon ground cinnamon
1 teaspoon salt
1 teaspoon ground cloves
½ teaspoon ground nutmeg
1 teaspoon sugar
1¼ cups (300 ml) warm water
1 packet (¼ ounce, or 7 g) active
    dry yeast
1 tablespoon (15 ml) extra-virgin
    olive oil
Oil, for frying

1. In a medium bowl, whisk together the flour, cinnamon, salt, cloves, and nutmeg. Set aside.

2. In the bowl of a stand mixer fritted with the dough hook attachment, dissolve the sugar in the warm water. Add the yeast and let sit until the mixture begins to bubble, 3 to 5 minutes. Add the olive oil.

3. With the mixer running on low speed, gradually add the dry ingredients to the wet ingredients. Increase the speed to medium and mix until a dough begins to form, about 3 minutes. The dough will be sticky. Cover the bowl with plastic wrap and let sit in a warm place to rise for about 1 hour (see Nonna Teresa Says).

4. Lightly flour a work surface and turn the dough out onto it. Knead the dough for 5 minutes and then divide the dough into 12 or 13 equal pieces.

5. Flour your hands and roll each piece into 2-inch-thick (5 cm) ropes, 10 to 12 inches (25 to 30 cm) long. Create a fish or cross shape with the dough, crossing one end over the other.

6. Heat about 3 inches (7.5 cm) of oil in a small heavy-bottomed stockpot over high heat. Working in batches of 2 or 3 at a time, carefully drop the dough into the hot oil and fry until brown, about 2 minutes per batch. Serve immediately.

Nonna Teresa Says
If you cannot find a warm spot in the house to let the dough rise, place the bowl inside your oven with the light on. The oven should be a constant 80 to 85°F (27 to 30°C)—the perfect environment to let dough rise.

FRIED CALAMARI

Calamari Fritti

PREP TIME: 15 MINUTES • COOK TIME: 20 MINUTES • YIELD: 4 TO 6 SERVINGS

Fried calamari hits everyone's Italian comfort-food spot. The plate never makes it more than one round around the dinner table! Nonna Romana's calamari are coated in refined semolina flour, which gives them a little more texture and a gorgeous golden color. In Italy, fried calamari aren't quite as crunchy as they are here in the States. The outside coating is light and delicate, and doesn't overpower the seafood. These can be served Italian-American style with marinara sauce, but my favorite is simply with a squeeze of fresh lemon.

2 cups (334 g) refined semolina flour

2 tablespoons (30 ml) salt, plus more for sprinkling

Oil, for frying

2 pounds (907 g) cleaned calamari, bodies cut into ½-inch (13 mm) rings and tentacles left whole

Nonna Romana Says
Calamari need room! Don't overcrowd the pan when you're frying, or the calamari won't brown.

1 In a large mixing bowl, whisk together the semolina and salt, breaking up any lumps.

2 Heat about 2 inches (5 cm) of oil in a large heavy-bottomed skillet over high heat.

3 With a paper towel, pat the calamari dry. Try and get them as dry as possible or else they will be soggy.

4 Dredge the calamari in the semolina mixture and transfer to a fine-mesh strainer to shake off any excess. Make sure all the pieces have an even coating.

5 Line a plate with paper towels.

6 Place the calamari in the oil and fry in 5 or 6 batches, for 3 to 4 minutes per batch, or until lightly golden brown. Transfer to the paper towel–lined plate to drain.

7 Sprinkle with extra salt. Serve immediately.

STUFFED CALAMARI WITH SPAGHETTI

Calamari Ripieni con Spaghetti

PREP TIME: 15 MINUTES • COOK TIME: 55 MINUTES • YIELD: 4 TO 6 SERVINGS

Helping Nonna Romana stuff calamari brings back so many memories from my childhood. She would ask me to help her because my little fingers were best for getting all the stuffing inside the calamari tube. Today, we still do it together but with demitasse spoons instead. We then cook them in a slightly spicy tomato sauce and say a prayer that the filling doesn't come out as the calamari shrink.

SAUCE

3 tablespoons (45 ml) extra-virgin olive oil

1 small onion, cut into a ¼-inch (6 mm) dice

42 ounces (1.25 L) crushed tomatoes

2 tablespoons (8 g) chopped fresh parsley

Pinch salt

¼ teaspoon red pepper flakes

CALAMARI

1 pound (454 g) whole fresh calamari

2 large eggs

¾ cup (75 g) grated Pecorino Romano cheese

⅓ cup (38 g) plain bread crumbs

3 tablespoons (45 ml) extra-virgin olive oil

2 tablespoons (8 g) chopped fresh parsley

3 cloves garlic, finely chopped

Salt, to taste

Black pepper, to taste

1 to 2 tablespoons (30 to 45 ml) milk, as needed

16 ounces (454 g) dried spaghetti

1 **To make the sauce:** Heat the olive oil in a large skillet over medium heat. Add the onion. Cook for 3 to 5 minutes, until translucent. Stir in the tomatoes, parsley, and salt. Add the red pepper flakes and bring the sauce to a boil. Reduce the heat to a simmer. Cook for 15 to 20 minutes.

2 **To make the calamari:** Cut a very small hole at the tips of the tails, as it will enable you to run fresh water through the calamari and completely clean them.

3 In a medium bowl, stir together the eggs, cheese, bread crumbs, olive oil, parsley, and garlic. Season with salt and pepper. Mix well until you have a semisoft stuffing. If the mixture looks dry, add 1 to 2 tablespoons (30 to 45 ml) of milk as needed.

4 Using a teaspoon, fill the bodies of the calamari with the stuffing up to ½ inch (13 mm) from the top. Be careful not to overfill. Secure the calamari with toothpicks, if necessary. (The calamari will shrink as they cook, so it's normal to have some filling come out.)

5 Add the calamari to the sauce and cover the pan. Continue to cook over low heat for 25 to 30 minutes. From time to time, stir the sauce and the calamari to prevent them from sticking to the bottom. Transfer the calamari and sauce to a rimmed serving plate.

6 Bring a medium stockpot of generously salted water to a boil. Drop in the spaghetti. Cook until the pasta is al dente. Add the spaghetti to the sauce and toss for 1 to 2 minutes over medium heat.

7 Serve the spaghetti in bowls with the stuffed calamari.

LINGUINE IN WHITE CLAM SAUCE

Linguine alle Vongole

PREP TIME: 10 MINUTES • COOK TIME: 20 MINUTES • YIELD: 4 TO 6 SERVINGS

Okay, so I have a confession to make: Nonna Romana learned this recipe from none other than my dad, Vito! In our family, he is undoubtedly the king of the clam sauce, and it's so good, we usually demand he make it for nearly every holiday. Over the years, Nonna has battled with him over who makes it best, and while her original clam sauce was quite good, the version she makes today is more my father's. The secret to a good white clam sauce, which is more popular in Italy than the red variety, lies in its simplicity. The fewer ingredients, the better, and you must always—always!—use fresh clams. For this dish, you will want to use the smallest clams possible, which pack in a lot more flavor, so if you can find cockles, use them.

36 littleneck clams or 3 pounds (1.4 kg) cockles, scrubbed and rinsed

Salt, to taste

16 ounces (454 g) dried linguine

¼ cup (60 ml) extra-virgin olive oil

5 cloves garlic

¼ teaspoon red pepper flakes

2 tablespoons (8 g) chopped fresh parsley, divided

½ cup (120 ml) dry white wine, such as Pinot Grigio

1 Put a large saucepan with a lid over high heat and add the clams. Cover the pan and cook for 5 to 7 minutes, until the clams open completely. Separate the meat of the clams from the shells and discard most of the shells; you can reserve a few for garnish if you desire. Discard any clams that do not open. Transfer the meat to a medium bowl. Strain the juice from the clams through a fine-mesh strainer lined with cheesecloth into a glass. Set aside. Rinse out the pan used for the clams.

2 Bring a medium stockpot of generously salted water to a boil. Drop the linguine into the water.

3 Heat the olive oil in the rinsed saucepan over medium heat. Add the garlic and red pepper flakes. Cook for 1 minute. Add the strained clam broth and 1 tablespoon (4 g) of the parsley. Bring to a boil and add the wine. Cook for 2 to 3 minutes, until the alcohol evaporates. Add the shelled clams. Cook for 3 to 4 minutes.

4 Scoop out 1 cup (240 ml) of pasta water and set aside. Once the pasta is just shy of al dente, scoop it out and add it to the pan with the clams. Cook, tossing, for 1 to 2 minutes over medium heat. Add a bit of the reserved pasta water if the pasta looks a bit dry. Sprinkle with the remaining 1 tablespoon (4 g) parsley and serve immediately.

CHRISTMAS DAY

NONNA ANTOINETTE CAPODICCI'S

RICE TIMBALLO

Sartù di Riso

PREP TIME: 20 MINUTES • COOK TIME: 2 HOUR 30 MINUTES • YIELD: 10 SERVINGS

When Nonna Antoinette wants to make something super special that will impress her holiday guests, she makes her Nonna's famous *sartù di riso alla Napoletana*. The first time I ever saw a sartu, I was completely mesmerized. Nonna Antoinette makes a mold of meat sauce–flavored rice in a Bundt pan and fills it with sautéed peas, pancetta, and hard-boiled eggs. And did I mention tiny meatballs?

SAUCE

¼ cup (60 ml) extra-virgin olive oil

1 small onion, cut into ¼-inch
   (6 mm) dice

1 clove garlic, cut into ¼-inch
   (6 mm) dice

6 ounces (170 g) sweet Italian
   sausage links (2 or 3 links)

2 cans (28 ounces, or 794 g, each)
   crushed tomatoes

1 cup (240 ml) water

Salt, to taste

4 fresh basil leaves

MEATBALLS

1 slice day-old Italian bread,
   crust removed

¼ cup (60 ml) whole milk

1 large egg, beaten

½ teaspoon salt

¼ teaspoon black pepper

⅛ teaspoon garlic powder

¼ cup (25 g) grated Parmigiano-
   Reggiano cheese

4 ounces (115 g) ground beef

Olive oil, for frying

1   **To make the sauce:** Heat the olive oil in a small stockpot over medium-high heat. Add the onion, garlic, and sausage. Cook for 7 to 10 minutes, stirring often, until the sausage has browned nicely and the onion is soft.

2   Stir in the crushed tomatoes, water, and salt. Reduce the heat to a simmer. Cover the pan and cook until the sauce thickens and is slightly reduced, about 1 hour.

3   Remove from the heat and stir in the basil. Remove the sausage from the sauce and slice the links into ¼-inch-thick (6 mm) slices. Transfer to a plate. Set the sauce aside, uncovered, while you make the meatballs.

4   **To make the meatballs:** In a small bowl, combine the bread and milk. Let sit for 2 to 3 minutes.

5   Meanwhile in a medium bowl, combine the egg, salt, pepper, garlic powder, cheese, and ground beef. Squeeze the excess moisture out of the bread and add it to the meat mixture. Using your hands, mix everything until well combined. With damp hands, roll the mixture into little balls about ½ inch (13 mm) in diameter.

6   Line a plate with paper towels and set aside. Heat about 1 inch (2.5 cm) of olive oil in a medium heavy-bottomed skillet over high heat. Working in batches, fry the meatballs until browned on all sides, about 2 minutes per batch. Transfer to the paper towel–lined plate. Set aside.

continued

RICE

3 quarts (2.8 L) water

2 teaspoons salt

16 ounces (454 g) Arborio rice, rinsed

3 large eggs, beaten

2 cups (200 g) grated Parmigiano-Reggiano cheese

PEAS

1 ounce (28 g) dried porcini mushrooms (optional)

2 tablespoons (30 ml) extra-virgin olive oil

½ small onion, cut into ¼-inch (6 mm) dice

2 ounces (55 g) pancetta, cut into ¼-inch (6 mm) dice

1 cup (130 g) frozen peas, thawed

ASSEMBLY

2 tablespoons (30 g) butter, at room temperature, divided

¼ cup (30 g) plain bread crumbs

2 large hard-boiled eggs, peeled and cut into small chunks

8 ounces (225 g) fresh mozzarella cheese, cut into ½-inch (13 mm) dice

¼ cup (25 g) grated Parmigiano-Reggiano cheese, divided

Nonna Antoinette Says
If you don't love some of the filling ingredients, feel free to leave them out.

7 **To make the rice:** In a small stockpot over high heat, combine the water and salt, and bring to a boil. Add the rice. Cook for 20 to 25 minutes, until the rice is al dente. Drain and transfer to a medium bowl.

8 Add 2 cups (475 ml) of the sauce to the rice and stir well to combine. Spread the rice in an even layer on a baking sheet and let cool for 10 to 15 minutes. When cool, put the rice back into the bowl and mix in the beaten eggs and cheese. Set aside.

9 **To make the peas:** If using the dried porcini, place them in a medium bowl with 1 cup (240 ml) of warm water and let soak for 10 to 15 minutes to rehydrate. In the meantime, cook the peas.

10 Put a small skillet over medium-high heat. Add the olive oil, onion, and pancetta. Cook for 3 to 5 minutes, until the pancetta is crisp and the onion is soft. Add the peas. Cook for 5 minutes, stirring often.

11 Drain and finely chop the rehydrated porcinis. Add them to the peas. Cook for 2 to 3 minutes. Remove from the heat and set aside.

12 **To assemble:** Preheat the oven to 350°F (180°C). Grease a 12-cup (2.8 L) Bundt pan with 1 tablespoon (15 g) of the butter. Dust the pan evenly with bread crumbs, making sure there are no bare spots.

13 Press half of the rice mixture into the bottom of the prepared pan. Wet your hands and press the rice firmly to coat the bottom and all the way up the sides and middle of the pan. Use the back of a wet spoon to make a well in the rice. Fill the well with the sliced sausage, meatballs, peas, hard-boiled egg pieces, and mozzarella, evenly packing the filling down. Cover with 2 tablespoons (30 ml) of sauce and 2 tablespoons (12.5 g) of the Parmigiano-Reggiano.

14 Put the remaining rice over the filling. Wet your hands and firmly pack the filling down. Add 2 tablespoons (30 ml) of sauce on top and sprinkle with the remaining 2 tablespoons (12.5 g) Parmigiano-Reggiano. Dot the top with the remaining 1 tablespoon (15 g) butter.

15 Bake for 40 to 45 minutes. Let rest for 15 to 20 minutes before inverting and cutting.

16 To invert, wearing oven mitts, place a large plate over the bottom of the Bundt pan. Place one hand over the top of the pan and flip the pan over onto the plate. Place the plate on the counter and lift the pan off. Serve warm.

NONNA MARIA'S ZUCCHINI FRITTERS

Polpette di Zucchine

PREP TIME: 5 MINUTES • COOK TIME: 12 MINUTES • YIELD: ABOUT 24 FRITTERS

Try as you might, it is simply impossible to have just one of Nonna Maria's zucchini fritters. She mixes finely chopped zucchini into a thick batter and fries them until they're golden brown and irresistible, making them the perfect holiday finger food.

1 medium zucchini, finely minced

1 small onion, minced

6 tablespoons (38 g) grated Pecorino Romano cheese

2 tablespoons (15 g) plain bread crumbs

2 tablespoons (8 g) minced fresh parsley

3 large eggs

2 tablespoons (30 ml) all-purpose or 00 flour

1 teaspoon salt

¼ teaspoon black pepper

Oil, for frying

1 In a medium bowl, add the zucchini, onion, cheese, bread crumbs, parsley, eggs, flour, salt, and pepper. Mix well with a spoon until all the ingredients are fully combined. The batter should be thick enough to drop by spoonfuls.

2 Line a plate with paper towels and set aside.

3 Heat about 1½ inches (4 cm) of oil in a medium skillet over medium-high heat. Working in batches, drop the batter by tablespoonfuls (15 g each) into the hot oil. Fry until the fritters are golden brown, about 2 minutes per batch. Transfer to the paper towel–lined plate to drain. Serve hot.

EGG DROP CHICKEN SOUP

Stracciatella

PREP TIME: 15 MINUTES • COOK TIME: 2 HOURS • YIELD: 4 TO 6 SERVINGS

Stracciatella is one of those things that is so super simple to make that you would wonder why you even need a recipe. Nonna Annita has been making this soup since her childhood in Lazio's Ciociaria and swears that the mastery of this iconic Italian egg drop soup is a combination of technique and high-quality ingredients. Sure, you can use store-bought chicken stock, but her homemade recipe really takes it to the next level. In her home, this is the perfect Christmas Day first course that doesn't fill her guests up too much.

4 quarts (3.8 L) cold water

2 teaspoons salt, plus more
   to taste

2 celery ribs, ends trimmed

10 baby carrots

½ whole chicken or 2 pounds
   (907 g) bone-in chicken thighs
   (you can use any chicken with
   a bone, as long as you choose
   fatty pieces), rinsed under cold
   running water

Black pepper, to taste

3 large eggs

1 In a small stockpot, combine the cold water, 2 teaspoons salt, celery, and carrots. Bring to a boil.

2 Add the chicken and reduce the heat to a simmer. Cover the pot halfway and simmer for 1 hour and 30 minutes.

3 Remove from the heat and transfer the chicken and vegetables to a bowl. Once the chicken is cool enough to handle, pull the meat apart and reserve for a different use. Discard the vegetables.

4 Pour the broth through a fine-mesh strainer into another pot. Bring to a boil. Taste and season with more salt and pepper as desired. Reduce the heat to low.

5 Crack the eggs, one at a time, into a small bowl and beat. With a fork, stir the broth in a circular motion while drizzling the eggs into the moving broth. Stir the eggs gently with a fork until strings form, about 1 minute. Bring to a boil once more and serve immediately.

NONNA DOROTEA CRISTINO'S

RIB-EYE ROAST

Costata di Manzo

PREP TIME: 18 MINUTES • COOK TIME: 4 HOURS • YIELD: 6 TO 8 SERVINGS

A good rib-eye roast is a safe bet to serve for any holiday. Nonna Dorotea's secret to a good roast is inserting whole garlic cloves into the meat as it cooks, so it absorbs the garlic's amazing flavor. If you're reading this recipe and think it sounds like a lot of garlic, it is! But Nonna knows best!

SPICE RUB

¼ cup (34 g) minced garlic (about 10 cloves)

3 tablespoons (11 g) Italian seasoning

3 tablespoons (54 g) coarse kosher salt

3 tablespoons (26 g) peppercorns

½ cup (120 ml) extra-virgin olive oil

ROAST

1 boneless beef rib eye (7 pounds, or 3.2 kg), do not trim the fat

30 cloves garlic

1 Preheat the oven to 400°F (200°C).

2 **To make the spice rub:** In a small bowl, mix together all the rub ingredients. Set aside.

3 **To make the roast:** Using a sharp knife, make 30 cuts all over the roast, about 2 inches (5 cm) deep. Insert 1 whole garlic clove into each cut. If a clove is too large, cut it in half.

4 Rub the spice rub all over the roast, coating the entire surface well. Massage the rub into the roast for 2 to 3 minutes. Place the roast, fatty side up, on the rack of a large roasting pan. Roast for 30 minutes.

5 Reduce the oven temperature to 325°F (170°C) and roast for 3 hours and 30 minutes to 4 hours, until an instant-read meat thermometer reads 150°F (66°C) for medium-rare or 160°F (71°C) for medium. Let the roast rest for 15 to 20 minutes before slicing.

6 Using a very sharp knife, slice the roast into 1-inch-thick (2.5 cm) slices. Pour the juices from the pan through a fine-mesh strainer and serve with the roast.

POTATO GNOCCHI WITH TOMATO SAUCE

Gnocchi con Sugo di Pomodoro

PREP TIME: 40 MINUTES • COOK TIME: 1 HOUR • YIELD: MAKES 4 POUNDS (1.8 KG)
GNOCCHI; 6 TO 8 SERVINGS (SEE NONNA LAURA SAYS)

Nonna Laura's ninety-year-old hands still work faster than someone a third of her age. "The gnocchi very eass', you see?" she says as she looks up at me, smiling while she rolls gnocchi horizontally across a wooden board so that they sort of resemble rigatoni. The light, pillowy dough isn't sticky to the touch when coated in flour, but it's moist on the inside, which will result in perfectly soft gnocchi. The general rule is the softer the dough, the softer the gnocchi, so try to resist adding too much flour if you can help it. She dresses them with a simple tomato sauce that really soaks into the gnocchi and hits that delicious Italian comfort-food spot.

SAUCE

3 tablespoons (45 ml) extra-virgin
  olive oil

3 cloves garlic, sliced

1 small onion, cut into ¼-inch
  (6 mm) dice

1 small carrot, cut into ¼-inch
  (6 mm) dice

3 ounces (85 g) tomato paste

24 ounces (680 g) passata or
  tomato puree

1 teaspoon salt

4 or 5 fresh basil leaves

GNOCCHI

3 pounds (1.3 kg) Idaho potatoes
  (about 4 potatoes), scrubbed
  and unpeeled

1 large egg

1 tablespoon (15 g) salted butter

1 teaspoon salt

3 cups (360 g) all-purpose or
  00 flour, plus more for dusting

Grated Parmigiano-Reggiano
  cheese, for serving

1 **To make the sauce:** Heat the olive oil in a large skillet over medium heat. Add the garlic, onion, and carrot. Cook for 7 to 10 minutes, until the onion is translucent and the carrot is soft.

2 Add the tomato paste. Cook for 1 to 2 minutes, stirring with a wooden spoon. Stir in the passata, salt, and basil. Reduce the heat to low and cook, uncovered, for 15 to 20 minutes.

3. **To make the gnocchi:** With a sharp knife, make a slit all the way around the skin of the potatoes. (Doing this will make the skin easier to remove after boiling.)

4 In a small stockpot, combine the potatoes with enough cold water to cover them. Bring the pot to a boil. Cook the potatoes, uncovered, for 25 to 30 minutes, until they are easily pierced with a fork. Drain and set aside to cool.

5 Once the potatoes are cool enough to handle, peel off the skins. Immediately rice the potatoes into a large bowl. Add the egg, butter, and salt, and mix well. Transfer the potato mixture to a floured surface. With your hands, incorporate the flour into the potatoes until they absorb all the flour and a supple dough forms. The dough should not stick to your hands.

continued

6 Take a chunk of dough and roll it into a rope about ½ inch (13 mm) thick. Line up 4 or 5 ropes of the same length and cut them into pieces 1½ inches (4 cm) long. To give the gnocchi texture, they can be rolled over a gnocchi board, the back of a fork, or simply make an indentation with your finger. (Nonna Laura rolls them horizontally down a floured gnocchi board using her index and middle fingers so that the texture resembles a rigatoni noodle.) Lay the gnocchi on a floured baking tray or kitchen cloth, making sure they do not touch one another.

7 **To freeze:** Place the gnocchi on a baking sheet in a single layer. Place the tray in the freezer. Once the gnocchi are frozen they can be transferred to resealable plastic bags and kept frozen for 2 to 3 months. Do not thaw before cooking; simply drop them frozen into the salted boiling water and cook until the gnocchi bob to the surface.

8 **To cook the gnocchi:** Bring a large stockpot of generously salted water to a boil. Drop the gnocchi in the boiling water. Cook just until the gnocchi bob to the surface, 3 to 4 minutes. With a large slotted spoon, scoop out the gnocchi and add them to the tomato sauce. Cook, tossing in the sauce over medium-high heat, for 1 to 2 minutes.

9 Serve in warm bowls with a generous sprinkle of grated Parmigiano-Reggiano cheese.

"I don't know why I love cooking. Maybe because I love eating!"

"I don't gotta nothing for hide! Everything open!" Nonna Laura exclaims to me with wide eyes and a burst of energy. She flashes a pearly white smile that makes me forget she is in her early nineties. She throws her hands up before resting them on the floral print vinyl tablecloth that covers the massive table in the basement of her home in Astoria, Queens, which has hosted many family dinners over the past sixty years. "When I used to do the holidays, one holiday would usually last for four days because we would always be eating the leftovers. The last holiday I had here, I had thirty-five people and we were eating for three days. This was before dishwashers and paper plates." Everything in her basement seems as though it has been frozen in time. The Formica countertops in the second downstairs kitchen are sparklingly clean, and the tile floor still shines as if someone meticulously scrubs it every day.

"I don't know why I love cooking. Maybe because I love eating!" she says with a big laugh. "My mother made sure I learned to do everything. In Orsogna, we were always cooking, and we had to make do with anything we had. There were lots of gnocchi (see recipe on page 167) to make because there were just so many potatoes!" Nonna Laura smiles as she recalls the simplicity of the times. "Even though I don't feel as strong now, I try to do

what I can. For the Padre Pio church festival, I helped cook sixty pounds (27 kg) of pasta at a time and five hundred to six hundred meatballs. Fuhgeddaboudit! Last year I didn't feel up to it, but when they heard I wasn't coming, they begged me to come anyway and just sit, because they would miss me. I went and I helped make meatballs. Padre Pio gave me the strength that day, but the love of my family gives me strength every day. *Con la buona volontà tutto si fa!* (With goodwill you can do anything!)"

Nonna Laura recalls, "I still remember both of my Nonne. When you think about it, they weren't educated at all, but the things they would say were all true, all real, all good, important lessons. . . . When I was growing up, things were all so bad. But we had never seen good, so we were content with it. We just didn't realize how bad it actually was. It was all good for us," Nonna Laura says, as she recounts her early childhood in Orsogna, Abruzzo, which would later be ravaged during World War II. "I was born in 1925, and my father was already working in America. I remember him and I don't," she says laughing. "Every five years he would come home and make another baby with my mother until there were three girls. We lived off the money from America, because in Italy there was nothing."

With the end of the war came Nonna Laura's marriage to her sweetheart, which led to her renouncing the chance to go to to America with her mother and sisters to join her father. "I had the papers ready, but I couldn't go if I was married and had a different last name," she says before telling me about the most difficult struggle in her life. "I had been only married eight months and I came down with typhus. I was in the hospital for forty-five days. And not a hospital like they have here—we would have to walk hours to a hospital. *Il tifo è malamente!* (Typhus is misery!) All I could eat was fresh milk. I lost my hair. My parents were in America and I didn't want to tell them I was sick. What could they have done?" she continues, as I sit anticipating a happy ending to the story.

"A friend of mine had gone to America and told them I was sick. It was different then. It wasn't easy to telephone. Letters were transported by ship, and it all took so long. When my parents found out I was sick, they sent syringes full of medicine to me through a friend. After forty-five days I was well again. It was hard because I had no one else in Italy at the time.

"Eventually, my husband was able to go to America because President Eisenhower had finally opened the borders. I followed him three years later with our two children. We were on the boat to New York for eight days. One day, someone came to get me because a person wanted to speak to me. The man brought me to a cabin and gave me the phone. I had never talked on a telephone before! I didn't even know how to use it. There was someone speaking on the other end. It was my father, and it was the first time I had ever heard his voice because I didn't remember him from when I was little. I was twenty-nine years old. When the boat docked in New York, I was walking down the ramp holding the hands of my two children. One of my *paesani* (someone from the same town) was walking in front of me, and she said, 'Laura, that's your father!' I had never seen him before. That was the first time. My cousin told me he had a car and I thought he meant a *carretto* (cart) with a horse, because hardly anyone in Orsogna had a real car." Laura laughs at the absurdity of it all, and she seems downright amused at my astonishment.

When I ask whether she has a stronger bond with her children or her grandchildren, she answers quickly, with zero hesitation. "My grandchildren. I don't know why. *Le creature sentono quando qualcuno gli vogliono bene.* (Children know when someone loves them.) But they're still innocent. It's beautiful. I have four grandchildren and five great-grandchildren. I love all of them and they're so sweet. The youngest is two years old and he's so affectionate!" She looks down at the table, where photos of her children and grandchildren lie. "There were so many hard things in my life. War, sickness, poverty. I barely knew my father until late in life, and I worked hard in a factory for thirty dollars a week. But I made a family full of love. *È bello fare le cose belle.* (It's nice to do nice things.)"

Nonna Laura simply won't let me go home until after I have Sunday dinner with her and her family. I sit on her stoop as I watch the rain come down, waiting for a car to take me back to my own borough. I think of just how remarkable Nonna Laura is and how she weathered so many storms before eventually seeing light in her life. I had spent the day in the presence of a living, breathing example of what was perhaps the greatest generation that will ever exist. She made the best of every difficult situation where I can just imagine it would have been so easy to crumble and give up. The sky above me begins to clear as my car arrives. I can see Nonna Laura watching me through the window as I get in. I hope the sun shines for her for the rest of her days. She has earned it.

NONNA ROMANA SCIDDURLO'S

LASAGNA WITH TINY MEATBALLS

Lasagne con Polpettine

PREP TIME: 30 MINUTES • COOK TIME: 1 HOUR 35 MINUTES • YIELD: 6 TO 8 SERVINGS

In my family, a happy Christmas is one spent together at the dinner table, even if it means we're all talking over one another and fighting over who gets the last piece of lasagna. If you've ever had Nonna Romana's lasagna with tiny meatballs, you'd understand that it's worth fighting over. Her variation is a classic recipe from Puglia that uses a delicious sausage meat sauce and lots of little meatballs that I've helped roll every Christmas morning since I was a little girl. You can make and fry the meatballs the night before, but if you do, some of them may disappear. (See the photo for this recipe on page 158.)

SAUCE

3 tablespoons (45 ml) extra-virgin
    olive oil
3 cloves garlic, finely chopped
1 small onion, cut into ¼-inch
    (6 mm) dice
Red pepper flakes, to taste
1 pound (454 g) sweet Italian
    sausage
½ cup (120 ml) red wine, such as
    Merlot
2 cans (28 ounces, or 794 g, each)
    crushed tomatoes
1½ teaspoons salt
4 fresh basil leaves

MEATBALLS

1 pound (454 g) ground meatloaf
    mix (veal, pork, and beef)
2 large eggs
¾ cup (75 g) grated Pecorino
    Romano cheese
¾ cup (75 g) grated Parmigiano-
    Reggiano cheese

1   **To make the sauce:** Heat the olive oil in a large saucepan over medium heat. Add the garlic, onion, and red pepper flakes. Cook for about 5 minutes, until the onion is soft.

2   Add the sausage. Cook and stir for 5 to 7 minutes, breaking up the sausage with a wooden spoon, until nicely browned.

3   Add the wine to the pan. Cook for about 2 minutes, until the alcohol evaporates. Stir in the tomatoes and salt. Fill each empty crushed tomato can about halfway with water and swish them around. Add the tomato water to the pan as well. Tear the basil leaves and add them to the sauce. Bring the sauce to a boil and reduce the heat to low. Simmer for 20 to 30 minutes. Remove the sauce from the heat and set aside.

4   **To make the meatballs:** In a large bowl, combine all the meatball ingredients except the oil. Mix with your hands until you have a uniform mixture. Roll the meat mixture into meatballs about ½ inch (13 mm) in diameter.

5   Line a plate with paper towels and set aside. Heat 1½ inches (4 cm) of oil in a large skillet over medium-high heat. Working in batches, fry the meatballs until golden brown, 1 to 2 minutes each. Transfer to the paper towel–lined plate. Set aside.

continued

¾ cup (81 g) plain bread crumbs

3 tablespoons (12 g) minced
    fresh parsley

2 cloves garlic, shaved

Oil, for frying

LASAGNA

Salt, to taste

24 lasagna pasta sheets

16 ounces (454 g) fresh mozzarella,
    shredded

½ cup (50 g) grated Parmigiano-
    Reggiano cheese

6 **To make the lasagna:** Bring a large stockpot of generously salted water to a boil. Add the lasagna sheets and cook for about half the time than what it says on the package. Drain and run the pasta sheets under cold running water. Lay the pasta sheets flat on a baking sheet or hang them over a colander.

7 **To assemble:** Preheat the oven to 400°F (200°C).

8 Spread 1½ cups (350 ml) of sauce over the bottom of a large lasagna pan. Arrange a layer of lasagna sheets, slightly overlapping one another, about 5 vertically and 1 horizontally, over the sauce. Cut any pieces that do not fit.

9 Begin the layering by spreading about 1 cup (240 ml) of sauce over the pasta sheets. Top with one-third of the meatballs. Add about ¼ cup (30 g) of the mozzarella and 2 tablespoons (12.5 g) of the Parmigiano-Reggiano. Repeat the layering 2 more times.

10 Top the third layer of meatballs with a final layer of pasta sheets, 1½ cups (350 ml) of sauce, and the remaining Parmigiano-Reggiano.

11 Bake for 30 minutes. Sprinkle on the remaining mozzarella and bake for 10 minutes more, until the cheese melts.

LITTLE HATS FILLED WITH CHEESE AND MORTADELLA IN BROTH

Cappelletti in Brodo

PREP TIME: 1 HOUR 30 MINUTES • COOK TIME: 1 HOUR 35 MINUTES • YIELD: 4 TO 6 SERVINGS

At Nonna Rina's house, Christmas is a big event and warrants a very special fresh pasta from her beloved Emilia Romagna. Watching her skilled hands roll out the dough into paper-thin sheets is a thing of absolute magic. This step can be a bit tricky, so don't feel bad if you need to use the stand mixer. The word *cappelletti* in Italian means "little hats," and Nonna Rina fills hers with a delicious mix of mortadella, ricotta, and stracchino cheese, which is a young and super creamy cow's milk cheese, typical of northern Italy. If stracchino is hard to find, substitute it with more ricotta.

BROTH

1 pound (454 g) bone-in chicken thighs

1½ pounds (680 g) bone-in beef short ribs

2 small carrots, cut into large chunks

2 celery ribs, cut into large chunks

1 Roma tomato, halved

1 small onion, halved

4 quarts (3.8 L) cold water

Salt, to taste

Black pepper, to taste

FILLING

6 ounces (170 g) mortadella

¾ cup (185 g) ricotta impastata

6 ounces (170 g) stracchino cheese (or more ricotta cheese)

9 tablespoons (56 g) grated Parmigiano-Reggiano cheese, plus more for serving

1 large egg yolk

Dash ground nutmeg

1. **To make the broth:** Put a small stockpot over high heat. Add the chicken, short ribs, carrots, celery, tomato, onion, and cold water. Bring to a boil. Skim off any foam that forms on top. Once you have removed all the foam and the pot is at a rolling boil, reduce the heat to a simmer and cook, uncovered, until the broth reduces by one-fourth, 1 hour to 1 hour and 30 minutes.

2. Transfer the meat to a bowl. Remove and discard the vegetables. Cool the meat until it is easy to handle. Pull it from the bones and reserve for another use. Pour the broth through a fine-mesh strainer into a large bowl. Taste and season with salt and pepper as desired. Reserve the broth for cooking the pasta.

3. **To make the filling:** In a food processor, pulse the mortadella until coarsely chopped. Transfer to a medium bowl and add the ricotta, stracchino, Parmigiano-Reggiano, egg yolk, and nutmeg. Stir until all the ingredients are fully incorporated and the mixture is smooth. Set aside.

continued

PASTA DOUGH

2½ cups (300 g) all-purpose or
    00 flour

3 large eggs, at room temperature,
    well beaten

1 large egg yolk, at room
    temperature, well beaten

¼ teaspoon salt

Nonna Rina Says
*You must work with very small
pieces of dough at a time or the
pasta can dry out and crack.*

4 **To make the pasta dough:** In the bowl of a stand mixer fitted with the dough hook attachment, combine the flour, eggs, egg yolk, and salt. Mix on low speed for 5 to 6 minutes, until the ingredients are incorporated and a dough begins to form. Turn out the dough onto a clean work surface and knead with your hands, picking up any particles of dough as you go. If the dough feels dry, add 1 tablespoon (15 ml) of tepid water at a time until it comes together. Continue to knead by hand for 8 to 10 minutes, or until the dough is smooth and supple and has the consistency of play dough. Wrap the dough ball in plastic wrap and let rest at room temperature for 30 minutes.

5 Take a golf ball–size piece of dough at a time and roll it out with a rolling pin as thinly as possible. Alternatively, use a pasta roller on a #3 setting and pass the pasta through 2 or 3 times. Set the pasta roller to the #6 setting and roll out each piece of dough 2 or 3 times more into sheets as thin as possible. The sheets should be opaque enough that you can almost see through them. Cover any pasta not being used with a clean, damp kitchen towel.

6 With a knife or a ravioli cutter, trim the pasta pieces of any jagged ends into a clean square or rectangle. Cut out 2-inch (5 cm) squares of pasta. Place any scraps immediately under a damp kitchen towel so they do not dry out and reroll.

7 Place 1 teaspoon of filling in the center of each square. Wet your finger with some water and dampen one corner. Close the square by folding one of the points over the filling to the opposite (wetted) point to create a little triangle. Wrap the pasta around your index finger so the two points of the triangle meet and overlap. Press them firmly together, making sure they are sealed. Repeat until all the squares are filled and shaped.

8 Lay your cappelletti in a single layer on a baking sheet or a clean kitchen towel. They may be cooked in the reserved broth immediately or frozen.

9 **To freeze:** Lay the cappelletti on a baking sheet and place the baking sheet in the freezer. Once frozen, put them in resealable plastic bags and keep frozen for up to 3 months. Do not thaw before cooking.

10 **To cook:** Bring the broth to a boil. Drop the cappelletti into the boiling broth. Cook for 1 to 2 minutes, until they bob to the surface. Serve with an extra sprinkle of grated Parmigiano-Reggiano cheese.

RICOTTA AND MEAT-FILLED MANICOTTI

Manicotti con Ricotta e Carne

PREP TIME: 35 MINUTES • COOK TIME: 2 HOURS 30 MINUTES • YIELD: ABOUT 24 CRÊPES; 8 TO 10 SERVINGS

At Nonna Dorotea's house, there is never a unanimous decision on what kind of manicotti filling to make. "Nobody can make up their minds, so I always make both because I want to make everybody happy." Making two fillings might seem like a lot of work, but they're both a breeze, and the two trays of Italian comfort food will put a smile on everyone's face for your Christmas feast.

SAUCE

3 tablespoons (45 ml) extra-virgin olive oil

½ small onion, cut into ¼-inch (6 mm) dice

1 clove garlic, minced

2 cans (28 ounces, or 794 g, each) tomato puree

2 tablespoons (8 g) minced fresh parsley

1½ teaspoons salt

Black pepper, to taste

CRÊPES

4 large eggs

2 cups (475 ml) whole milk

1 cup (240 ml) water

3 cups (360 g) all-purpose or 00 flour

Vegetable shortening, for cooking

1 **To make the sauce:** Heat the olive oil in a small stockpot with a lid over medium heat. Add the onion and garlic. Cook for 5 to 7 minutes, until the garlic is golden and the onion is translucent.

2 Add the tomato puree and parsley. Fill each empty tomato puree can with 2 inches (5 cm) of water, swish them around, and add the tomato water to the pan. Add the salt and pepper, and bring the sauce to a boil. Reduce the heat to a simmer, cover the pan, and cook for 45 minutes to 1 hour. When the sauce is finished, uncover and let cool. In the meantime, make the crêpes.

3 **To make the crêpes:** In a blender, combine the eggs, milk, water, and flour. Process until smooth, about 10 seconds. Transfer to a bowl.

4 Put a small nonstick skillet over low heat and melt ½ teaspoon of shortening. Add ¼ cup (60 ml) of batter to the pan and spread it in a circular motion with a fork. Cook each crêpe until set in the middle, 1 to 2 minutes. Do not flip. Keep adding a bit of shortening every other crêpe to prevent sticking. Transfer the cooked crêpes to baking sheets in a single layer until cool. Once cooled, the crêpes can be stacked and frozen in a resealable plastic bag for up to 3 months.

continued

RICOTTA FILLING

12 ounces (340 g) whole-milk
ricotta

1 large egg

½ cup (50 g) grated Pecorino
Romano cheese, plus more
for sprinkling

1 cup (115 g) shredded fresh
mozzarella cheese

MEAT FILLING

12 ounces (340 g) ground sirloin

¼ cup (25 g) grated Pecorino
Romano cheese

1 large egg

½ teaspoon salt

¼ teaspoon black pepper

¼ cup (29 g) shredded fresh
mozzarella cheese

ASSEMBLY

2 tablespoons (13 g) grated
Pecorino Romano cheese

¼ cup (29 g) shredded fresh
mozzarella cheese

5   **To make the ricotta filling:** In a large bowl, combine the ricotta, egg, ¼ cup (60 ml) of the sauce, Pecorino Romano, and mozzarella. Mix well and set aside.

6   **To make the meat filling:** Put a medium skillet over medium heat. Add the meat. Cook until well browned. Remove from the heat and stir in 6 tablespoons (90 ml) of the sauce, the Pecorino Romano, egg, salt, pepper, and mozzarella. Mix well and set aside.

7   Preheat the oven to 380°F (193°C).

8   **To assemble:** Spread 1 cup (240 ml) of the sauce over the bottom of each of two 13 × 9-inch (33 × 23 cm) pans.

9   Fill half the crêpes with 1½ tablespoons (23 g) of the ricotta filling in each crêpe and the other half with 1½ tablespoons (23 g) of the meat filling in each crêpe. Roll to close, and place, seam sides down, in the pan. Do not pack them too tightly. You should be able to fit 12 crêpes in each pan. Ladle about 1 cup (240 ml) of the sauce over the crêpes in each pan and sprinkle each with the Pecorino Romano and mozzarella.

10 Cover each baking dish with aluminum foil and bake for 25 to 30 minutes, or until the cheese is bubbling. Let rest for 15 minutes before serving.

GENOVESE MEAT SAUCE WITH SWISS CHARD-FILLED PASTA

U Tuccu di Carne con Pansotti alla Ligure

PREP TIME: 1 HOUR • COOK TIME: 4 HOURS • YIELD: 6 TO 8 SERVINGS

When I asked Nonna Vivian about her favorite Ligurian Christmas recipes, *u tuccu* immediately came to her mind. The meat sauce is perfect served over fresh *pansotti*, which are filled with a mixture of Swiss chard and hard-boiled eggs. To save time, you can make the pansotti beforehand and freeze them.

SAUCE

1½ pounds (680 g) boneless bottom round beef (must be in 1 piece)

Salt, to taste

Black pepper, to taste

1 ounce (28 g) dried porcini mushrooms

1 cup (240 ml) warm water

5 tablespoons (75 ml) extra-virgin olive oil

1 large onion, cut into ¼-inch (6 mm) dice

1 clove garlic

1 celery rib, cut into ¼-inch (6 mm) dice

1 medium carrot, cut into ¼-inch (6 mm) dice

2 tablespoons (4 g) minced fresh rosemary

¼ cup (34 g) pinoli (pine nuts), plus more for garnishing

½ cup (120 ml) dry red wine, such as Merlot

2 bay leaves

3 ounces (85 g) tomato paste

1 can (28 ounces, or 794 g) can crushed tomatoes

1 cup (240 ml) beef broth

1 **To make the sauce:** Season the beef well on all sides with salt and pepper.

2 In a small bowl, combine the mushrooms with the warm water. Let soak for 10 to 15 minutes to rehydrate. With a slotted spoon, transfer the mushrooms to a cutting board and finely chop. Pour the soaking water through a fine-mesh strainer lined with paper towels into a small bowl. Set aside.

3 In a Dutch oven or large heavy-bottomed pot over medium-high heat, combine the olive oil, onion, garlic, celery, carrot, and rosemary. Cook for 3 to 5 minutes.

4 Add the meat and brown on all sides, 8 to 10 minutes. This is the most important step, as the meat must brown very well on the outside. Once the meat is nicely browned on all sides, add the chopped mushrooms and pinoli to the pan, stirring with a wooden spoon. Cook for 2 to 3 minutes.

5 Add the wine and the bay leaves. Cook until the alcohol evaporates, 2 to 3 minutes. Stir in the tomato paste and cook for 1 minute. Stir in the crushed tomatoes, broth, and the reserved mushroom soaking water. Bring to a boil, then reduce the heat to the lowest level possible. Cover the pan and cook until the meat is easily shredded with a fork, about 3 hours and 30 minutes. Check on the sauce often, stirring with a wooden spoon and turning the meat over to prevent it from sticking. In the meantime, make the pasta.

continued

PASTA FILLING

Salt, to taste

1 bunch Swiss chard, washed and ends trimmed

1 cup (100 g) grated Pecorino Romano cheese, plus more for serving

¼ cup (34 g) pinoli (pine nuts)

2 large hardboiled eggs, peeled

1 teaspoon dried marjoram

PASTA DOUGH

2½ cups (300 g) all-purpose or 00 flour

3 large eggs, at room temperature, well beaten

1 large egg yolk, at room temperature, well beaten

¼ teaspoon salt, plus more to taste

Nonna Vivian Says
Sprinkle a few extra pinoli nuts around the dishes when serving for an effortlessly elegant presentation.

6 **To make the pasta filling:** Bring a large stockpot of lightly salted water to a boil. Drop in the Swiss chard and boil for 15 to 20 minutes, until tender. Drain and run under cold water. Squeeze out the excess water and transfer it to a food processor. Add the remaining filling ingredients and process until smooth, about 10 seconds. Transfer to a medium bowl. Set aside.

7 **To make the pasta dough:** In the bowl of a stand mixer fitted with the dough hook attachment, combine the flour, eggs, egg yolk, and salt. Mix on low speed for 5 to 6 minutes, until the ingredients are incorporated and a dough begins to form.

8 Turn out the dough onto a clean work surface and begin kneading with your hands, picking up any particles of dough as you go. If the dough feels dry, add 1 tablespoon (15 ml) of tepid water at a time until it comes together. Continue kneading for 8 to 10 minutes, or until the dough is smooth and supple, and has the consistency of play dough. Wrap the dough ball in plastic wrap and let rest at room temperature for 30 minutes.

9 Divide the dough into 4 equal pieces. Working with one piece at a time, with a rolling pin, roll it into a rectangle as thin as possible, $\frac{1}{8}$ or $\frac{1}{16}$ inch (3 or 1 mm) thick. The sheets should be opaque enough that you can almost see through them. Cover any dough not being used with a clean, damp kitchen towel.

10 Begin working on the longer horizontal edge of one rectangle. Dot 1 teaspoon of filling along the dough about 1½ inches (4 cm) apart, leaving at least a ½-inch (13 mm) border on all sides. Dip your finger in water and dampen the area around the filling. Fold the dough over, away from you, to cover the filling. Press down on the edges of the dough and press together the areas around the filling with your fingers to create separate pockets of filling. Cut out 2-inch (5 cm) squares with a ravioli cutter. Lay the filled pasta squares on a floured baking sheet or a clean kitchen towel.

11 **To freeze:** Place the filled pasta squares on a baking sheet in a single layer. Place the tray in the freezer. Once frozen, transfer to resealable plastic bags and keep frozen for 2 to 3 months. Do not thaw before cooking; simply drop them frozen into the boiling water and cook until they bob to the surface.

12 **To cook the pasta:** Bring the sauce to a simmer in a large skillet over medium heat.

13 Bring a large stockpot of generously salted water to a boil. Drop the pasta into the boiling water. Cook for about 5 minutes, until al dente. Scoop the pasta out and add it to the sauce. Cook, tossing, for 1 to 2 minutes.

14 Serve in warm bowls with an extra sprinkle of Pecorino Romano and garnish with a few pinoli. Break up the meat and either serve atop the pasta or traditionally as an entrée.

LOBSTER OREGANATA

Astice Gratinato al Forno

PREP TIME: 15 MINUTES • COOK TIME: 40 MINUTES • YIELD: 2 TO 4 SERVINGS

This easy yet impressive lobster dish is a great way to make your guests feel special on Christmas. Nonna Dorotea learned this recipe from her husband, Leonardo, who worked in an Italian-American restaurant while he was growing up in Brooklyn. "I had just come to America and this was a very popular dish in all the restaurants at the time. I remember the first time Lenny showed me how to split the lobster because I had never done it before, and I was a little scared. I worked on the bread-crumb topping for years, trying to get the right balance of oregano and garlic and cheese. I always like to make something special for Christmas, and this dish never disappoints."

2 live lobsters

6 tablespoons (42 g) plain bread crumbs

2 tablespoons (13 g) grated Pecorino Romano cheese

3 cloves garlic, minced

2 tablespoons (8 g) minced fresh parsley

¼ cup (60 ml) extra-virgin olive oil

2 tablespoons (30 ml) dry white wine, such as Pinot Grigio

¾ cup (180 ml) water

Lemon wedges, for serving

1 Place the lobsters, belly sides down, on a cutting board. Using a sharp knife, split the lobsters in half, straight down the middle, beginning with the point of the knife in the middle of the head and running it down the tail. Remove the eggs and the innards. Transfer the lobster halves, cut side up, to a rimmed baking sheet.

2 Preheat the oven to 400°F (200°C).

3 In a small bowl, mix together the bread crumbs, cheese, garlic, parsley, and olive oil. Spread the bread-crumb mixture over the lobsters. Drizzle each lobster half with ½ tablespoon (7.5 ml) of wine.

4 Pour the water into the bottom of the baking sheet. Cover the sheet with aluminum foil and bake until the shells are red and the meat is firm, about 30 minutes. Uncover and bake for 10 minutes more.

5 Serve with lemon wedges for squeezing.

BABY ARTICHOKES

Carciofini

PREP TIME: 10 MINUTES • COOK TIME: 40 MINUTES • YIELD: 6 SERVINGS

Because my Nonno was an artichoke farmer in Italy, my family has always had a visceral connection to the vegetable. My Zia Rosa braises these babies in a white wine broth with a little garlic until they're tender and delicious, making them the perfect side dish or antipasto for a big family gathering.

2 pounds (907 g) baby artichokes (about 16)

2 lemons, halved, plus wedges for serving

½ cup (120 ml) extra-virgin olive oil

8 cloves garlic, sliced

½ cup (120 ml) dry white wine, such as Pinot Grigio

2 cups (475 ml) chicken broth

1 teaspoon salt

2 tablespoons (8 g) minced fresh parsley

Nonna Rosa Says

It is very important to use fresh artichokes for this recipe, as frozen ones will break down too much and become a little mooshad *(mushy).*

1 Fill a large bowl with cold water and set aside.

2 Clean the artichokes by removing the outer leaves until you reach the yellow or light green part of the artichoke. Remove the artichokes' stems and discard. Quarter the artichokes and add them to the bowl of cold water. Add the lemon halves to the bowl to prevent browning.

3 Heat the olive oil in a large skillet with a lid over medium heat. Add the garlic. Cook for 1 to 2 minutes, until golden.

4 Drain the artichokes and add them to the pan. Cook and stir for 5 minutes.

5 Add the wine. Cook until the alcohol evaporates, about 2 minutes.

6 Add the chicken broth and salt to the pan. Bring to a boil. Reduce the heat to low, cover the pan, and cook for 25 to 30 minutes, until the artichokes are tender.

7 Serve at room temperature with a sprinkle of parsley and a squeeze of fresh lemon juice.

ALMOND SPICE COOKIES WITH CHOCOLATE

Mostaccioli

PREP TIME: 15 MINUTES • COOK TIME: 12 MINUTES • YIELD: ABOUT 40 COOKIES

Mostaccioli are a popular Christmas cookie in southern Italy, especially among those who hail from the Campania region. Nonna Rosetta's are the perfect blend of spicy and chocolatey goodness, with a pop of crunch from the toasted almonds. She garnishes them with a swipe of melted semisweet chocolate that dries to a shiny finish and adds some sparkle to every Christmas cookie tray!

COOKIES

½ cup (73 g) whole almonds

2 cups (240 g) plus 1 tablespoon (8 g) all-purpose or 00 flour, plus more for dusting

2½ tablespoons (13 g) unsweetened cocoa powder

1½ teaspoons baking powder

¾ teaspoon ground cinnamon

½ teaspoon ground cloves

2 large eggs

½ cup (170 g) honey

½ cup (100 g) sugar

Zest of 1 orange

Zest of 1 lemon

Nonstick baking spray, for coating the baking sheet

GLAZE

8 ounces (225 g) good-quality semisweet chocolate

1 **To make the cookies:** Preheat the oven to 400°F (200°C). Spread the almonds on a baking sheet and toast until fragrant, 7 to 8 minutes. Coarsely chop the toasted almonds and set aside.

2 In a large bowl, whisk together the flour, cocoa, baking powder, cinnamon, and cloves. Add the chopped almonds and whisk to combine.

3 In another large bowl, whisk together the eggs, honey, sugar, and zests. Add this mixture to the dry ingredients and mix with a wooden spoon or spatula until a dough forms. Cover the bowl with plastic wrap and let rest for 30 minutes at room temperature.

4 Preheat the oven to 350°F (180°C). Line a baking sheet with parchment paper or aluminum foil and lightly spray it with nonstick baking spray.

5 Flour the work surface and turn the dough out onto it. Flour a rolling pin and roll out the dough ¼ inch (6 mm) thick. If the dough is sticky, keep dusting the surface and the dough with flour.

6 Using a 2½ × 3-inch (6 × 7.5 cm) rhomboid-shaped cookie cutter, cut out the cookies. Reroll any scraps and continue cutting cookies until all the dough is used. Place the cookies on the prepared baking sheet.

7 Bake for 10 to 12 minutes, or until the bottoms of the cookies color. Cool completely before dipping in the glaze.

8 **To make the glaze:** Melt the chocolate in a double boiler or a microwave. Dip the tops of each cookie into the melted chocolate and cool on a wire rack.

PUGLIESE CHRISTMAS FRITTERS

Cartellate

PREP TIME: 1 HOUR • COOK TIME: 6 HOURS 30 MINUTES • YIELD: ABOUT 48 CARTELLATE

"Se non facciamo le cartellate, non mi sembra che è Natale (If we don't make cartellate, it doesn't feel like Christmas),*"* my Nonna Romana declares every year the day after Thanksgiving. These traditional fritters are the most popular Christmas dessert from the region of Puglia, and my experiences learning to make them in my Nonna's basement apartment in Brooklyn are some of my fondest childhood memories.

CARTELLATE

3 cups (360 g) all-purpose or 00 flour

1 cup (240 ml) white wine, such as Pinot Grigio or Chablis

¼ cup (60 ml) olive oil

Oil, for frying

DIPPING SAUCE

1 cup (240 ml) Vin Cotto (page 14)

Ground cinnamon, for sprinkling

OR

1½ cups (510 g) honey

Rainbow sprinkles, for decorating

Nonna Romana Says

Cartellate with vin cotto *are best when made and dipped a day or so before serving, as the flavor of the vin cotto intensifies. Undipped, the cartellate can be kept in an airtight container for a few weeks. Perfect for the holiday season.*

1 **To make the cartellate:** Place the flour on a clean work surface and make a well in the center Add the wine and oil to the well and begin incorporating the flour into the liquid until fully absorbed. Knead with your hands until a supple dough forms, 8 to 10 minutes.

2 Using a pasta roller, begin passing golf ball–size chunks of dough through it at a #3 setting. Fold the dough over and keep passing it through until the sheets no longer have holes. Once you achieve smooth sheets of dough, transfer them to a clean work surface. Using a ravioli cutter, cut strips of dough about 1½ inches (4 cm) wide and 10 to 12 inches (25 to 30 cm) long. Cover any unused dough with a clean, damp kitchen towel. (Once the sheets dry too much, they will be difficult to pinch together.)

3 Flip the strips of dough to the wetter side and fold the end up at one side, about 1 inch (2.5 cm), pinching it together. Pinch the dough together the same way, every inch (2.5 cm) or so, creating little pockets. Roll the strip into a pinwheel and pinch the pockets together as you roll. This creates the pockets that will hold the vin cotto or honey. Place the rolled cartellate on a clean kitchen towel.

4 Line a plate with paper towels and set aside. Heat 2 inches (5 cm) of oil in a small stockpot over high heat. Working in batches, fry the cartellate until golden brown, about 2 minutes per batch. Transfer to the paper towel–lined plate.

5 **To dip:** In a large saucepan, bring the vin cotto or the honey to a simmer over medium heat. Using a fork, dip the cartellate until completely coated. Transfer to a serving dish and sprinkle the cartellate dipped in vin cotto with a dash of cinnamon; sprinkle the honey-dipped cartellate with sprinkles as desired.

✦

NONNA ROSA VIRONE'S

CALABRESE HONEY BALLS

Turdilli

PREP TIME: 30 MINUTES • COOK TIME: 30 MINUTES • YIELD: ABOUT 200 HONEY BALLS

Turdilli are small fritters of dough made with wine, and are typical of Calabria. They are fried and then dipped in warm honey, and decorated with colorful sprinkles. You can make these with white or red wine, but Nonna Rosa prefers red because it gives the dough a purple tint.

1 cup (240 ml) sweet red wine

½ cup (120 ml) vegetable oil

½ teaspoon lemon extract

¼ teaspoon sugar

Pinch salt

1 large egg

3 cups (360 g) all-purpose or
   00 flour, plus more for dusting

¼ teaspoon baking powder

Oil, for frying

3 cups (1 L) honey, plus more
   as needed

Rainbow nonpareils, for decorating

1 In a small saucepan over high heat, combine the wine, vegetable oil, lemon extract, sugar, and salt. Bring to a boil. Remove from the heat and let cool for 15 minutes.

2 Pour the wine mixture into the bowl of a stand mixer fitted with the paddle attachment. Add the egg. Mix on medium speed until combined.

3 Reduce the speed to low. Add the flour and baking powder. Mix until a soft dough forms. The dough should be a bit tacky, but not sticky. Lightly flour the work surface and turn the dough out onto it. Knead the dough by hand for 5 minutes, until smooth and supple. Cover the dough with a clean kitchen towel and let rest for 10 minutes.

4 Divide the dough in 8 pieces. Roll each piece into a ½-inch-thick (13 mm) rope. Cut the rope into pieces about 1½ inches (4 cm) long. Roll each piece on the back of a fork or a gnocchi board.

5 Line a plate with paper towels and set aside. Heat about 2½ inches (6.5 cm) of oil in a large saucepan over high heat. Working in batches, fry the balls until golden brown, 2 to 3 minutes per batch. With a slotted spoon, transfer to the paper towel–lined plate.

6 In a small saucepan over low heat, warm the honey until liquid.

7 Toss the balls, a handful at a time, in the honey to coat. With a slotted spoon, transfer to a serving dish. Sprinkle with the nonpareils.

"I believe cooking and feeding people are the best ways to show love."

I arrive at Nonna Rosa Virone's home in southern New Jersey, and before she opens the door to her small tract house, I can already hear the Italian music blaring inside. "Hallo, *bella*!" Nonna Rosa greets me as she opens the door and gives me a great big hug. She is dressed in a floral sweater that is very Nonna, and she wears a small pin with a photo of Jesus on it that she later told me she puts on every day. Her enormous smile lights up her entire face, which only bears a few wrinkles.

I make my way past the small living area where photos hang displaying a much younger Nonna Rosa with her family. "I gotta five grandchildren and one great-grandchild on the way!" she declares proudly, pointing to the photos. "And look at this!" she says, pointing to a photo of a baby boy. "After four granddaughters, the prince was born! I retired with the birth of my grandson, because I wanted to raise him. I wanted to be with my grandchildren, it was so important to me," she says happily. "When my first grandchild was born, the nurse handed me the baby in the hospital and I felt so much joy. It's different. You love your kids, but you love your grandchildren more. You feel like you've made it."

I make my way into the quaint kitchen where she has laid out a wonderful spread of freshly baked goods and coffee on a lace tablecloth.

"I know you come from far away, so I wanna make you something." She walks over to her small radio with both a CD and a cassette player to change the music. She opens a cabinet above the radio to reveal stacks of cassette tapes I haven't seen in twenty years, full of Italian love songs from the 1960s. "I love music. We had no movie theater in my town in Calabria until 1950, so music was all I had." She begins to hum the lyrics to one of the songs and closes her eyes, as if remembering something wonderful. After a piece of cake and coffee, we move our conversation to her antique sofa, which stands out in the recently constructed home. She's had this furniture set since she got married, and it still looks brand new. She begins to tell me a bit about her life.

"I was born in Satriano, Calabria, in the province of Catanzaro. Then I go to New York, then Philadelphia, and now I'mma right here!" she says with a giggle. "In Calabria, the life was hard. The Germans came to Satriano when my mother was pregnant with my younger brother. They knocked at the door and they wanted my mother's pots to melt down the metal. My mother quickly hid me and my sister under her long skirt and told them to take whatever they wanted. They took most of the pots, but they left one, and I still have it!" She excuses herself and runs to get the pot to show me. Quickly, the smile disappears from her face as she recalls the moment of struggle. "See this? I brought this from Italy. It will stay with me as long as I'm here, and then someone will take it. My mother begged the Germans to let her keep this pot so she could make rice for her children."

Shortly after the birth of her brother, her mother passed away, leaving her to be responsible for the day-to-day chores until her father remarried. She remembers having the help of her Nonna, whom she was very close with growing up. "My Nonna Rosa was such an important person in my life. I still see her when I close my eyes, with her rosary beads in hand. She would pray four or five times a day. She would always look at me and say, 'Bella di Nonna! (Love of Nonna!) Come here!' And she would send me to the store to buy a liter of wine. Back then, everyone had a little wine. It wasn't a big deal."

At nineteen, she and her family boarded the ship *Christopher Columbus*, bound for New York. Although she knew she would be leaving behind a much harder life in Italy, life in America didn't excite her one bit. "I didn't want to come. I didn't want to have to learn a whole new language, I was so shy! I'mma not shy now!" she says, laughing. "I don't know what happened. *Questa e' la vita!* (This is life!)" It was on the ship that Nonna Rosa got her first taste of America. "The food was nothing we had ever seen before, with a formal dining room and banquet tables with cookies my brothers and sisters and I had never seen in our entire lives! My sister Clara turned to me and said, 'We're rich tonight!' We stuffed our faces with cakes and cookies like we had never eaten before, but then we paid for it. We got so sick! In bed for seven days and seven nights. From then on, all we ate was soup and an apple that the waiters would bring us. He would smile and ask, *'Come stanno le gallinette bionde?'* How are the blonde chickens? Because I had this blonde hair."

In America, Rosa suffered even more. "For two months, I cried and said I wanted to go back to Italy. I didn't like this country, but my father said that I had to stay. In fifty years, I still haven't been back." Here in the States and with the passing of time, Rosa managed to make a life and a family full of love. "I was married in St. Nicholas' church in Philadelphia. Marriage is about the way you take it on. There's ups and down, *sta sopra e sotto*. You gotta give and take." We both look up at a framed photograph of Rosa and her husband, taken at a friend's wedding before they were married. "We were married fifty-eight years," she says, making the sign of the cross with her hands.

Over the years, Nonna Rosa has found happiness spreading her love of cooking in the kitchen of a Philadelphia high school's cafeteria. "I worked in a kitchen for twenty years, but I still love to cook at home. At work, I used to make so many different things. It was the only school that ever tasted risotto. I would take the leftover peas and beans and make *pasta e piselli, pasta e fagioli*, things no one would think to make. Now everything is frozen. When I retired, they were all so sad. I was sad too. I cried. I really loved my work." She pauses to fight back some tears and I think about how lucky those students were to have Nonna Rosa. She is the kind of woman who views cooking and feeding people as a noble calling, something she was born to do. "Until my father died, we had Sunday lunch at 12 p.m. every week. Right before he died, he looked at me and said, 'You are the oldest, you carry the tradition.' I accepted that as my duty. It didn't matter that I cooked for twenty-seven people for the holidays. I did it with love. Now the holidays are at my daughter's house, but I still go over there and cook everything. Only the house changed."

WINE COOKIES

Biscotti al Vino

PREP TIME: 10 MINUTES • COOK TIME: 15 MINUTES • YIELD: ABOUT 35 COOKIES

"When you bake the wine cookies, the whole house smells beautiful!" Nonna Annita says, as I help her dip a little bagel-shaped cookie into granulated sugar, while the intoxicating aroma of sweet wine and fennel seeds waft past me from the baking sheet in the oven. These simple, slightly sweet wine cookies are typical of Nonna Annita's hometown of Ciociaria, and their mild flavor makes them perfect for dipping in a glass of wine or in your morning coffee. You can use red or white wine for this recipe, but Nonna Annita prefers to use white wine (which she makes herself) for a lighter flavor.

2 cups (240 g) all-purpose or 00 flour

2 teaspoons baking powder

½ cup (120 ml) white wine, any kind you like

6 tablespoons (90 ml) extra-virgin olive oil, plus more for working the dough

½ cup (100 g) sugar, plus more for dipping the cookies

1 tablespoon (6 g) fennel seeds

1   Preheat the oven to 400°F (200°C). Line 2 baking sheets with parchment paper. Set aside.

2   In a medium bowl, whisk together the flour and baking powder. Set aside.

3   In the bowl of a stand mixer fitted with the paddle attachment, add the wine, olive oil, and sugar. Mix on medium-high speed until the sugar dissolves. Add the fennel seeds and mix until combined.

4   Add half of the dry ingredients to the bowl and mix on low speed until absorbed. Add the remaining dry ingredients. Mix again on low speed, just until absorbed.

5   Pour some granulated sugar into a shallow dish.

6   Oil your hands and roll a chunk of dough into a rope about ½ inch (13 mm) thick and 4 inches (10 cm) long. Bring the ends together to form a ring. Roll one side of the ring in the sugar and place it, sugar side up, on the prepared baking sheets. Continue with the remaining dough, placing the cookies 2 inches (5 cm) apart on the baking sheets.

7   Bake for about 15 minutes until the cookies are golden.

NONNA MICHELINA GAGLIARDO'S

SICILIAN FIG COOKIES

Cucciddati

PREP TIME: 1 HOUR • COOK TIME: 24 MINUTES • YIELD: ABOUT 48 COOKIES

No self-respecting Sicilian can let a Christmas go by without making these delightful fig-filled cookies that everyone loves. All throughout Sicily, you will find slight variations on this cookie's filling and shape. Every family seems to have their own precious recipe that they safeguard against outsiders. Luckily, Zia Michelina was sweet enough to give up the goods: *"Ti do questa ricetta che è beautiful troppo assai, bedda Mia!* (I'll give you this recipe that is too beautiful, my love!)" At her house, making *cucciddati* is a family event, where all her daughters and granddaughters pitch in. Zia Michelina says you can make the filling up to two weeks in advance and chill it in the refrigerator: *"Cosi pigghia u sappuri.* (So it absorbs the flavor.)" The cookies are wonderful eaten plain—as is more common in Italy—as well as coated with a sweet glaze and sprinkled with rainbow nonpareils.

FILLING

14 ounces (395 g) dried figs, stemmed

1¼ cups (180 g) raisins

½ cup (90 g) mini semisweet chocolate chips

1 tablespoon (15 ml) Grand Marnier, Cointreau, or another orange-flavored liqueur

1 tablespoon (15 ml) cold espresso coffee

1 teaspoon ground cinnamon

Zest of 1 orange

DOUGH

2½ cups (300 g) all-purpose or 00 flour

1¼ cups (205 g) semolina flour

2 teaspoons baking powder

1 cup (200 g) granulated sugar

1 cup (225 g) shortening

2 large eggs, at room temperature

¼ cup (60 ml) whole milk

1   **To make the filling:** In a large saucepan, combine the figs with enough cold water to cover completely. Bring to a boil and cook for about 10 minutes, until the figs are soft. Drain and cool to room temperature. In the meantime, make the dough.

2   **To make the dough:** In a large bowl, whisk together the all-purpose flour, semolina, and baking powder. Set aside.

3   In the bowl of a stand mixer fitted with the paddle attachment, cream together the granulated sugar and shortening on medium speed until fluffy, about 5 minutes. Add the eggs, one at a time, and beat on medium speed to combine. Add the milk and combine. Reduce the speed to low and add the dry ingredients. Mix on low speed until a dough forms that pulls away from the sides of the bowl. Divide the dough into 4 pieces and flatten each piece into a disk. Wrap each disk with plastic wrap and refrigerate until firm, about 1 hour. In the meantime, finish the filling.

4   Place the cooled figs in a food processor along with the raisins, chocolate chips, Grand Marnier, coffee, cinnamon, and orange zest. Process until smooth, about 20 seconds.

continued

GLAZE

2 cups (240 g) confectioners' sugar
½ teaspoon vanilla extract
2 tablespoons (30 ml) whole milk
Rainbow nonpareils, for decorating

Home for the Holidays
Back in Corleone, Sicily, I would help my mother make dozens of cucciddati *for Christmas, but they were not usually for us to enjoy until Christmas Eve. We were eight children, and if she let us at the cookies, we would have certainly eaten them all. She would want to save them in case guests came over, so she would put them all in a basket and keep them on a high windowsill out of reach. One day when she was in the other room, I tried to be sneaky and put two chairs on top of one another to get to the basket and eat the cookies. I managed to grab a few before falling to the ground, and my mother rushed in and asked how I fell. I told her I was trying to dust the windowsill, and I don't think she ever found out the truth!*
—Nonna Michelina Gagliardo

5 **To assemble:** Preheat the oven to 375°F (190°C). Line 2 baking sheets with parchment paper.

6 Unwrap one disk of chilled dough, keeping any unused dough chilled. Take a chunk of dough and roll the dough into a rectangle about ⅛ inch (3 mm) thick, 3½ inches (9 cm) wide, and 14 inches (36 cm) long.

7 Place a 1-inch-wide (2.5 cm) log of filling in the center of the dough, leaving about a 1-inch (2.5 cm) border at the top and bottom. Take one side of the dough and roll it over, enclosing the filling to make a log. (Don't worry if there are a few cracks in the cookies; they will be covered when you ice them.) Pinch the ends together to seal.

8 Using a sharp floured knife, cut out cookies 2 inches (5 cm) long, making, diagonal cuts so each cookie is shaped like a diamond. Place them, seam side down, 1 inch (2.5 cm) apart on the prepared baking sheets. Continue with the remaining dough and filling.

9 Bake the cookies for 12 to 14 minutes, or until the bottoms are nicely browned. Cool completely before glazing.

10 **To make the glaze:** In a small bowl, whisk together the confectioners' sugar, vanilla, and milk. Drizzle the glaze over the cooled cookies and sprinkle with rainbow nonpareils.

CREAM CHEESE KNOT COOKIES

Biscotti con Formaggio Cremoso

PREP TIME: 15 MINUTES • COOK TIME: 45 MINUTES • YIELD: ABOUT 60 COOKIES

While these delectable little knot cookies aren't an example of traditional Italian baking, they are highly addictive! All of Nonna Annita's grandchildren look forward to the holiday season, when they help her make hundreds of cookies for her church group in Jersey City. The cookies themselves are lightly sweetened and flavored with a tiny bit of anise liqueur (she's partial to Marie Brizard), which she also adds to the glaze for a little kick. It is the holiday season, after all!

COOKIES

3 cups (360 g) all-purpose or 00 flour

1 tablespoon (15 ml) baking powder

4 ounces (113 g) cream cheese, at room temperature

½ cup (1 stick, or 120 g) unsalted butter, at room temperature

½ cup (100 g) granulated sugar

2 large eggs

2 tablespoons (30 ml) anisette liqueur or anise extract

1 packet (½ ounce, or 15 g) Italian vanilla powder or 1 teaspoon vanilla extract

GLAZE

3 cups (360 g) confectioners' sugar

3 tablespoons (45 ml) anisette liqueur or anise extract

¼ cup (60 ml) whole milk

Nonpareils, for decorating

1 Preheat the oven to 350°F (180°C). Line an 18 × 13-inch (46 × 33 cm) baking sheet with parchment paper. Set aside.

2 **To make the cookies:** In a large bowl, whisk together the flour and baking powder. Set aside.

3 In the bowl of a stand mixer fitted with the paddle attachment, add the cream cheese, butter, and granulated sugar. Mix on medium speed until fluffy, about 5 minutes.

4 Stir in the eggs, one at a time, until each one is fully incorporated. Add the anisette and vanilla. Mix to combine. Reduce the speed to low. Add the flour–baking powder mixture, and mix until fully absorbed. The dough should be soft but not sticky.

5 On a clean work surface, roll a chunk of dough into a rope ½ inch (13 mm) wide. Cut the rope into 4- to 5-inch-long (10 to 12.5 cm) pieces. Shape into little knots and place on the prepared baking sheet 2 inches (5 cm) apart.

6 Bake for 10 to 15 minutes, or until the cookies just begin to color. Cool completely before glazing.

7 **To make the glaze:** In a small bowl, whisk together the confectioners' sugar, anisette, and milk until smooth. Drizzle the glaze over the cooled cookies and decorate with the nonpareils.

CALABRESE FRUIT AND NUT PASTRY

Pitta 'Mpigliata

PREP TIME: 45 MINUTES • COOK TIME: 45 MINUTES • YIELD: ONE 9-INCH (23 CM) PITTA

This traditional pastry from Calabria goes by many different names depending on your location; *pitta 'nchiusa* or *pitta chjina* are dialect words that mean "stuffed" or "filled." In Nonna Rosa's family, they call this Christmas confection *rosette*, or "little roses," because strips of shortbread are spread with a layer of prunes, raisins, and walnuts, and rolled up into rosettes. Nonna Rosa loves this recipe because it's forgiving when it comes to the fruits and nuts used. "You can use whateva you like-a!"

DOUGH

1 cup (240 ml) dry white wine
¼ cup (60 ml) olive oil
¼ cup (50 g) sugar
1 packet (½ ounce, or 15 g) Italian
    vanilla powder or 1 teaspoon
    vanilla extract
3 large eggs, divided
3¾ cups (450 g) all-purpose
    or 00 flour, plus more for
    dusting
2 teaspoons baking powder

FILLING

1 cup (100 g) walnuts
½ cup (87.5 g) pitted prunes
½ cup (75 g) raisins
Zest of 1 orange
1 tablespoon (20 g) honey
1 tablespoon (15 ml) vermouth
½ teaspoon ground cinnamon
¼ teaspoon ground cloves

ASSEMBLY

Nonstick baking spray, for
    preparing the pie plate

1 **To make the dough:** In the bowl of a stand mixer fitted with the paddle attachment, combine the wine, olive oil, sugar, and vanilla. Mix on medium speed until combined. Add 2 of the eggs. Mix on medium speed until incorporated.

2 Change the attachment to the dough hook. Add the flour and baking powder. Mix again on medium speed until a smooth dough comes together, 3 to 5 minutes.

3 Lightly flour a work surface and turn the dough out onto it. Knead by hand for 2 to 3 minutes. Cover the dough with a clean kitchen towel and let rest while you make the filling.

4 **To make the filling:** In a food processor, add the walnuts, prunes, raisins, orange zest, honey, vermouth, cinnamon, and cloves. Process for 20 to 30 seconds, or until no large chunks remain. Transfer to a medium bowl.

5 **To assemble:** Preheat the oven to 350°F (180°C). Spray a 9-inch (23 cm) pie plate with baking spray.

6 With a rolling pin, roll one-third of the dough into a 10-inch (25 cm) circle about ⅛ inch (3 mm) thick. Roll the dough onto the rolling pin and transfer it to the pie plate. Trim any excess dough to the height of the pie plate.

BRUSHING
¼ cup (80 g) apricot preserves
2 tablespoons (30 ml) water
Rainbow nonpareils, for decorating

 Home for the Holidays
I love Christmas. In Italy, I looked forward to Christmas for the zeppole and a little torrone. We were poor, so we knew not to hope for Santa Claus, but the sweets we could hope for. We went to Mass at midnight and we would come home and play bingo, but we didn't have the real game, so we would use pieces of orange zest to mark our cards. It was so different then.
—Nonna Rosa Virone

7 Roll the remaining dough ⅛ inch (3 mm) thick. Using a ravioli cutter, cut strips of dough about 2 inches (5 cm) wide and 10 to 12 inches (25 to 30 cm) long. Spread the filling along each strip and roll into a rosette. Place the first rosette in the middle of the crust. Repeat the process, placing each additional rosette around the first one. You should be able to make about 12 to 13 rosettes. Fold in the surrounding dough.

8 Beat the remaining egg and brush the entire pastry with it.

9 Bake for 40 to 45 minutes, until golden brown.

10 **For brushing:** In a small saucepan over medium heat, combine the apricot preserves and water. Heat until liquid. Brush the pitta with the preserves and decorate with the nonpareils.

STRUFFOLI CONES

PREP TIME: 1 HOUR • COOK TIME: 15 MINUTES • YIELD: ABOUT 8 TO 10 CONES

Struffoli are Neapolitan honey balls that are synonymous with celebrating Christmas, Italian-style. But let's be real: they can be a bit messy to eat. One year, the ever-clever Nonna Antoinette had the brilliant idea of serving them in ice-cream cones to cut down on the sticky factor and give them a festive presentation, perfect for any holiday dessert bar. The kids are sure to love them too!

STRUFFOLI

3 cups (360 g) all-purpose or
    00 flour, plus more for dusting
½ teaspoon baking powder
Pinch salt
2 tablespoons (30 g) unsalted
    butter, softened
2 tablespoons (30 ml) sugar
4 large eggs, at room temperature
1 teaspoon vanilla extract
1 tablespoon (15 ml) white wine
Zest of ½ lemon
Zest of ½ orange
Olive oil, for frying (or use any
    frying oil you like)
Small ice cream cones
Rainbow Jimmies or nonpareils,
    to decorate

HONEY SYRUP

1½ cups (510 g) honey
½ cup (100 g) sugar
2 tablespoons (30 ml) water

1   **To make the struffoli:** In a medium bowl, whisk together the flour, baking powder, and salt. Set aside.

2   In the bowl of a stand mixer fitted with the paddle attachment, beat the butter and sugar on medium speed until combined. Reduce the speed to low and add the eggs, one at a time, until each one is fully incorporated.

3   Add the vanilla, wine, and zests. Add the dry ingredients and mix until a slightly firm dough comes together, 3 to 4 minutes.

4   Flour the work surface and a baking sheet. Take a small chunk of dough, and with your hands, roll it into a long rope about ½ inch (13 mm) thick. With a knife, cut the rope into ¼-inch (6 mm) pieces. Roll the pieces into balls and place them on the prepared baking sheet. Repeat with the rest of the dough.

5   Line a plate with paper towels. Set aside.

6   Heat about 1½ inches (4 cm) of olive oil in a large saucepan over medium-high heat until it reaches about 350°F (180°C). Fry the struffoli in small batches until light golden brown, 2 to 3 minutes per batch. Transfer them to the paper towel–lined plate to drain.

7   **To make the honey syrup:** Place a second large saucepan over medium heat and bring the honey, sugar, and water to a boil.

8   Drop in the struffoli in small batches, just as you did when you fried them. With a slotted spoon, stir them in the honey until they are completely coated, then transfer them to a serving plate.

9   Allow the struffoli to become a little bit tacky before shaping them into small mounds using 2 spoons and filling the cones. Sprinkle the struffoli with the sprinkles.

NONNA ROMANA SCIDDURLO'S

ITALIAN CHRISTMAS BREAD

Panettone

PREP TIME: 30 HOURS • COOK TIME: 45 MINUTES • YIELD: ONE 6-INCH (15 CM) PANETTONE

There are a few things Italians could possibly live without at Christmastime, but *panettone* is not one of them. This lightly sweetened fruit and nut bread is, without a doubt, the official symbol of an Italian Christmas. Nonna Romana's panettone isn't too sweet, making it perfect for a little after-dinner snack or with morning coffee after it dries out a bit. Making your own panettone is a bit of a labor of love and will take up some time, but it will leave you with a sense of accomplishment and the house smelling like Christmas.

BIGA

2 tablespoons (24 g) active dry yeast
¼ cup plus 3 tablespoons (105 ml) lukewarm water
¾ cup (98 g) Manitoba flour

FIRST MIX

3 large egg yolks
1 large egg
1½ cups (195 g) Manitoba flour, plus more for dusting
¼ cup (50 g) sugar
⅓ cup (80 ml) whole milk
1 tablespoon (20 g) molasses
3½ tablespoons (53 g) unsalted butter, cut into pieces, at room temperature

1 **To make the biga:** In a small bowl, dissolve the yeast in the lukewarm water, stirring for 5 minutes. Add the flour and mix with your hands until you achieve a very sticky dough ball. Transfer the dough to a clean bowl and cover with plastic wrap. Refrigerate for 5 hours.

2 Remove the bowl from the refrigerator and let stand at room temperature for 2 hours.

3 **To make the first mix:** Measure 3 ounces (85 g) of biga. Refrigerate the remaining biga to use as a starter for other baking.

4 In a small bowl, whisk together the egg yolks and egg. Measure the volume of the eggs and reserve half in the refrigerator for the second mix.

5 In the bowl of a stand mixer fitted with the dough hook attachment, combine the biga, half the whisked eggs, the flour, sugar, milk, and molasses. Mix on medium speed for 5 minutes. Add the butter, 1 tablespoon (15 g) at a time, mixing on medium speed after each addition until it is fully absorbed before adding the next.

6 Lightly flour a work surface and turn the dough out onto it. Flour your hands and knead the dough by hand for 5 minutes. If the dough feels sticky, continue to flour the work surface. Transfer the kneaded dough to a large bowl and cover it with plastic wrap. Let rise in a warm place for 12 hours.

SECOND MIX

½ cup (75 g) golden raisins

½ cup (75 g) raisins

1 cup (240 ml) water

3 tablespoons (45 ml) white rum

Dough, from the first rising

Remaining eggs, from the first mix

⅓ cup plus 1 tablespoon (80 g)
    sugar

1 packet (½ ounce, or 15 g) Italian
    vanilla powder or 1 teaspoon
    vanilla extract

Zest of 1 orange

Zest of 1 lemon

Zest of 1 tangerine

1 cup plus 2½ tablespoons (150 g)
    Manitoba flour

¼ cup (½ stick, or 60 g) unsalted
    butter

7 **To make the second mix:** In a small bowl, combine the raisins, water, and rum. Soak for 2 hours. Drain, discarding the soaking liquid. Pat the raisins dry with paper towels. Set aside.

8 Punch down the dough and transfer it to the bowl of a stand mixer fitted with the dough hook attachment. Add the reserved half of the whisked eggs, the sugar, vanilla, zests, and flour. Mix on medium speed for 5 minutes.

9 Add the butter, 1 tablespoon (15 g) at a time, mixing on medium speed after each addition until it is fully absorbed before adding the next. Once the butter is fully absorbed, add the soaked raisins. Mix on medium speed for 5 minutes.

10 Lightly flour a wooden board and transfer the dough to it. Knead by hand for 7 to 10 minutes, until the dough is elastic. Shape the dough into a ball and place it, smooth side down, in a panettone paper mold. Cover the mold with plastic wrap and let rise in a warm place until the dough doubles in size, about 2 inches (5 cm) below the top of the mold, 6 to 7 hours.

11 When the dough has just about doubled, remove the plastic wrap and let sit, uncovered, for 30 minutes.

12 Preheat the oven to 350°F (180°C).

13 Score a cross across the top of the dough. Place the panettone mold onto a baking sheet. Bake for 45 minutes, or until golden brown and springy in the middle.

PUGLIESE CANDIED ALMONDS

Torrone di Mandorle

PREP TIME: 20 MINUTES • COOK TIME: 30 MINUTES • YIELD: ABOUT 36 SQUARES

Every holiday season, Nonna Romana and my Zia Rosa turn my Nonna's basement-apartment kitchen into a veritable commercial bakery, producing enough holiday sweets that seem to last until New Year's Eve. One of their most popular confections is a classic Pugliese *torrone di mandorle*, which differs greatly from a classic nougat found in many regions of Italy. This torrone is actually more of an almond brittle—super crunchy, not too sweet, and a gorgeous deep-amber color. The secret ingredient is a little bit of white vinegar, which my great-grandmother Regina began adding because she swore it made the torrone better. I'm going to be totally real with you guys: to this day we have no idea what the vinegar exactly does, but no one wants to mess with tradition, and if it's not broken . . . don't fix it.

2 cups (290 g) raw almonds

1 cup (200 g) sugar

¼ cup (60 ml) water

2 tablespoons (30 ml) white vinegar

Zest of 1 lemon

1 Line a flat surface with a large sheet of aluminum foil.

2 Place all the ingredients in a small stockpot and put the pot over medium heat. Cook, stirring with a wooden spoon. The sugar will melt, but you must keep stirring continuously for 10 to 15 minutes, until the sugar crystalizes again. Continue to stir for 10 to 15 minutes more, until the sugar melts once again and turns a dark amber color.

3 Remove from the heat and pour the contents onto the foil. With a spatula, quickly flatten the hot almonds to form a sheet about ¾ inch (2 cm) thick. Let cool for about 5 minutes.

4 With a large knife, cut the entire sheet into 2-inch (5 cm) squares. Remove the aluminum foil from all the pieces and cool completely before serving.

ITALIAN LEMON WAFFLE COOKIES

Pizzelle al Limone

PREP TIME: 10 MINUTES • COOK TIME: 1 HOUR • YIELD: ABOUT 50 COOKIES

In Italian-American culture, *pizzelle* have become synonymous with Christmastime. Nonna Laura hails from the region of Abruzzo, where pizzelle originate, and there, they are made year-round using a simple batter that can have different flavorings, the most popular being anise. Nonna Laura flavors hers with her homemade Sweet Lemon Zest (page 13) and makes them two at a time using her trusty electric iron in her Queens basement. They're exquisite with a simple dusting of powdered sugar, and no matter how many she makes, they don't last long.

6 large eggs

¾ cup (150 g) plus 1 tablespoon (13 g) sugar

½ cup (120 ml) vegetable oil, plus more for greasing the iron

1 teaspoon vanilla extract

Zest of 1 lemon

Juice of 1 lemon or 1 tablespoon (15 ml) Nonna Laura's Sweet Lemon Zest (page 13)

1¾ cups plus 1 tablespoon (310 g) all-purpose or 00 flour

2 teaspoons baking powder

1 In a large bowl, add the eggs, sugar, oil, vanilla, lemon zest, and lemon juice. Using a handheld electric mixer, beat on high speed until smooth.

2 Add the flour and baking powder. Mix on high speed for 30 seconds. Give the batter a good stir with a spoon or a spatula.

3 Preheat a pizzelle iron until very hot. Moisten a paper towel with vegetable oil and carefully grease the hot iron.

4 Add 1 tablespoon (15 ml) of batter to each cavity and close the iron. Cook for 1 to 2 minutes, until the cookies are golden. Using a fork, carefully lift the cookies off the iron and transfer to a baking sheet in a single layer until cooled.

🥄 **Nonna Laura Says**
The pizzelle are very soft when you first make them, but as they cool, they have a nice, crispy texture, like waffles. It's best if you leave them to cool in a single layer to prevent them from getting soggy.

LIGURIAN BUTTER COOKIES

Canestrelli di Torriglia

PREP TIME: 20 MINUTES • COOK TIME: 18 MINUTES • YIELD: ABOUT 36 COOKIES

When it comes to Christmas cookies, Nonna Vivian keeps it simple and chic with these classic Ligurian butter cookies. *Canestrelli* is an easy shortbread recipe that has a hint of lemon and white rum. The cookies are then cut into a lovely daisy shape with a cookie cutter and dusted with a light coating of powdered sugar.

1 cup (2 sticks, or 240 g) unsalted butter, at room temperature, plus more for greasing

6 tablespoons (75 g) granulated sugar

2 large egg yolks, at room temperature

Zest of ½ lemon or 2 teaspoons Nonna Laura's Sweet Lemon Zest (page 13)

1 packet (½ ounce, or 15 g) Italian vanilla powder or 1 teaspoon vanilla extract

1 tablespoon (15 ml) white rum

1½ cups (180 g) all-purpose or 00 flour

¾ cup (96 g) cornstarch

Confectioners' sugar, for dusting

1 In the bowl of a stand mixer fitted with the paddle attachment, combine the butter and granulated sugar. Mix on high speed until fluffy, about 5 minutes.

2 Add the egg yolks, one at a time. Mix on medium speed until fully incorporated before adding the next. Add the lemon zest, vanilla, and rum. Mix again on medium speed to combine.

3 Reduce the speed to low. Add the flour and cornstarch. Mix until a soft dough forms. Spread the dough onto a piece of plastic wrap and flatten into a disk. Chill until firm, about 1 hour.

4 Preheat the oven to 340°F (171°C). Grease a baking sheet with butter.

5 Place the dough between two pieces of parchment paper and roll it ¼ inch (6 mm) thick, using rolling guides to help, if you have them. Chill any dough not being used.

6 Using a 2½-inch (6 cm) daisy-shaped cookie cutter, cut out the cookies and place them 1 inch (2.5 cm) apart on the prepared baking sheet. Optionally, cut out the centers with a small circular cookie cutter. Place the baking sheet in the freezer for 5 minutes before baking.

7 Bake for 15 to 18 minutes, until the cookies have just slightly colored on the bottom and the tops are still quite pale. Cool completely. Dust with confectioners' sugar.

Home for the Holidays

I remember the first time my mother, Elsie, tried making canestrelli *at her restaurant, the original Beatrice Inn in the West Village. When she gave them to my father to taste, she would ask him if they were as good as her friend's, and he would always tease her by responding, 'Nei tuoi sogni! (In your dreams!)' They were actually delicious, and I still make them with her recipe every Christmas.*

—Nonna Vivian Cardia

CHOCOLATE-ORANGE-HAZELNUT BISCOTTI

Biscotti al Cioccolato e Arancia con Nocciole

PREP TIME: 20 MINUTES • COOK TIME: 1 HOUR 10 MINUTES • YIELD: ABOUT 40 BISCOTTI

An excellent chocolate biscotti recipe is a necessity for holiday baking. Nonna Nina's have some hazelnuts and a hint of orange, and are delectable when dipped in strong espresso or some Vin Santo for dessert.

2 cups (240 g) all-purpose or 00 flour

⅓ cup plus 2 tablespoons (39 g) unsweetened cocoa powder

1½ tablespoons (8 g) ground espresso powder

1 teaspoon baking soda

½ teaspoon salt

¼ cup (½ stick, or 60 g) unsalted butter, at room temperature

1 cup (225 g) packed brown sugar

1 packet (½ ounce, or 15 g) Italian vanilla powder or 1 teaspoon vanilla extract

3 large eggs

Zest of 2 oranges

1½ teaspoons orange extract

3 ounces (85 g) good-quality semisweet chocolate, finely chopped

1 cup (115 g) chopped hazelnuts

1 Preheat the oven to 300°F (150°C). Line a baking sheet with parchment paper. Set aside.

2 In a medium bowl, whisk together the flour, cocoa powder, espresso powder, baking soda, and salt. Set aside.

3 In the bowl of a stand mixer fitted with the paddle attachment, combine the butter, brown sugar, and vanilla. Beat on medium-high speed until fluffy, about 5 minutes.

4 Add the eggs, one at a time, beating on medium speed until each one is fully incorporated. Add the orange zest and extract. Beat to combine.

5 Add half the dry ingredients. Mix on low speed until absorbed. Add the chocolate and hazelnuts, along with the remaining dry ingredients. Mix again until a dough forms. Divide the dough into 2 equal pieces. Place them on the prepared baking sheet and shape each piece into a log 2½ inches (6 cm) wide and about 14 inches (36 cm) long.

6 Bake for about 30 minutes, until the logs feel firm to the touch. Cool for 15 minutes. Cut the logs crosswise into 1-inch-thick (2.5 cm) slices. Transfer the slices, cut side down, onto 2 baking sheets.

7 Bake for 15 to 20 minutes. Flip the biscotti and bake for 15 to 20 minutes more. The longer you bake the biscotti, the crispier they will be.

PANDORO CHRISTMAS TREE CAKE WITH LIMONCELLO CREAM

Albero di Pandoro con Crema al Limoncello

PREP TIME: 15 MINUTES • COOK TIME: 15 MINUTES • YIELD: 8 TO 10 SERVINGS

If you're looking for a showstopping Christmas dessert, then look no further than this Christmas tree cake. *Pandoro* is a classic leavened cake from northern Italy that many Italians enjoy from Christmas to New Year's Day. Its lovely star shape is perfect for layering with some delicate pastry cream that Nonna spikes with limoncello, for a dessert that can double as a gorgeous table centerpiece.

LIMONCELLO CREAM

1¾ cups plus 2 tablespoons (450 ml) whole milk

1¾ cups plus 2 tablespoons (450 ml) limoncello liqueur

½ cup (120 ml) heavy cream

1½ cups (300 g) sugar

¾ cup (90 g) cornstarch

1 teaspoon vanilla extract

10 large egg yolks

Peel of 1 lemon, in 1 long piece

PANDORO

1 store-bought pandoro

1 cup (240 ml) limoncello liqueur

DECORATION

Fresh berries, for decorating (you can also use candied cherries, if you like), plus more for garnish

Confectioners' sugar, for dusting

1 **To make the limoncello cream:** In a medium saucepan, combine the milk, limoncello, heavy cream, granulated sugar, cornstarch, vanilla, egg yolks, and lemon peel. Whisk until smooth. Turn the heat to medium-low and cook, whisking continuously, until the mixture begins to thicken and bubbles are visible, about 15 minutes. Remove the pan from the heat and continue to stir for 30 seconds more. Strain any lumps, if necessary, and press plastic wrap directly onto the cream's surface to prevent a skin from forming. Let cool to room temperature before using.

2 **To make the pandoro:** Lay the pandoro on its side and, using a long serrated knife, cut slices about 2 inches (5 cm) thick. You should be able to get about 5 slices. If the bottom piece is uneven, cut it so it can sit flat.

3 Brush the cut sides of the bottom layer with about one-fifth of the limoncello and top with limoncello cream.

4 Put the next slice on top at an angle so the points of the star are staggered. Repeat with all layers.

5 **To decorate:** Add a fresh berry to each point and dust with confectioners' sugar. Garnish with fresh berries.

ITALIAN SPRINKLE COOKIES

Dolci con Confettini

PREP TIME: 45 MINUTES • COOK TIME: 30 MINUTES • YIELD: ABOUT 48 COOKIES

The Italian sprinkle cookie has become a cult holiday favorite and Nonna Angelina's are some of the best I've ever had. Her secret is a powdered vanilla extract that comes in packets called Vanillina by the Italian brand Paneangeli ("bread of angels"). Unlike many recipes that require you to cool the cookies completely before glazing, Nonna Angelina glazes them while they're nice and hot, resulting in the sugar drying a pure white color that really makes the sprinkles pop!

COOKIES

4 large eggs, at room temperature

2 packets (½ ounce, or 15 g, each) Italian vanilla powder or 4 teaspoons (20 ml) vanilla extract

1 cup (200 g) granulated sugar

½ cup (1 stick, or 120 g) unsalted butter, melted

4 teaspoons (20 g) baking powder

3 cups (360 g) all-purpose or 00 flour

GLAZE

2 cups (240 g) confectioners' sugar

¼ cup (60 ml) whole milk

1 packet (½ ounce, or 15 g) Italian vanilla powder or 1 teaspoon vanilla extract

1 teaspoon fresh lemon juice or lemon extract (optional)

2 tablespoons (30 g) unsalted butter, melted

Nonpareils, for decorating

Nonna Angelina Says
Don't confuse Vanillina with vanilla-flavored baking powder.

1 **To make the cookies:** In a large bowl, add the eggs, vanilla, and granulated sugar. Using a handheld electric mixer, beat on high speed until pale yellow, about 3 minutes. Add the melted butter and beat on high speed to combine.

2 Reduce the speed to low. Add the baking powder and beat to combine. Add the flour, 1 cup (120 g) at a time, and beat on low speed until fully absorbed. Do not overmix. Cover the bowl with plastic wrap and refrigerate for 45 minutes.

3 Preheat the oven to 375°F (190°C). Line a baking sheet with aluminum foil or parchment paper.

4 Take a tablespoon-size (15 g) chunk of dough and roll it between your hands into a 1-inch-thick (2.5 cm) log. Roll the log into a pinwheel and place on the prepared baking sheet. Continue rolling the dough, placing the cookies on the baking sheet 2 inches (5 cm) apart. If the dough feels sticky, place it back in the fridge to chill for a few minutes.

5 Bake the cookies until the swirls on the tops have nearly disappeared and the bottoms have slightly browned, 12 to 15 minutes. While the cookies bake, make the glaze.

6 **To make the glaze:** In a small bowl, whisk together the confectioners' sugar, milk, vanilla, and lemon juice (if using). Whisk in the melted butter.

7 Let the cookies cool for 2 minutes. While they are still hot, dip them into the glaze and sprinkle with the nonpareils. Place on a wire rack to cool completely.

CHOCOLATE-COVERED ROCOCO

Rococo al Cioccolato

PREP TIME: 30 MINUTES • COOK TIME: 20 MINUTES • YIELD: 12 COOKIES

Nonna Antoinette is as creative as she is tenacious. One year, she began dreaming up a way to revamp her family's classic *rococo* recipe, which is a yummy spiced cookie from the Campania region—it can fill you with nostalgia, but also leave you needing dental work after eating it. Being the clever Nonna that she is, she added some more dried fruit for softness and covered them in dreamy chocolate for a modern touch. The result is delicious rococo you can't wait to sink your teeth into (pun intended).

ROCOCO

2 cups (290 g) whole almonds, toasted

1 cup (130 to 150 g) dried fruit, such as figs, raisins, or apricots

4 cups (480 g) all-purpose or 00 flour

1 cup (200 g) sugar

½ cup (120 ml) water

¼ cup (80 g) honey

1 tablespoon (15 ml) allspice

2 teaspoons baking powder

1 teaspoon vanilla extract

1 teaspoon orange extract

1 teaspoon lemon extract

Pinch salt

CHOCOLATE DIP

1½ pounds (679 g) bittersweet chocolate chips

1 tablespoon (13 g) shortening

1 Preheat the oven to 350°F (180°C). Line a baking sheet with parchment paper. Set aside.

2 **To make the rococo:** In a food processor, grind the toasted almonds. Add the dried fruit and process until a paste forms. Transfer to the bowl of a stand mixer fitted with the paddle attachment. Add the flour, sugar, water, honey, allspice, baking powder, extracts, and salt. Mix on low speed until a dough forms and is well mixed. The dough will be hard.

3 Lightly flour a work surface and turn the dough out onto it. Divide the dough into 12 equal pieces. Roll each piece into a rope 8 inches (20 cm) long and form a bagel-shaped cookie. Place the cookies on the prepared sheet about 2 inches (5 cm) apart. Bake for 18 minutes. Transfer to a wire rack to cool.

4 **To make the chocolate dip:** In a double boiler over low heat or in a microwave, melt the chocolate and shortening, stirring to combine.

5 Dip each cooled cookie in the melted chocolate until evenly coated. Gently place on a wire rack until the chocolate solidifies.

GLAZED ALMOND S COOKIES

Dolci S alle Mandorle

PREP TIME: 10 MINUTES • COOK TIME: 15 MINUTES • YIELD: ABOUT 24 COOKIES

Nonna Romana's classic olive-oil S cookies got jazzed up for the holidays, and the result is an impossibly delicious, almond-scented cookie, covered with the dreamiest almond glaze imaginable. When topped with lovely holiday sprinkles, they will be a favorite on your cookie tray.

COOKIES

Nonstick baking spray, for preparing
    the baking sheet
4¾ cups (570 g) all-purpose or
    00 flour, plus more for dusting
2 teaspoons baking powder
1½ cups (218 g) blanched almonds
6 large eggs, divided
1 cup (200 g) granulated sugar
¾ cup (180 ml) olive oil
Zest of 1 lemon
2 teaspoons vanilla extract
2 tablespoons (30 ml) almond extract

GLAZE

2 cups (240 g) confectioners' sugar
2 tablespoons (30 ml) whole milk
1 tablespoon (15 ml) almond extract
½ teaspoon vanilla extract
Sprinkles, for decorating

Home for the Holidays

My mother, Regina, taught so many people how to make traditional cookies for holidays. Even now, I still meet people who learned from my mother when they were young. They stop me and say, 'Regina teach me everything!' It's so nice.

—Nonna Romana Sciddurlo

1 **To make the cookies:** Preheat the oven to 375°F (190°C). Line a baking sheet with aluminum foil or parchment paper. Spray with baking spray. Set aside.

2 In a large bowl, whisk together the flour and baking powder. Set aside.

3 In a food processor, process the almonds for 20 to 30 seconds. Transfer to another large bowl and add 5 of the eggs, the granulated sugar, olive oil, lemon zest, and extracts. Using a handheld electric mixer, mix on medium speed until smooth.

4 Add the flour, little by little, mixing on low speed until just absorbed.

5 Lightly flour a work surface and your hands. Take a golf ball–size piece of dough and roll it into a 1-inch-thick (2.5 cm) rope. If the dough is sticky, coat your hands with more flour. Continue making ropes until all the dough is used. Cut the ropes into 4- to 5-inch (10 to 13 cm) pieces and shape each into an S shape. Place the cookies 2 inches (5 cm) apart on the prepared baking sheet. Flatten each cookie slightly with the palm of your hand.

6 In a small bowl, beat the remaining egg. Brush each cookie with the egg wash.

7 Bake for 15 minutes, or until the cookies have browned nicely on the bottom. Cool completely before glazing.

8 **To make the glaze:** In a medium bowl, mix together the confectioners' sugar, milk, and extracts. For a thicker glaze, add more sugar; for a thinner, glaze add more milk. Drizzle the glaze over the cookies and decorate with sprinkles. Let the glaze dry for at least 2 hours.

CHESTNUT CREAM-FILLED COOKIES

Pastatelle

PREP TIME: 1 HOUR • COOK TIME: 1 HOUR 30 MINUTES • YIELD: ABOUT 72 COOKIES

Nonna Rosetta looks forward to Christmas every year so she can make her favorite chestnut cream–filled *pastatelle*. Across the region of Campania, traditional sweets that resemble ravioli are made with a puree of chestnuts or chickpeas mixed with chocolate and stuffed into a lightly sweet dough that is fried until golden brown. Nonna Rosetta prepares these in her kitchen in the most traditional way she was taught back in Aquilonia. When I first asked her to show me how to make these, she warned me: *"Questo e' un procedimento molto lungo! (This is a long process!)"* You can save time by using roasted chestnuts and a pasta roller machine.

FILLING

10 ounces (280 g) roasted chestnuts, peeled

1 ounce (28 g) good-quality semisweet chocolate

2 tablespoons (40 g) honey

1½ teaspoons unsweetened cocoa powder

Zest of 1 orange

¼ teaspoon ground cinnamon

DOUGH

3 large eggs, beaten

½ cup (100 g) granulated sugar

¼ cup (60 ml) olive oil

Pinch baking powder

2½ cups (300 g) all-purpose or 00 flour, divided, plus more for dusting

Oil, for frying

Confectioners' sugar, for dusting

1 **To make the filling:** In a medium saucepan, combine the chestnuts with enough cold water to cover completely. Place the pan over high heat and bring to a boil. Cook for 25 to 30 minutes, until the chestnuts are tender. Using a slotted spoon, transfer the chestnuts to a food processor. Process until smooth. Transfer to a large bowl and set aside.

2 In another medium saucepan over low heat, combine the chocolate, honey, cocoa powder, orange zest, and cinnamon. Cook just until the chocolate melts. Stir in the chestnuts. Cook for 3 to 5 minutes more, stirring until very smooth. Transfer to a medium bowl and set aside to cool.

3 **To make the dough:** In a large bowl, using a fork, beat the eggs and granulated sugar for 2 minutes. Add the olive oil and mix until combined. Add the baking powder and mix until combined. Add 2 cups (240 g) of the flour. Mix until a dough begins to form and the flour is absorbed. Generously flour a work surface and turn the dough out onto it. Add the remaining ½ cup (60 g) flour, kneading it in by hand until the dough is smooth and supple, 5 to 7 minutes. Cover the dough with plastic wrap and let rest for 10 minutes.

continued

Home for the Holidays

For Christmas in Aquilonia, we would get gifts like a new coat or a new pair of shoes, or maybe some chocolate. Not like today. We would decorate our Christmas tree with little Mandarin oranges and little chocolates. There would be a little nativity under the tree. When I came to America, I saw these big trees and lots of Christmas lights. It was so pretty. Like a dream. —Nonna Rosetta Rauseo

4 Using a pasta roller on a #3 setting, begin passing the dough through until no holes remain and you have a sheet about 3 inches (7.5 cm) wide.

5 Lay the dough sheet on a work surface. Dot teaspoons of filling about 1½ inches (4 cm) apart, leaving a border of at least ½ inch (13 mm) on all sides. Fold the dough over toward you to cover the filling. Press down on the edge of the dough and press the areas around the filling together to create pockets that resemble ravioli. Cut out squares with a ravioli cutter to seal. Place the filled dough squares on a clean kitchen towel, making sure they do not touch one another. You can fry or bake these cookies.

6 To fry: Line a plate with paper towels and set aside. Heat about 2 inches (5 cm) of oil in a small stockpot over high heat. Working in batches, fry the cookies until golden brown, 2 to 3 minutes per batch. Transfer to the paper towel–lined plate. To bake: Preheat the oven to 375°F (190°C). Place the pastatelle on an ungreased baking sheet 1 inch (2.5 cm) apart. Bake for 15 to 18 minutes, until lightly golden.

7 Dust with confectioners' sugar while warm.

SEVEN LAYER COOKIES

Dolci Tricolore

PREP TIME: 2 HOURS 15 MINUTES • COOK TIME: 12 MINUTES • YIELD: SEVERAL DOZEN

I don't think I've ever met a person who didn't like seven layer cookies, also called rainbow cookies. Nonna Cecilia learned to make this Italian-American classic cookie from her Commara Maria, who had come to America before her, and it quickly made its way into her repertoire.

4 large eggs, separated

1 cup (2 sticks, or 240 g) unsalted butter, at room temperature

1 cup (200 g) sugar

12 ounces (340 g) almond paste

2 cups (240 ml) all-purpose or 00 flour

Red and green food coloring

½ cup (160 g) apricot jam

4 ounces (113 g) good-quality semisweet chocolate

Nonna Cecila Says

Some recipes say you should weight the cookies down overnight to make sure they're pressed together. I used to put encyclopedias on them! But over time, I found that it wasn't really necessary and just giving them a good press with your hands is all you need.

Home for the Holidays

In Italy, we would hang our stockings and hope for presents. My brother always got nice gifts because my mother said he was a good little boy. I wasn't always a perfect child; I was kind of a tomboy and I didn't like to listen too much. I always got charcoal. —Nonna Cecilia DeBellis

1 Preheat the oven to 375°F (190°C).

2 In the bowl of a stand mixer fitted with the paddle attachment, beat the egg yolks and butter on medium speed until combined. Add the sugar and mix until incorporated. Break up the almond paste into small chunks. Add to the mixer and mix until smooth. Reduce the speed to low and add the flour.

3 In a small bowl, whisk the egg whites with a fork until foamy and add them to the mixer. Mix for a few minutes until a soft, uniform dough forms.

4 Divide the dough into 3 equal parts in 3 separate bowls. Leave one of the parts of dough the natural white color. Add the food coloring to the 2 remaining bowls to achieve your desired colors.

5 Spread the dough into 3 separate 12 × 8-inch (30 × 20 cm) baking pans. Bake for 10 to 12 minutes and let cool completely.

6 Line a clean work surface with parchment paper. Flip the green sheet out of the baking pan and lay it down first. Spread half the apricot jam over the green sheet. Place the white sheet on top of the green sheet and spread the remaining apricot jam. Place the red sheet over the white and press the sheets firmly together with your hands.

7 With a serrated knife, trim all 4 edges of the sheets to even them out.

8 Melt the chocolate in a double boiler or microwave, and then spread it over the top. Place in the refrigerator until the chocolate is dry, about 1 hour, or preferably overnight. Turn over to the other side so that the chocolate side is facing the parchment paper and spread the bottom with chocolate. Refrigerate until the chocolate is set, about 1 hour.

9 Cut into 1½ × ½-inch (4 × 1.5 cm) cookies and serve.

CANNOLI COOKIES

Dolci al Cannolo

PREP TIME: 20 MINUTES • COOK TIME: 12 MINUTES • YIELD: ABOUT 48 COOKIES

I didn't think it was possible to get all the flavors of a cannoli in a single cookie, but guess what? It is! Nonna Romana and I jazzed up her classic ricotta cookie recipe with notes of orange and cinnamon, before adding some yummy pistachios and chocolate chips to the batter for crunch and texture. I love decorating these with a gorgeous, thick white glaze and different-colored candied cherries to put everyone in the holiday mood.

COOKIES

1 cup (125 g) unsalted pistachios

2 cups (240 g) all-purpose or 00 flour

1½ teaspoons baking powder

½ teaspoon salt

1 cup (200 g) granulated sugar

½ cup (1 stick, or 120 g) unsalted butter, at room temperature

2 teaspoons vanilla extract

1¼ teaspoons ground cinnamon

Zest of 1 orange

1 large egg, at room temperature

8 ounces (227 g) whole-milk ricotta, at room temperature

1 cup (180 g) mini semisweet chocolate chips

GLAZE

2 cups (240 g) confectioners' sugar

3 tablespoons (45 ml) milk, plus more as needed

¼ teaspoon vanilla extract

DECORATING

Crushed pistachios

Candied cherries

1 Preheat the oven to 350°F (180°C). Line a baking sheet with parchment paper.

2 **To make the cookies:** In a food processor, process the pistachios until coarsely chopped, 15 to 20 seconds. Transfer to a small bowl and set aside.

3 In a large bowl, whisk together the flour, baking powder, and salt. Set aside.

4 In the bowl of a stand mixer fitted with the paddle attachment, combine the granulated sugar, butter, vanilla, cinnamon, and orange zest. Beat for about 5 minutes on medium-high speed until fluffy.

5 Add the egg and ricotta. Beat again on medium-high speed to combine.

6 Add the dry ingredients, little by little, and beat on medium-high speed until a dough forms. Mix in the pistachios and chocolate chips.

7 Using a tablespoon (15 g), portion the dough, roll it into balls, and place 2 inches (5 cm) apart on the prepared baking sheet.

8 Bake for 10 to 12 minutes. The bottoms of the cookies should be slightly brown. Cool completely before glazing.

9 **To make the glaze:** In a medium bowl, mix together the confectioners' sugar, milk, and vanilla until a smooth glaze forms. Add less milk for a thicker glaze or more for a thinner glaze. Spoon the glaze over the cookies and decorate with chopped pistachios and candied cherries as desired.

SAINT DAYS AND CELEBRATIONS

Home for the Holidays

Ever since I got married, I have always written the details of the holiday dinners that I've hosted in a little notebook. I would write down everything from the number of guests to the menu to any special ingredients and shopping lists. Years later, I would look at them and reading them inspires so many memories. Sometimes you host a holiday and you ask yourself, 'Oh my God! What am I going to make this year?' But this helps you look back and put all the pieces together. One day I'm going to give the books to my daughters. —Nonna Liliana Barone

Epiphany (January 6)

NONNA ROMANA SCIDDURLO'S

SWEET COAL

Carbone della Befana

PREP TIME: 3 HOURS • COOK TIME: 20 MINUTES • YIELD: ABOUT 12 PIECES OF COAL

In an Italian household, the Epiphany officially marks the end of the Christmas season. Ever since I was a little girl, Nonna Romana would tell me stories of the good witch La Befana, who would visit children on the eve of January 6 to give the good little boys and girls gifts of candy and treats, while anyone who misbehaved (you can guess which list I was usually on) received coal. She would recite the famous Befana poem to me until I knew it by heart: *"La Befana viene di notte, con le scarpe tutte rotte, il vestito alla Romana, viva viva la Befana!"* When I woke one Epiphany morning many years ago and walked over to the fireplace to see what La Befana had left me, to my shock and surprise, it looked like there were lumps of coal in a dish! Upon further inspection, I found that it wasn't coal at all, but candy that looked exactly like the real thing—my father, Vito, had teamed up with Nonna Romana to trick me. This recipe is perfect for your little ones who are a little naughty, a little nice, and very sweet.

ICING
1 large egg white
¾ cup (150 g) granulated sugar
1 tablespoon (15 ml) Everclear
　　or vodka
2 teaspoons fresh lemon juice
¾ cup (90 g) confectioners' sugar
3 or 4 drops black food coloring

SUGAR SYRUP
1⅓ cups (265 g) granulated sugar
2 cups (475 ml) water

1　Line a loaf pan with parchment paper. Set aside.

2　**To make the icing:** In a large bowl, beat the egg white with a handheld electric mixer until stiff peaks form.

3　Add in the granulated sugar, vodka, and lemon juice, and continue mixing. Add in the confectioners' sugar and food coloring, and mix until you reach the consistency of a thick icing. Set aside.

4　**To make the sugar syrup:** In a small heavy-bottomed saucepan, combine the granulated sugar and water. Bring the mixture to a boil over high heat and reduce the heat to medium-low until the sugar reaches a light caramel color.

5　Reduce the heat to medium-low and add the egg white mixture to the pan, quickly mixing it in until well combined.

6　Transfer the mixture to the prepared loaf pan and let rest at room temperature until hardened, about 3 hours or overnight.

7　Turn it out of the pan and break into irregularly shaped pieces of coal.

International Women's Day (March 8)

NONNA ROMANA SCIDDURLO'S

CHAMPAGNE AND STRAWBERRY MIMOSA CAKE

Torta Mimosa

PREP TIME: 3 HOURS • COOK TIME: 55 MINUTES • YIELD: 10 TO 12 SERVINGS

International Women's Day is celebrated all over the world on March 8. In Italy, people celebrate by giving mimosa flowers and mimosa cakes to the women they love . . . because when Italians want to show their appreciation for something or someone, there should always be a cake or a pastry to go with it! For this cake, an entire extra sponge cake is baked in order to be cut or broken up to mimic the lovely yellow mimosa blossoms. Talk about dedication! Dreamy whipped cream and rich diplomat cream, which is a delicate mix of pastry cream and whipped cream, are layered with airy Italian sponge cake soaked in champagne and layered with vibrant strawberries. While it may look like a labor of love, this cake is actually pretty easy to make, and so worth it!

PAN DI SPAGNA

Nonstick baking spray, for
    preparing the pans
12 large eggs, at room temperature
2 cups (400 g) granulated sugar
Pinch salt
1½ cups (180 g) all-purpose or
    00 flour
1½ cups (192 g) cornstarch
1 teaspoon vanilla extract

DIPLOMAT CREAM

4¼ cups (1 L) milk
10 large egg yolks, beaten
1 teaspoon vanilla extract
1½ cups (300 g) granulated sugar
¾ cup (96 g) cornstarch
Peel of 1 lemon
1½ cups (350 ml) heavy cream
2 tablespoons (15 g) confectioners'
    sugar

1   Preheat the oven to 350°F (180°C). Grease two 9-inch (23 cm) springform pans with nonstick baking spray.

2   **To make the pan di Spagna:** In the bowl of a stand mixer fitted with the paddle attachment, combine the eggs, granulated sugar, and salt. Mix for 15 to 20 minutes on high speed until ribbons form.

3   In a medium bowl, sift the flour and cornstarch 3 times. Stop the mixer and, little by little, sift the dry ingredients over the egg-sugar mixture. Very carefully, with a spatula, fold everything together. (Do this carefully so you don't deflate the egg mixture.) Fold in the vanilla. Pour the batter into the prepared pans. Bake for 40 minutes, or until the centers are firm. Cool completely.

4   Once cooled, trim the dark crusts from the tops and sides of the cakes and discard. Slice one cake into 3 layers about ½ inch (13 mm) thick. Slice the other cake into thin strips, then slice the strips into small cubes. These will be used to decorate the cake.

continued

ASSEMBLY

1½ cups (350 ml) champagne,
   prosecco, or spumante,
   divided

1½ cups (218 g) fresh
   strawberries, sliced

5 **To make the diplomat cream:** In a medium bowl, whisk together the milk, beaten egg yolks, and vanilla.

6 In a medium saucepan, whisk together the granulated sugar and cornstarch. Put the pan over medium heat and stir in the milk mixture with a wooden spoon. Keep stirring and add the lemon peel. Cook, stirring continuously. After 5 to 7 minutes, the mixture will begin to thicken and form a custard. Once thickened, remove the pan from the heat, remove and discard the lemon peel, and continue to stir for 30 seconds more.

7 Cool the custard by spreading it in a shallow baking dish. Cover the custard with plastic wrap, pushing the plastic against the cream to prevent a skin from forming. Place the baking dish in the refrigerator or freezer until cooled.

8 In a medium bowl, combine the heavy cream and confectioners' sugar. Using a handheld electric mixer, beat until stiff peaks form. Remove 6 tablespoons (18 g) of whipped cream and set aside.

9 Add the remaining whipped cream to the cooled custard. Using a handheld electric mixer, whip the custard and whipped cream for a smoother consistency.

10 **To assemble the cake:** Line a 2½-quart (2.4 L) glass bowl with plastic wrap. Press the first cake layer into the bowl and moisten with ½ cup (120 ml) of the champagne. Spread on a layer of the reserved whipped cream. Follow with a layer of diplomat cream. Top with a layer of half the strawberry slices, reserving a few slices for garnish.

11 Add the second cake layer and moisten with ½ cup (120 ml) of the champagne. Spread a layer of diplomat cream and follow with another layer of the remaining strawberry slices.

12 Add the third cake layer and moisten with the remaining ½ cup (120 ml) champagne. Wrap the top of the bowl in plastic wrap and freeze for 2 to 3 hours.

13 Place a plate over the bowl and invert the cake. Unwrap and frost the cake with the remaining diplomat cream. Stick the cake cubes all over the cake. Top with sifted confectioners' sugar. Chill before serving. Garnish with the reserved strawberry slices.

Saint Joseph's Day (March 19)

NONNA LILIANA BARONE'S

BUCATINI WITH SARDINES

Bucatini con le Sarde

PREP TIME: 30 MINUTES • COOK TIME: 40 MINUTES • YIELD: 4 TO 6 SERVINGS

Nothing will spark a heated Sicilian conversation like the question "How do you make your *pasta con sarde*?" Every family has their own recipe, which they hold dear to their hearts, but Nonna Liliana stole mine with her incredible recipe for this iconic Saint Joseph's Day pasta dish. The typical preparation involves a combination of wild fennel, or *finocchietto selvatico* as Nonna Liliana calls it; fresh sardines, which have to be cleaned and deboned, one by one; and a mix of pine nuts and tomato concentrate, all tossed over saffron yellow–tinted bucatini pasta. While *bucatini con le sarde* seems exotic by today's standards, it's important to remember that it is part of Italy's *cucina povera* (peasant food) and utilizes ingredients that were quite abundant in the Sicilian landscape. If you have a hard time finding the wild fennel, regular fennel is an adequate substitute, although milder in flavor.

2 pounds (907 g) fresh sardines

¼ cup (38 g) currants

1 cup (240 ml) warm water

6 tablespoons (90 ml) extra-virgin olive oil, divided

½ cup (55 g) plain bread crumbs

¼ cup (22 g) fennel stems, cut into ¼-inch (6 mm) dice

2 tablespoons (30 ml) salt, plus more to taste

5 ounces (140 g) fresh wild fennel fronds or regular fennel if you cannot find wild fennel

1 large onion, cut into ¼-inch (6 mm) dice

¼ cup (34 g) pinoli (pine nuts)

1 tablespoon (16 g) tomato concentrate or tomato paste

0.016 ounce (0.5 g) saffron threads (about 2 packets), divided

1 Rinse the fresh sardines under cold running water. On a clean work surface, remove the heads and the dorsal fins with a sharp paring knife. Scrape the bodies of the sardines with the knife blade to remove the scales. Rinse the sardines once more under cold running water to remove any remaining loose scales. Beginning at the point where the tail meets the body, slice open the belly of the sardines and scrape out the entrails with your knife and discard. Fillet the fish in half and remove the center bone and discard. Set aside.

2 In a small bowl, combine the currants with the warm water to rehydrate. Let soak while you continue with the recipe.

3 In a medium skillet over medium heat, combine 2 tablespoons (30 ml) of the olive oil and the bread crumbs. Cook for 5 to 7 minutes, stirring constantly with a wooden spoon, until the bread crumbs just begin to turn lightly golden. Remove from the heat and immediately transfer to a medium bowl. Set aside.

4 In a large stockpot, combine the fennel stems, 4 quarts (3.8 L) of water, and 2 tablespoons (30 ml) salt. Bring to a boil.

continued

¼ cup (37 g) sardines or anchovies packed in salt (about 4 fish)

16 ounces (454 g) dry bucatini pasta

Nonna Liliana Says
Domani è più buono di oggi! *(This is one of those dishes that is even better the next day!) We all look forward to San Giuseppe so we can enjoy this dish for two straight days, because it's that good!*

Home for the Holidays
I remember many wonderful holidays spent in Sicily, but to tell the truth, we celebrate them almost the exact same way here. We froze the traditions in time, and in Italy, they already don't do certain traditions the way we as Italian-Americans continue to do.
—Nonna Liliana Barone

5 Fill a small stockpot halfway with water and bring it to a boil. Add the fennel fronds. Cook, uncovered, for 10 minutes. With a slotted spoon, transfer the fennel to a bowl. Reserve the cooking water.

6 Heat the remaining 4 tablespoons (60 ml) olive oil in a large skillet over medium heat. Add the onion and cook for 5 to 7 minutes, until soft and translucent. Add the pinoli and cook until toasted, 2 to 3 minutes. Drain the currants and add to the pan; discard the soaking water.

7 Stir in the tomato concentrate and 1 cup (240 ml) of the reserved fennel-frond cooking water.

8 Coarsely chop the fennel fronds. Add them to the pan along with another 1 cup (240 ml) of the reserved fennel-frond cooking water.

9 In a small cup, combine half the saffron threads with 2 tablespoons (30 ml) of the reserved fennel-frond cooking water. Stir and add to the pan. Cook for 1 minute.

10 Add the fresh sardines and salt-packed sardines, along with another ¼ cup (60 ml) of the reserved fennel-frond cooking water to the pan. Cook for 4 to 5 minutes, until the flesh is just firm. Do not overcook. If the pan looks dry, add enough of the reserved fennel-frond cooking water so it just slightly pools at the bottom of the pan. Taste and season with salt as desired. Turn off the heat while you cook the pasta.

11 Drop the pasta into the boiling water with the fennel stems and cook until al dente.

12 In another small cup, combine the remaining half of the saffron threads with 2 tablespoons (30 ml) of the pasta cooking water. Stir and add to the pot with the pasta.

13 Scoop out the cooked pasta and add it to the sardine mixture. Turn the heat to medium and cook, tossing, for 1 to 2 minutes.

14 Transfer to a serving dish and top with the sautéed bread crumbs. Serve immediately.

❧

NONNA ROSA VELLA'S

TUSCAN RICE FRITTERS

Frittelle di San Giuseppe

PREP TIME: 1 HOUR 30 MINUTES • COOK TIME: 1 HOUR • YIELD: ABOUT 48 FRITTERS

The first time I ever met Nonna Rosa, she was frying these fritters on her stove in her kitchen and her whole house smelled like heaven! These *frittelle* are prepared in Tuscany and most of central Italy to celebrate Saint Joseph's Day on March 19, but Nonna Rosa doesn't need a calendar to tell her when to make something: "To tell the truth, I make all the time because everybody love-a!" These fritters are crispy on the outside and have soft, citrus-scented rice on the inside that takes on an almost creamy texture. Try your best, but it will be very hard to have just one! (I tried!)

RICE

2 cups (475 ml) whole milk
2 cups (475 ml) water
1 small navel orange, quartered
½ lemon, quartered
2 cups (370 g) long-grain rice
1¼ cups (250 g) sugar

FRITTERS

3 large eggs
2 large egg yolks
Zest of 1 orange
Zest of 1 lemon
1 packet (½ ounce, or 15 g) Italian
    vanilla powder or 2 teaspoons
    vanilla extract
¼ cup (60 ml) Vin Santo
¼ cup (30 g) all-purpose or
    00 flour
1½ teaspoons baking powder
Olive oil, for frying

1 **To make the rice:** In a medium saucepan over medium-high heat, combine the milk, water, orange, and lemon. Bring to a boil. Do not worry if the milk begins to separate a little.

2 Drop in the rice and reduce the heat to low. Cook, uncovered, for 10 minutes.

3 Stir in the sugar. Cook, uncovered, for 10 to 15 minutes, until the rice is tender but still has some bite. Remove from the heat. Remove and discard the lemon and orange. Pour the rice into a shallow baking dish and spread it into an even layer. Cover with a clean kitchen towel and cool for 1 hour.

4 **To make the fritters:** Transfer the cooled rice to a large bowl. Add the eggs, egg yolks, zests, vanilla, and Vin Santo. Stir until well combined. Add the flour and baking powder and stir until just combined.

5 Line a plate with paper towels and set aside. Heat about 1 inch (2.5 cm) of olive oil in a large heavy-bottomed skillet over high heat.

6 Working in batches, with a small ice cream scoop, carefully drop scoops of the fritter mixture into the hot oil. Flatten each scoop with the back of a spoon. Fry for about 3 minutes per side until very golden brown. With a slotted spoon, transfer to the paper towel–lined plate. Serve hot or warm.

SAINT JOSEPH'S DAY MINESTRONE

Minestra di San Giuseppe

PREP TIME: 20 MINUTES • COOK TIME: 1 HOUR 5 MINUTES • YIELD: 8 TO 10 SERVINGS

Saint Joseph's Day in Sicily is a day of great celebration, but to many Sicilians, it is also a day to give back. Nonna Angelina's flavorful minestrone is traditionally made to mark the holiday and perform an act of charity. Nonna Angelina recalls that many families in Sicily who felt they had been blessed by Saint Joseph would prepare large pots of this vegetable stew to give to the less fortunate. The traditional *minestra* would be made with any seasonal vegetables and legumes they could find at home or growing in nearby fields. It's very easy to make, and a beautiful example of Sicily's *cucina povera* (peasant food).

1 teaspoon salt, plus more for cooking the vegetables

10 ounces (280 g) broccoli florets

½ head escarole, washed and cut into 1-inch (2.5 cm) strips

1 bunch chicory, washed and cut into 2-inch (5 cm) pieces

1 bunch red Swiss chard, washed, ends trimmed, and cut into 2-inch (5 cm) pieces

3 tablespoons (45 ml) extra-virgin olive oil

3 cloves garlic, sliced

1 small onion, cut into ¼-inch (6 mm) dice

1 cup (149 g) cherry tomatoes, halved

¼ teaspoon black pepper

4 to 5 fresh basil leaves

1 can (15 ounces, or 425 g) chickpeas, drained and rinsed

1 can (15 ounces, or 425 g) lentils, drained and rinsed

1 can (15 ounces, or 425 g) cannellini beans, drained and rinsed

1½ cups (350 ml) vegetable broth

1 Bring a large stockpot of lightly salted water to a boil over high heat. Drop in the broccoli and boil until tender, 7 to 10 minutes. Scoop the broccoli out and transfer to a large bowl. Bring the water back to a boil.

2 Drop in the escarole and boil until tender, 12 to 15 minutes. With a large slotted spoon or tongs, transfer to the bowl with the broccoli. Bring the water back to a boil.

3 Add the chicory and red Swiss chard to the water. Boil until tender, 17 to 20 minutes. Transfer to the bowl with the other vegetables. Set aside.

4 Put a small stockpot over medium heat and add the olive oil, garlic, and onion. Cook for 5 to 7 minutes, until the onion is translucent. Add the cherry tomatoes, 1 teaspoon salt, pepper, and basil. Cook and stir for 2 minutes, stirring with a wooden spoon.

5 Add the chickpeas, lentils, cannellini beans, and broth. Bring to a boil. Cook for 7 to 10 minutes, until heated through.

6 Transfer the vegetables to a casserole dish. Pour the legume mixture on top and mix well to combine.

7 Serve in warm bowls with some crusty semolina bread, if desired.

NONNA ROMANA SCIDDURLO'S

SAINT JOSEPH BREAD ROLLS

Rosette di San Giuseppe

PREP TIME: 1 HOUR 30 MINUTES • COOK TIME: 25 MINUTES • YIELD: 22 ROLLS

Many Italians in America have maintained the beautiful tradition of making an altar to honor Saint Joseph, the patron saint of Sicily. The first altars were created to give thanks for a rainstorm after a very long drought, which had caused intense famine throughout Sicily. As the rain fell and nourished the people, they began to make altars full of food to show their gratitude to Saint Joseph. Over the years, the altars have become more and more ornate, involving breads made into intricate shapes, like staves and chalices.

⅔ cup (160 ml) whole milk

1 packet (¼ ounce, or 7 g) active dry yeast

2¾ cups (385 g) bread flour, divided

¼ cup (50 g) sugar

1 teaspoon salt

2 tablespoons (25 g) lard, melted

3 large eggs, divided

2 teaspoons anise extract

Extra-virgin olive oil, for brushing the bowl

Sesame seeds, for sprinkling

1 In a small saucepan over medium heat, heat the milk until warm but not hot. Transfer to the bowl of a stand mixer fitted with the dough hook attachment. Add the yeast and let stand for 10 minutes.

2 Add 1 cup (140 g) of the flour, the sugar, salt, and melted lard. Mix on low speed until the flour is absorbed. Add 2 of the eggs, the anise extract, and another cup (140 g) of the flour. Mix on low speed until the flour is absorbed. Add the remaining ¾ cup (105 g) flour. Mix on low speed until the flour is mostly absorbed and a ball of dough begins to form.

3 Turn the dough out onto a clean work surface and knead with your hands until all the flour is absorbed and the dough is smooth and supple, about 5 minutes. Brush a large bowl with olive oil and place the dough in it. Flip the dough to coat it in the oil. Cover the bowl with plastic wrap and let rise in a warm place for 1 hour.

4 Preheat the oven to 350°F (180°C). Line a baking sheet with parchment paper. Set aside.

5 Punch down the dough and knead it for 2 to 3 minutes. Take a chunk of dough and roll it into a 1-inch-thick (2.5 cm) rope about 8 inches (20 cm) long. With a knife, make cuts about halfway through the rope, ½ inch (13 mm) apart. Roll the rope into a pinwheel and pinch the ends together to form a rose shape. Place on the prepared baking sheet. Repeat with the remaining dough.

6 Beat the remaining egg in a small bowl with a fork. Brush the rolls with the egg wash and sprinkle with sesame seeds.

7 Bake for 20 to 25 minutes, until golden brown.

MAFALDINE PASTA WITH ANCHOVIES

Lagane di San Giuseppe

PREP TIME: 5 MINUTES • COOK TIME: 15 MINUTES • YIELD: 4 TO 6 SERVINGS

For my Nonna Romana, the feast of Saint Joseph on March 19 is particularly special. Geppino, her son and my uncle, is named for one of the many Italian variations on the name Giuseppe, or Joseph. When the big day approaches, she invites over Geppino and everyone else she knows who has a name derived from Joseph or Giuseppe to celebrate the feast of Saint Joseph, Pugliese-style! *Lagane di San Giuseppe* is the traditional Pugliese dish only prepared for Saint Joseph's Day, and the ingredients are selected to honor Saint Joseph's profession as a carpenter. The *mafaldine*, which look like tiny lasagna noodles, represent curled wood shavings, while the toasted bread crumbs evoke sawdust. This dish is very simple but requires excellent timing, as adding water to hot oil and anchovies can be a bit explosive, but the aromatic pasta comes together quickly and is delicious when topped with the toasted bread crumbs. You'll want to make it more than once a year!

1 cup (108 g) plain bread crumbs

3 tablespoons (45 ml) plus ½ cup (120 ml) extra-virgin olive oil, divided

Salt, to taste

16 ounces (454 g) dried mafaldine

1 can (2 ounces, or 56 g) anchovies, drained and broken into small pieces

Nonna Romana Says

The trick to this recipe is not letting the anchovies cook too much before adding the water. As soon as they begin to break apart, be ready with the ladle.

1. Put a large high-sided skillet over medium heat. Add the bread crumbs and 3 tablespoons (45 ml) of the olive oil to the pan together, stirring constantly with a wooden spoon until the bread crumbs just begin to turn lightly golden, 5 to 7 minutes. Remove from the heat and immediately transfer them to a medium bowl to prevent burning. (Bread crumbs will continue to cook if left in the pan.)

2. Bring a medium stockpot of generously salted water to a boil. Drop in the pasta and return to a boil.

3. When the pasta has 2 to 3 minutes to go before it is al dente, heat the remaining ½ cup (120 ml) olive oil in a medium saucepan over medium-high heat. Once the oil is very hot, add the anchovies and stir carefully with a wooden spoon for about 5 seconds. There may be some spatter but it will calm down when you add the water in the next step.

4. Scoop out about 1 cup (240 ml) of the pasta water and add it to the skillet, stirring until the anchovies have dissolved.

5. Drain the pasta and transfer it to a large serving bowl. Add the anchovy mixture and toss well to coat the pasta. Sprinkle with the toasted bread crumbs, reserving some for garnish. Serve the pasta in warm bowls and garnish with some extra bread crumbs on top.

SAINT JOSEPH SFINCI AND ZEPPOLE

Sfinci e Zeppole di San Giuseppe

PREP TIME: 1 HOUR • COOK TIME: 45 MINUTES • YIELD: MAKES 14 SFINCI OR 8 ZEPPOLE

Italians and Italian-Americans rejoice in the weeks leading up to Saint Joseph's Day on March 19, as bakeries begin to stock *zeppole* and *sfinci* galore. Nonna Lydia's recipe is from her brother's bakery in Queens, and he learned it from his Sicilian Mamma. Many would line up early in the morning on Saint Joseph's Day in hopes of getting a warm pastry to start the day Italian-style. The classic zeppole is a piped choux dough that can be baked or fried and filled with Pastry Cream (page 11), and sfinci, their Sicilian cousins, can only be fried and are filled with sweetened Cannoli Cream (page 12). If the pressure of choosing between team zeppole and team sfinci is too much to handle, Nonna Lydia has a solution: "Have one of each!" (See the photo for this recipe on page 222.)

DOUGH

1 cup (240 ml) water
¼ cup (50 g) shortening
Pinch salt
1 cup (120 g) all-purpose or 00 flour
4 large eggs
Oil, for frying

SFINCI FILLING AND DECORATION

1 Cannoli Cream recipe (page 12)
14 pieces candied orange peel
14 candied cherries
Crushed pistachios, for sprinkling

ZEPPOLE FILLING AND DECORATION

1 Pastry Cream recipe (page 11)
8 Amarena cherries
Confectioners' sugar, for dusting

1 **To make the dough:** In a medium saucepan, combine the water, shortening, and salt. Bring to a boil. Add the flour. Reduce the heat to low. Mix with a wooden spoon, continually, for about 30 seconds, until all the flour is incorporated and a soft dough forms that pulls away from the sides of the pan. Turn off the heat and continue stirring for 30 seconds more. Remove from the heat and transfer the dough to a medium bowl. Let sit until the dough is cool enough to handle.

2 Once cooled, mix the dough with your hands for 5 minutes. If you find any clumps of flour that did not dissolve, remove and discard them. Cool the dough to room temperature.

3 Add 1 egg. Mix with your hands until completely absorbed. Add the second egg. Repeat the hand mixing. Add the third egg. Using a handheld electric mixer, mix on medium speed until the egg is fully absorbed. Add the final egg and mix again until the dough is very smooth.

4 **If making sfinci:** Line a plate with paper towels and set aside. Heat about 2½ inches (6 cm) of oil in a small stockpot over high heat. Use a thermometer to maintain the temperature between 375° and 400°F (190° and 200°C).

5   Fill a small bowl with olive oil. Using a small ice cream scoop or a spoon, dip the scoop in the olive oil, scoop the dough, and immediately drop the dough into the hot oil, working in batches (3 per batch). The dough will continue popping and expanding as the sfinci cook. Fry the sfinci until golden brown and they no longer pop and expand, about 5 minutes. With a slotted spoon, transfer to the paper towel–lined plate. Cool before slicing and filling. The sfinci will be hollow on the inside.

6   Slice the sfinci three-quarters of the way through and fill with about 2 tablespoons (30 g) of cannoli cream. Top each sfinci with a candied orange peel, a candied cherry, and crushed pistachios.

7   **If making zeppole and frying:** Cut out eight 4-inch (10 cm) squares of parchment paper. Fill a disposable pastry bag fitted with a large star tip with the dough. Carefully pipe a circle of dough about 3 inches (7.5 cm) in diameter on each parchment piece. Overlap the dough by no more than 1 inch (2.5 cm).

8   Line a plate with paper towels and set aside. Heat about 2½ inches (6 cm) of oil in a small stockpot over high heat. Use a thermometer to maintain the temperature between 375° and 400°F (190° and 200°C). Working in batches, carefully drop about 3 pieces of parchment paper with the dough circles attached into the hot oil. Using tongs, remove the pieces of parchment paper from the oil. Fry the zeppole until golden brown, about 5 minutes per batch. With a slotted spoon, transfer to the paper towel–lined plate. Cool completely before slicing and filling.

9   **If making zeppole and baking:** Preheat the oven to 425°F (220°C). Line a baking sheet with parchment paper. Carefully pipe 8 circles of dough about 3 inches (7.5 cm) in diameter and 2 inches (5 cm) apart on the prepared baking sheet. Overlap the dough by no more than 1 inch (2.5 cm). Bake for 18 to 20 minutes, until the zeppole are golden. Cool completely before slicing and filling.

10 Slice the zeppole in half horizontally.

11 Transfer the pastry cream to a disposable pastry bag fitted with a star tip. Pipe the cream onto the bottom half of the zeppole and top with the other half. Pipe a bit of cream in the center of the zeppole and top with an Amarena cherry. Dust with confectioners' sugar.

Saint Rocco's Day (August 16)

NONNA ANTOINETTE CAPODICCI'S

BREAD OF SAINT ROCCO

Frese di San Rocco

PREP TIME: 3 HOURS 3 MINUTES • COOK TIME: 20 MINUTES • YIELD: 3 FRESE

In Nonna Antoinette's hometown of Morcone, just outside Naples, this traditional bread is baked to honor Saint Rocco on August 16. These loaves would be traditionally baked a few days before the holiday, so they could dry out a bit. On the feast day of Saint Rocco, they would be taken into the country for a picnic where there was a natural spring. According to tradition, using the spring water to moisten your *frese* could bring you good fortune.

1 packet (¼ ounce, or 7 g) active dry yeast

1¼ cups (300 ml) warm water, divided

4 large eggs, at room temperature, divided

2 ounces (55 g) lard, at room temperature

¼ cup (60 ml) extra-virgin olive oil, plus more for brushing the bowl and greasing the pans

4 cups (560) bread flour, plus more for dusting

2 teaspoons salt

¼ teaspoon black pepper

❦ Nonna Antoinette Says
Break off a small piece of dough and put it in a glass of warm water. When the dough rises to the top that usually means your dough has finished rising. A little trick I learned from my Nonna!

1 In the bowl of a stand mixer fitted with the dough hook attachment, dissolve the yeast in 1 cup (240 ml) of the warm water. Let stand until the mixture bubbles, about 3 minutes.

2 Add 3 of the eggs and the lard to the bowl. Mix on low speed. With the mixer running, stream in the olive oil. Gradually, add the flour. Continue mixing until incorporated. Add the salt, pepper, and the remaining ¼ cup (60 ml) warm water. Increase the speed to medium and mix until a smooth, supple dough forms that no longer sticks to the sides of the bowl. The dough should be very wet but not stick to your hands.

3 Brush a large bowl with olive oil. Place the dough inside the bowl. Cover the bowl with plastic wrap and let rise in a warm place until the dough doubles in size, about 1 hour and 30 minutes to 2 hours.

4 Grease 2 baking sheets with olive oil and set aside.

5 Lightly flour a work surface and turn the dough out onto it. Divide the dough into 3 equal pieces. Roll each piece into a 2-inch-thick (5 cm) rope and shape each rope into a ring. Arrange the rings on the baking sheets, making sure the frese do not touch one another. Cover the baking sheet with a clean kitchen towel and let rise in a warm place until doubled in size, about 1 hour.

6 Preheat the oven to 400°F (200°C).

7 In a small bowl, beat the remaining egg. Brush the tops of each ring with the beaten egg. Bake for 18 to 20 minutes, until the frese are golden brown.

NONNA CARMELA TORNATORE'S

EGGS IN PURGATORY WITH POLENTA

Uova in Purgatorio con Polenta

PREP TIME: 15 MINUTES • COOK TIME: 30 MINUTES • YIELD: 4 SERVINGS

It is said that on All Souls' Day we also honor our faithfully departed souls who are in purgatory. Leave it to Italians to make suffering into an excuse to eat a delicious meal! This recipe consists of eggs cooked in a fiery tomato sauce that will awaken your taste buds and feed your soul.

EGGS IN PURGATORY

3 tablespoons (45 ml) extra-virgin olive oil

½ teaspoon red pepper flakes (optional)

¼ teaspoon black pepper

1 small onion, cut into ½-inch (13 mm) dice

½ medium green bell pepper, cut into ½-inch (13 mm) dice

2 cloves garlic, sliced

1 can (14 ounces, or 395 g) crushed tomatoes

½ teaspoon salt

4 large eggs

1 tablespoon (3 g) chopped fresh basil

POLENTA

3 cups (720 ml) water

¼ cup (60 ml) whole milk

1 chicken bouillon cube

Salt, to taste

1 cup (140 g) quick-cooking polenta

2 tablespoons (30 g) unsalted butter

Black pepper, to taste

1 **To make the eggs in purgatory:** Put a large skillet with a lid over medium heat. Add the olive oil, red pepper flakes (if using), black pepper, onion, bell pepper, and garlic. Cook for 2 to 3 minutes. Reduce the heat to low. Cook for 5 to 7 minutes more, stirring occasionally with a wooden spoon, until the onion softens.

2 Add the tomatoes and salt. Return the heat to medium and bring the mixture to a boil. Reduce the heat to low, cover the pan, and cook for 10 minutes. In the meantime, make the polenta.

3 **To make the polenta:** In a large saucepan over high heat, combine the water, milk, and bouillon cube. Bring to a boil. Taste and season with salt, if desired. While whisking to avoid clumps, stream in the polenta. Reduce the heat to a simmer. Cook for 2 to 3 minutes, stirring occasionally. Whisk in the butter.

4 **To finish the eggs in purgatory:** Carefully crack each egg, trying not to break it, into a small bowl, ramekin, or even an espresso cup, keeping them separate. You don't want to crack the eggs directly into the sauce because the jagged edges of the shells can break the eggs.

5 Increase the heat under the sauce to medium. Make 4 small wells, one at a time, in the sauce with your wooden spoon. Pour 1 egg into each well. Sprinkle the eggs with the basil. Cover the pan and cook for 2 to 3 minutes, until the egg whites are white and the yolks are firm. Cook for less time if you like your eggs a bit runnier. Season with pepper and serve the eggs and sauce over the warm polenta.

STUFFED ESCAROLE

Scarola Ripiena

PREP TIME: 20 MINUTES • COOK TIME: 1 HOUR • YIELD: 4 SERVINGS

Roman-born Nonna Teresa learned this recipe that honors All Souls' Day from her Neapolitan mother-in-law. "My wonderful mother-in-law would say that stuffing the escarole and wrapping it up represented our loved ones' eternal rest." Nonna Teresa warns not to remove the base of the escarole, which will make tying the leaves down with kitchen twine difficult.

2 small escarole heads, washed

2 to 3 slices day-old bread

1 cup (155 g) Kalamata or Gaeta olives, pitted and halved

2 teaspoons capers

⅔ cup (67 g) grated Parmigiano-Reggiano cheese

⅔ cup (77 g) plain bread crumbs

½ cup (68 g) pinoli (pine nuts)

¼ cup (16 g) minced fresh parsley

2 large eggs, beaten

¼ cup (35 g) raisins

5 anchovy fillets packed in oil, broken up into little pieces

3 tablespoons (45 ml) extra-virgin olive oil

3 cloves garlic, sliced

1⅓ cups (320 ml) chicken broth

1 Remove any brown outer leaves from each escarole head and trim about ¼ inch (6 mm) off the bottom—you want to trim away any brown. Pull the leaves open and cut out the 2-inch-wide (5 cm) center bulb in each head, leaving only the large outer leaves. This will make room for the filling. Pat the escarole dry and set aside while you make the filling.

2 In a small bowl, combine the day-old bread with enough cold water to cover it. Soak for 2 minutes. Squeeze out the excess moisture from the bread and transfer it to a large bowl.

3 Add the olives, capers, cheese, bread crumbs, pinoli, parsley, eggs, raisins, and anchovies to the bowl. Mix until you have a homogenous mixture that holds its shape. Divide the filling in half and place it in the center of each escarole head, but do not spread it out.

4 Holding all the leaves tightly together with one hand, wrap kitchen twine around one of the escarole heads, from the base up, tying it together. Repeat on the second head.

5 Heat the olive oil in a large skillet with a lid over medium heat. Add the garlic and cook for 1 minute. Add the stuffed escarole to the pan and cover. Cook for 3 minutes, or until the escarole begins to wilt. Turn the escarole with tongs and reduce the heat to low. Cover and cook for 15 minutes more.

6 Add the chicken broth to the pan and increase the heat to medium. Cover the pan and bring to a boil. Cook until the escarole has wilted to half its size and the broth has reduced by half, about 15 minutes. Uncover and turn the escarole once more. Cook, uncovered, for 15 minutes more.

7 Remove the twine from the escarole, cut each head in half, and serve.

BUTTERNUT SQUASH WITH POTATOES AND FAVA BEANS

Minestra dei Morti

PREP TIME: 1 HOUR* • COOK TIME: 45 MINUTES • YIELD: 4 TO 6 SERVINGS

*REQUIRES 24 HOURS OF SOAKING

In Nonna Anna's hometown of Mola di Bari, this hearty minestrone with autumnal flavors was made to commemorate the dead on All Souls' Day. The sweetness of the butternut squash mingles beautifully with the fried onions, while the skin of the fava beans adds wonderful texture to this dish. It's perfect for an evening when there's a little chill in the air.

16 ounces (454 g) dried fava beans

2 pounds (907 g) Yukon Gold potatoes (about 7 small potatoes), scrubbed, peeled, and cut into 1-inch (2.5 cm) chunks

1 pound (454 g) butternut squash, peeled and cut into 1-inch (2.5 cm) chunks

½ cup (120 ml) plus 5 tablespoons (75 ml) extra-virgin olive oil, divided

2 teaspoons salt

5 cups (1.2 L) boiling water

1 medium onion, sliced

1 In a large saucepan, combine the dried fava beans with enough cold water to cover completely. Cover the pan with plastic wrap and let the beans soak for 24 hours.

2 Drain the beans. Using a small knife or your fingernail, peel the black line off each fava bean. Do not peel off all the skin. Transfer to a medium bowl.

3 Put a large skillet with a lid over medium-high heat. Add the fava beans, potatoes, butternut squash, 5 tablespoons (75 ml) of the olive oil, and the salt. Cook for 5 to 7 minutes, turning frequently with a wooden spoon.

4 Pour in the boiling water so that it just barely covers everything. Reduce the heat to medium, cover the pan, and cook for 25 to 30 minutes, until the fava beans begin to break down and the potatoes and butternut squash are tender.

5 Heat the remaining ½ cup (120 ml) olive oil in another large skillet over medium heat. Add the onion. Cook for 6 to 7 minutes, until the edges of the onion just begin to turn golden brown.

6 Pour the browned onion and olive oil over the fava beans, potatoes, and butternut squash, and gently stir to combine. Serve in warm bowls with some crusty Italian bread, if desired.

NONNA CHIARA TAPINO'S

WITCH FINGER COOKIES

Le Dita della Strega

PREP TIME: 1 HOUR 15 MINUTES • COOK TIME: 15 MINUTES • YIELD: ABOUT 24 COOKIES

My Zia Chiara has always loved to bake and she became particularly adventurous when her first grandchild, Chiara, was born. They began celebrating Halloween in Italy a few years ago, and while it's not quite the same as Halloween in America, they've created a few themed treats to get into the spirit of things. These deliciously spooky almond shortbread cookies are made to look like real witch fingers! The strawberry jam enables the whole-almond nails to stick to the cookies and gives them a ghoulish feel that all the kids will love!

1½ ounces (43 g) slivered almonds

½ cup (1 stick, or 120 g) unsalted butter, at room temperature

⅓ cup (40 g) confectioners' sugar

1 large egg yolk

½ teaspoon almond extract

1½ cups (180 g) all-purpose or 00 flour

½ teaspoon baking powder

24 whole almonds

Strawberry jam, for brushing

1. In a food processor, process the slivered almonds until fine, 40 to 60 seconds. Transfer to the bowl of a stand mixer fitted with the paddle attachment.

2. Add the butter, confectioners' sugar, egg yolk, and almond extract. Mix on medium speed until combined. Add the flour and baking powder. Mix on medium speed until the flour is just absorbed. Scrape down all the dough and shape it into a disk. Wrap the disk in plastic wrap and refrigerate for 1 hour.

3. Preheat the oven to 350°F (180°C). Line a baking sheet with parchment paper.

4. Divide the dough into 24 equal pieces. Roll each piece into a rope 1 inch (2.5 cm) wide and about 4 inches (10 cm) long. With a knife, make a few lines in the rope that mimic the lines on a finger. Leave about 1 inch (2.5 cm) of space at each end and in the middle of the rope. Place a whole almond on the end of the rope. Place the cookies 1 inch (2.5 cm) apart on the prepared baking sheet and place the baking sheet in the freezer for 10 minutes before baking

5. Bake for 15 minutes, or until the bottoms of the cookies begin to brown. Cool for 15 minutes before handling.

6. Once cool, remove the almonds from the cookies. With your finger, brush the cavity with some strawberry jam and place the almond over the jam. You can also dip the other end of the cookie in jam, if desired.

BONES OF THE DEAD COOKIES

Ossa dei Morti

PREP TIME: 8 HOURS 30 MINUTES • COOK TIME: 22 MINUTES • YIELD: ABOUT 48 COOKIES

In Italy, All Souls' Day on November 2 is a day to remember those who have left us. In keeping with Sicilian tradition, Nonna Carmela bakes these unique cookies that literally translate to "bones of the dead." They are given to children as a way to explain how the people we love pass on. The process of preparing *ossa dei morti* can be a bit tricky. The cookie dough must rest for at least 8 hours so that the outside of the dough dries out and the sugar completely separates from the flour during the baking process. The result is a cookie with two distinct colors and textures. One side is dark, hard, and crunchy, and the other is white and meringue-like.

2½ cups (300 g) all-purpose or
  00 flour, plus more for dusting
1 pound (454 g) confectioners'
  sugar
1½ teaspoons baking powder
1 teaspoon ground cloves
Zest of 1 lemon
4 large eggs, beaten

1   Line 3 baking sheets with parchment paper and set aside.

2   In a large bowl, whisk together the flour, confectioners' sugar, baking powder, cloves, and lemon zest.

3   Add the eggs. With a spatula, mix until everything is well combined and the dry ingredients are absorbed.

4   Lightly flour a work surface and turn the dough out onto it. Flour your hands and the dough and knead by hand for about 5 minutes, until a ball of dough forms. The dough may be sticky. Divide the dough into 6 pieces. Working with one piece at a time, roll each into a rope about 1 inch (2.5 cm) thick. Cut it into 1½-inch-long (4 cm) pieces and place them 2 inches (5 cm) apart on the prepared baking sheets. (The sugar from the cookies will spread out, so you want to leave enough room.)

5   Cover the baking sheets with clean kitchen towels and let rest at room temperature for at least 8 hours or overnight.

6   Preheat the oven to 350°F (180°C).

7   Bake the cookies until the internal sugar of the cookie has come out and resembles white meringue, about 22 minutes. Cool before handling. The cookies will be very hard, but are perfect for dipping into coffee.

NONNA ROMANA SCIDDURLO'S

TARALLI OF SAINT LUCY

Occhi di Santa Lucia

PREP TIME: 3 HOURS OR OVERNIGHT • COOK TIME: 25 MINUTES • YIELD: ABOUT 120 TARALLI

Occhi di Santa Lucia are tiny, sweet taralli from Puglia made throughout the month of December, especially to celebrate Saint Lucy's Day on December 13. They are coated with a sugar glaze that Nonna Romana refers to as *u gilepp*, which gives them a white sugar finish as they dry. Santa Lucia is the patron saint of the blind, her name being a derivative of the word for light. She is often depicted holding a plate with eyes on it and a palm branch that symbolizes victory over evil. These taralli are made very small to resemble the eyes of Santa Lucia, using a simple dough typical of the region. (It's actually the same dough as *cartellate* on page 188!)

TARALLI

1 cup (240 ml) dry white wine,
    such as Pinot Grigio, at room
    temperature
¼ cup (60 ml) olive oil
3 cups (360 g) all-purpose or
    00 flour

GLAZE

½ cup (120 ml) water
1 cup (200 g) sugar

❙ Nonna Romana Says
The tinier these are, the better, so it's a good idea to enlist any available nipotini *(grandchildren) to help roll the dough around their little fingers for perfectly tiny* tarallini.

1 Preheat the oven to 375°F (190°C). Line a baking sheet with parchment paper. Set aside.

2 **To make the taralli:** In the bowl of a stand mixer fitted with the dough hook attachment, combine the wine and olive oil. Mix on low speed for 1 minute. Add the flour. Continue mixing on low speed until the flour is completely absorbed and a dough forms, about 5 minutes.

3 Lightly flour a work surface and turn the dough out onto it. Knead by hand for about 5 minutes, until the dough is supple.

4 Take a small chunk of dough and roll it into a rope about ¼ inch (6 mm) thick. Cut 2-inch (5 cm) pieces of dough from the rope. Connect the ends of each piece together by wrapping around your pinky finger to form a little ring. Arrange the taralli on the prepared baking sheet. Repeat with the remaining dough.

5 Bake for 20 to 25 minutes, or until the bottoms of the mini taralli are golden and the taralli are crunchy. Cool completely before glazing.

6 Place a large sheet of aluminum foil on a work surface and set a wire rack over it.

continued

7 **To make the glaze:** In a medium saucepan over medium-high heat, combine the water and sugar. Bring to a boil, stirring constantly with a wooden spoon. Boil for 5 minutes. Turn off the heat and transfer the sugar glaze to a large metal bowl.

8 Add all the taralli to the glaze. Tumble them with a wooden spoon so they become coated with the glaze. Continue stirring until the sugar becomes tacky and the mixture becomes difficult to stir, 7 to 10 minutes. The sugar will still be clear. Turn the taralli out onto the wire rack. Let rest for 10 minutes. Separate the taralli so they are not touching one another. Let the taralli dry until the sugar turns white, 2 to 3 hours or overnight.

SICILIAN WHEAT BERRY AND RICOTTA PUDDING

Cuccia

PREP TIME: 10 MINUTES • COOK TIME: 45 MINUTES • YIELD: 6 TO 8 SERVINGS

Nonna Lydia tells me that according to a Palermitano legend, there was a great famine in Sicily in the mid-1600s, and the people were desperate to find food to nourish their families. On December 13, which happened to be the feast day of Saint Lucy, a ship miraculously appeared in the port containing bundles of wheat, and the people rejoiced. Not having the patience to wait for the wheat to be brought to the mills and ground into flour, they decided to quickly cook the wheat with some oil and salt, and eat it right away. Over the years, *cuccia* has evolved into a pudding of cooked wheatberries and sweetened ricotta, eaten once a year on December 13 to celebrate the feast of Saint Lucy in Sicily.

1 cup (180 g) hulled wheat, rinsed

4 cups (960 ml) water

1 teaspoon salt

14 ounces (395 g) whole-milk ricotta

½ cup (100 g) sugar

¼ cup (36 g) citron, cut into ¼-inch (6 mm) dice

¼ cup (44 g) candied orange peel, cut into ¼-inch (6 mm) dice

Pinch ground cinnamon

Bittersweet chocolate, for shaving and garnishing

1   In a large saucepan over high heat, combine the hulled wheat, water, and salt. Bring to a boil. Reduce the heat to medium and cook for 40 to 45 minutes, until the wheat is tender. If you like your wheat a bit softer, continue cooking for an additional 10 minutes, or until the desired texture is reached. In the meantime, make the ricotta cream.

2   In a large bowl, combine the ricotta, sugar, citron, orange peel, and cinnamon. Mix until well combined.

3   Drain the wheat and let cool to room temperature.

4   Add the cooled wheat to the ricotta cream and mix until fully incorporated.

5   Spoon into bowls and garnish with chocolate shavings.

NONNA LYDIA PALERMO'S

THIN SPAGHETTI WITH PROSCIUTTO, SPINACH, AND RAISINS

Spaghettini con Prosciutto e Spinaci

PREP TIME: 15 MINUTES • COOK TIME: 15 MINUTES • YIELD: 4 TO 6 SERVINGS

This is Nonna Lydia's go-to pasta when she needs to feed a big group in a hurry, while still keeping things effortlessly chic (just like her). The simple savory and sweet flavors seamlessly blend together and make for an elegant presentation for any celebration, Italian-style!

Salt, to taste

3 tablespoons (45 ml) extra-virgin olive oil

3 cloves garlic, sliced

4 ounces (113 g) prosciutto, cut into ¼-inch (6 mm) dice

16 ounces (454 g) dried thin spaghetti

½ cup (75 g) golden raisins

½ cup (68 g) pinoli (pine nuts)

5 ounces (140 g) fresh baby spinach

Grated Pecorino Romano cheese, for serving

Home for the Holidays
I passed all my traditions to my daughter and my little grandsons. I see the way they watch me and they're so interested. I hope the traditions live on after me. —
Nonna Lydia Palermo

1 Bring a medium stockpot of generously salted water to a boil.

2 Heat the olive oil in a large skillet over medium heat. Add the garlic. Cook for 1 minute, until golden.

3 Add the prosciutto to the pan. Cook and stir for 2 to 3 minutes, stirring frequently with a wooden spoon.

4 Drop the pasta into the boiling water and cook until al dente.

5 Add the raisins and pinoli to the pan with the pancetta, and cook for 4 to 5 minutes.

6 Add the spinach to the pan along with ½ cup (120 ml) of the pasta cooking water. Cook until the spinach is just wilted.

7 Scoop out another ½ cup (120 ml) of the pasta cooking water and add it to the pan. Drain the pasta and add that as well. Cook, tossing everything together, for 1 minute.

8 Serve in warm bowls with a generous sprinkle of grated Pecorino Romano cheese.

CHERRIES IN SWEET WINE

Ciliegie con Vin Santo

PREP TIME: 5 MINUTES • COOK TIME: 10 MINUTES • YIELD: 4 TO 6 SERVINGS

When guests drop by Nonna Nina's fabulous Manhattan apartment on the Upper East Side, she likes to serve them something simple and sophisticated. This sweet cherry sauce is easy to prepare, especially if using frozen cherries, and is magical on top of gelato or even with some panna cotta. Vin Santo is a sweet wine from Tuscany, where Nonna Nina is from, and it is smooth and sweet when paired with the slightly sour cherries.

12 ounces (340 g) fresh or frozen cherries, thawed if frozen, pitted, and halved

5 tablespoons (75 ml) Vin Santo, divided

3 tablespoons (38 g) sugar

2½ tablespoons (38 ml) fresh lemon juice

1 packet (½ ounce, or 15 g) Italian vanilla powder or 2 teaspoons vanilla extract

Pinch salt

1½ tablespoons (23 ml) cornstarch

1 In a small saucepan over medium heat, combine the cherries, ¼ cup (60 ml) of the Vin Santo, the sugar, lemon juice, vanilla, and salt. Bring the mixture to a boil. Reduce the heat to low. Cook for 5 to 7 minutes, stirring with a wooden spoon, until thickened.

2 In a small bowl, whisk together the cornstarch and remaining 1 tablespoon (15 ml) Vin Santo. Add the cornstarch mixture to the cherries and remove from the heat. Stir until the mixture coats the back of a spoon, 1 to 2 minutes.

WEDDING PASTRIES

Dolci della Sposa

PREP TIME: 30 MINUTES • COOK TIME: 30 MINUTES • YIELD: 12 PASTRIES

If you peek into the pastry shops in Puglia, you will see many of these lovely cream cakes staring back at you. *Dolci della sposa* literally translates to "sweets of the bride." They are traditionally made to celebrate weddings and would be brought to a bride's house on her wedding day as friends and family would gather to watch her get ready for the big event. Nonna Romana starts with little domes of Italian sponge cake that she soaks in rum and fills with smooth Pastry Cream (page 11). Traditionally, the glaze would be prepared by melting sugar and water on the stove and then working in lemon juice on a piece of glass or marble, producing a thick white glaze that dries hard. Over the years, Nonna has come to prefer a simpler glaze made with confectioners' sugar, milk, and just a little vanilla. Candied cherries are used to decorate and make an elegant presentation.

CAKES

Nonstick baking spray, for preparing the pan
2 cups (240 g) all-purpose or 00 flour
1½ teaspoons baking powder
5 large eggs, at room temperature
1 cup (200 g) granulated sugar

SOAK

3 tablespoons (45 ml) white rum
3 tablespoons (45 ml) water

ASSEMBLY

1 Pastry Cream recipe (page 11)

1. Preheat the oven to 350°F (180°C). Coat an oven-safe 6-cavity silicone half-sphere pan with baking spray.

2. **To make the cakes:** In a small bowl, whisk together the flour and baking powder. Set aside.

3. In the bowl of a stand mixer fitted with the paddle attachment, beat the eggs and granulated sugar on medium speed for 30 seconds. Increase the speed to high and beat for 15 to 20 minutes, until the mixture is pale yellow, has doubled in volume, and ribbons form.

4. Reduce the speed to low. Spoon in the dry ingredients, a little at a time, mixing until they are fully absorbed. Pour ¼ cup (60 ml) of batter into each prepared cavity and place the pan on a baking sheet. (Note: For a total of 12 cakes, you will need to fill and bake the pan twice.)

5. Bake for about 20 minutes, until the cakes are golden and springy in the middle. Cool to room temperature.

6. **To make the soak:** In a small bowl, combine the rum and water.

7. **To assemble the pastries:** Transfer the pastry cream to a disposable pastry bag or a resealable plastic bag with a lower corner snipped off.

continued

GLAZE

4½ cups (540 g) confectioners' sugar

½ cup (120 ml) whole milk

1 packet (½ ounce, or 15 g) Italian vanilla powder or 1 teaspoon clear vanilla extract

DECORATION

12 candied cherries

8 Using a very sharp knife, slice the domes off the tops of the cakes so they have a straight edge. Discard or eat the domes. Slice the cakes in half horizontally, making sure the bottom piece is at least ½ inch (13 mm) thick. Brush both halves of each cake with the soak.

9 Pipe a thin layer of pastry cream on the bottom half of each cake and top with the other half of the cake. If any cream peaks out, smooth it out with a knife or a spatula so it's flush.

10 **To make the glaze:** In a medium bowl, whisk together the confectioners' sugar, milk, and vanilla until blended and smooth.

11 Position the cakes on top of a wire rack with some height to it. Spoon the glaze over the cakes, making sure all sides are well coated. Top each with a candied cherry. Let the glaze dry completely before handling.

12 Place the finished cakes inside jumbo paper cupcake liners.

INDEX

ACKNOWLEDGMENTS

I wish to thank the people who have worked so very hard to bring this book to life.

The Quarto Group editor Jeannine Dillon, who championed the *Cooking with Nonna* cookbooks from the very beginning. Thank you for making me believe I am a good writer and for reeling me in when my crazy Italian passion gets the best of me. Over the past few years, you've become the big sister who I never want to disappoint.

Erin Canning, for working tirelessly on the manuscript. I cherish every laugh that we share and I hope every *Cooking with Nonna* book you edit makes you feel a little more Italian.

Many thanks to Lydia Jopp, Kristine Anderson, and Jeff McLaughlin at The Quarto Group, for all their support and hard work.

Photographer Colin Cooke and food stylist Michaela Hayes, for capturing each Nonna's individual style in every yummy photograph and bringing the holidays to life for this book.

To all the Nonne who shared all their precious holiday recipes and memories with me: your extraordinary lives make this book magical, and I know they will inspire people everywhere to celebrate with the love that comes through its pages.

Great thanks to my partners in Cooking with Nonna, John and Leona Seazholtz, for giving so much love and energy to the Cooking with Nonna brand.

To the love of my life, Nick: Thank you for always encouraging me to dream bigger and work harder. You have made every holiday since we met so much sweeter.

Many thanks to everyone who took the time to proofread, recipe-test, give advice, and drink wine with me when I didn't think I would make my deadlines. I appreciate your love and friendship more than you will ever know. Special thanks to Francesca Cwynar, who did all of the above and provides never-ending comfort.

A big thank-you to Enza Cristino and Gabriella Trantino, who doubled as a hair and makeup team and set designers for the photo shoot. I am so fortunate to have such beautiful and talented friends.

Thank you to my wonderful, crazy Italian parents, Vito and Angela, who have hosted countless holidays and celebrations in every home they have lived in. People like you are so rare, and I'm so lucky I've gotten to make so many enchanting memories with you.

A huge thank-you to my brilliant big brother, Leo, for always finding the right words to help me make sense of things. I would be absolutely lost without you.

Finally, thank you to my incredible Nonna Romana, for always bringing our family together year after year. You are my greatest inspiration and every day with you feels like a holiday.

ABOUT THE AUTHOR

Rossella Rago is the host of the popular web TV series *Cooking with Nonna* (www.cookingwithnonna.com). For each episode of the show, Rossella invites an Italian-American *nonna* to cook with her and share traditional Italian recipes and fond memories of her childhood in Italy. Rossella, a graduate of St. John's University, has traveled the country and performed cooking demonstrations in numerous cities across the United States with local *nonne* as her partners.

Rossella spent her childhood in the kitchen with her maternal Nonna Romana, learning the long legacy of recipes from Puglia passed down through the generations. Launching *Cooking with Nonna* TV has allowed Rossella to expand her culinary expertise to much of the rest of Italy too. Rossella, together with her mother and her Nonna Romana, won the "Italiano Battle" episode of the Food Network's *24 Hour Restaurant Battle* in 2010. She is the author of *Cooking with Nonna* (Race Point Publishing, 2017) and lives in Brooklyn, New York.